A Decade of Dark Humor

A DECADE OF DARK HUMOR

How Comedy, Irony, and Satire Shaped Post-9/11 America

Edited by TED GOURNELOS and VIVECA GREENE

University Press of Mississippi / Jackson

www.upress.state.ms.us

The University Press of Mississippi is a member of the
Association of American University Presses.

First printing 2011

∞

Library of Congress Cataloging-in-Publication Data

A decade of dark humor : how comedy, irony, and satire
shaped post 9-11 America / edited by Ted Gournelos and
Viveca Greene.
p. cm.
Includes bibliographical references and index.
ISBN 978-1-61703-006-2 (cloth : alk. paper) — ISBN
978-1-61703-007-9 (ebook) 1. Political culture—United
States—History—21st century. 2. September 11 Terrorist Attacks, 2001—Influence. 3. Mass media—Political
aspects—United States. 4. United States—Politics and
government—2001–2009—Humor. 5. United States—Politics and government—2001–2009. 6. American wit and
humor—History and criticism. 7. Political satire, American. I. Gournelos, Ted, 1979– II. Greene, Viveca.
E902.D423 2011
973.931—dc22   2010053395

British Library Cataloging-in-Publication Data available

To the artists, authors, filmmakers,
and comedians who inspired this book,
and did what they could to keep us all sane.

Contents

Acknowledgments

The editors would like to thank Seetha Srinivasan for her early interest in this project, as well as Walter Biggins and the rest of the wonderful staff at the University Press of Mississippi for their work making it come together. In addition, we would like to thank our authors for their tireless work and good humor; it was truly a pleasure working with all of you. A special thank-you to Paul Lewis for his timely contribution and heartfelt advice. Ted Gournelos and Viveca Greene would also like to extend their deepest appreciation to Dr. Debra Wellman, Dean of Faculty at Rollins College, for her generous assistance in financing the index for this volume.

Ted Gournelos would like to thank David Monje for his editorial contributions early on in this project, and give love to the project David moved to instead: his amazing wife, Kumi, and the birth of their beautiful daughter, Ruby. Ted would also like to thank his family for . . . well, for everything . . . as well as the people closest to him both academically and personally: Anne Stone, Kent Ono, the Craig brothers (1 and 2, you know who you are), and the many other people in his life who have made this project possible.

Viveca Greene is grateful for the support and suggestions of many friends, colleagues, and students, especially Lawrence Douglas and Amelie Hastie at Amherst College, Brett Ingram at UMASS/Amherst, and Sam Butterfield and Anne Koehler at Hampshire College. Special recognition goes to the seraphic Erica Silva. Finally, Chris Perry and Jordy and Noe Perry-Greene lead even an ironically inclined person to offer the sincerest thank-you for their love and humor: fanks.

Introduction

Popular Culture and Post-9/11 Politics

—Ted Gournelos and Viveca Greene

When one looks back on the events of September 11, 2001, after almost a decade of social unrest teeming with political humor and satire, it seems more than a little strange that editorials and commentators initially called for an "end of irony." In its September 24, 2001, edition, for instance, *Time* magazine ran an article by its editor Roger Rosenblatt titled "The Age of Irony Comes to an End." Lambasting what he regarded as a thirty-year reign of ironists who in "seeing through everything, made it difficult for anyone to see anything," Rosenblatt bitterly asked his reader, "Are you looking for something to take seriously? Begin with evil." The world had been, reportedly, "forever changed," and others echoed Rosenblatt's prediction; *Vanity Fair* editor Graydon Carter remarked, "I think it's the end of the age of irony" (Allis 2001), and even a spokesperson for Comedy Central announced that "irony is dead—at least for the moment" (Hibbs 2001). Not only are these comments reminiscent of Theodor Adorno's suggestion that to "write poetry after Auschwitz is barbaric," but they also sound suspiciously like the neo-imperialistic desire for an "end of history," originally described by Fukuyama (1989) and developed by advocates of what are now known as "neoliberal" and "neoconservative" ideologies, and pursued through the myopic policies of the Bush administration.

There is, however, a counternarrative to 9/11 discourse, in which the past decade can be characterized as much by dissent—often in the form of ironic or humorous expression—as by acceptance of simplified notions of good and evil and of amplified state power. From this perspective, far from being an end to anything, 9/11 represents the beginning of a reinvigorated opposition movement to dominant media, industry, political, and economic interests. A moment after Rosenblatt advocated the "end of the age of irony," David Beers (2001) responded on Salon.com with a call for an "irony of engagement." Reflecting back on 9/11 five years after the attacks, Kevin Dettmar noted that "it now appears that 9/11 and the subsequent 'war on terror' may have shaken irony out of the lazy cynicism into which it had settled and, rather than rendering it obsolete, has made ironic critique more urgent than ever" (2006, 139). The chapters in this volume demonstrate that humor, irony, and satire were not only shaped *by* 9/11 and its aftermath, but were also pivotal in shaping responses to the events—especially as their practitioners combated the foreclosure and silencing of discourse and (re)opened and reinvigorated an active, contested public sphere.

Many humorists initially hesitated to critically address the 9/11 attacks and, in particular, the Bush administration's framing of them. The response of long-time New York City media landmark *Saturday Night Live* (*SNL*) offers an interesting case study. Although the failings and merits of the show are up for debate, and a number of cable programs are better known for offering harder-hitting political commentary, it is certainly the case that *SNL* has been a staple of network television and political humor since it debuted in 1975, and thus is a useful example of mainstream commentary and the politics of critique humorous programs offer.

Viewers who tuned in on September 29 to the first show that aired after the attacks found New York City mayor Rudolph Giuliani opening the night surrounded by city firefighters and police officers. After an earnest discussion of the attacks and the nature of heroism, followed by a musical performance by Paul Simon, *SNL*'s executive producer Lorne Michaels joined Giuliani on stage, and the mayor affirmed the significance of *SNL* to New York City as "one of our great New York City institutions." After an awkward pause, Michaels asked Giuliani, "Can we be funny?" The audience laughed anxiously, perhaps in anticipation of a restored play frame. Giuliani responded to Michael's question with one of his own: "Why start now?" Seemingly relieved, the live audience laughed again, harder, at the political comedian and the comedic politician.

It is significant that in seeking the mayor's permission, *SNL* rescripted Giuliani—a frequent target of lampooning on the show during his administration—as a credible authority. For those who support the unrepentant transformative social power of political satire, this introduction—as well as the political sketches *SNL* offered early in its 2001–2002 season—were troubling moments of compromise. As scholars as diverse as Joseph Boskin (1990) and Jeffrey Jones (2009) argue, humor divorced from engagement with divisive policies or structural inequalities reflects an older style of political humor in which the satiric aim of shows like *SNL* is political style rather than substance.

I.1   Tina Fey (left) imitating Sarah Palin (right).

Interestingly enough, seven years later it was a series of *SNL* episodes that reminded the country that there has been a real, tangible shift in social and political discourse in the United States from the period immediately following 9/11 to that of the present day. This shift does not reflect changes in the U.S. political system itself, but instead foregrounds an increasingly media-saturated and heavily managed and branded political atmosphere, one in which a president landing on an aircraft carrier to declare the end of a war and a speech at a political party's national convention are as meticulously choreographed as the Academy Awards and the Olympics. When logos, theme songs, and photo ops are as prevalent in politics as they are in sports and entertainment, attacking the constructed brand identity of a politician is a meaningful political act. And, just as importantly, due to the changed

media and industrial climate of the digital age, political performances—
humorous or otherwise—can iterate from a few thousand viewers to tens
of millions. There are many instances of such performances. Will.i.am's *Yes
We Can* video is in some ways paradigmatic of this shift, as are the YouTube
primary debates, and Tina Fey's renditions of Sarah Palin on *SNL* became
some of the most unforgettable moments of the 2008 campaign.

The Fey/Palin sketches also exemplify the power of irony and humor in a
political climate. Fey's first parody of the vice presidential hopeful appeared
in the 2008 season premiere on September 13, which garnered the highest ratings since the post-9/11 premiere discussed above (Seideman 2008a;
2008b), and this time *SNL*'s producer did not request anyone's permission to
be funny. The sketch was largely considered a success, and even Palin herself
(who allegedly watched it without sound) considered the parody to be spot
on. Fey appeared as Palin five more times before the November election;
however, it is the second of these appearances that most clearly illustrates
the shift from 9/11 politics to post-9/11 politics.

The second Fey/Palin sketch, from the September 27 episode, was viewed
on YouTube more than six million times within a week (as opposed to the
first sketch's five million views, itself a massive number for *SNL*). The premise of the sketch was a parody of Palin's disastrous interview with Katie Couric on CBS, in which Palin betrayed, among other things, that she did not
understand basic geography or the premises of Bush administration policy.
Although some of the sketch was hyperbolic in true *SNL* fashion, it was
largely faithful to the original transcript, even to the extent that some of
the responses were repeated verbatim. After the sketch, other major news
outlets, which had generally avoided overt criticism of the charismatic Palin,
were suddenly eager to—and, by the weight of public opinion and the viral
spread of the sketches over the internet, effectively forced to—address her
shortcomings via stories on the parody.

Commentators at ABC, CBS, NBC, CNN, Comedy Central, and Fox News
discussed the sketch, some showing it in its entirety, and some airing clips
back-to-back with corresponding segments from the original interview. In
many cases journalists used the sketch as a frame through which they could
discuss Palin's (un)suitability for the White House. By praising the Couric
interview sketch (and others involving Fey's Palin) for its verisimilitude as
well as its humor, and by discussing the extent to which the unflattering
portrayal could influence the election, mainstream news networks became
complicit in *SNL*'s critique of Palin's brand image. As a result, the sketches
essentially offered a source of anti-Palin commentary, often as short bursts

following coverage of Palin, and provided bias in a form inaccessible to "legitimate" journalists that did not follow the *O'Reilly Factor* model of infotainment.

◆ ◆ ◆

The significance of the Fey/Palin story does not only derive from the sketch itself, or even its coverage in mainstream news outlets, but also from its place in a specific cultural-industrial climate in which digital media production, distribution, and consumption have largely shifted. As Henry Jenkins (2006) argues about the significance and circulation of media texts in the contemporary mediascape, such a sketch's place in mainstream media and accessibility to the public was made possible by the convergence of the original interview with the ability of audiences to see it online, the subsequent negotiation of the text by *SNL*, audiences watching the *SNL* clip, and its continued life on news outlets, blogs, and comedy shows. The Fey/Palin sketches do not reflect a different form of political engagement on the part of the show itself; in fact it is not substantially different from other *SNL* parodies of politicians. We argue, however, that it is characteristic of the rise of what we call *post-9/11 politics*: the increased importance of negotiated media, image, and discourse through a rapid and complex interaction between politicians, media sources, texts, and audiences, wherein political action and activism are quantitatively and qualitatively different from simpler concepts of performance and consumption.[1]

What we should remember, however, is that the post-9/11 political climate may have been facilitated by these industrial and cultural shifts, but that it also indicates a new political reality that manifested in large part due to anger and fear in the United States. Corrupt industry (e.g., Halliburton and Enron), a failing economy, illegal domestic policies like warrantless wiretapping, a decreased standing in the world community, government lies that led to an unnecessary war (or two), an influx of hyperconservative judges and politicians, and Newscorp's increasingly powerful right-wing media conglomerate all contributed to this discontent. In a time of social unrest accelerated by an increasingly participatory mediascape, humor and irony can potentially organize—and disorganize—that anger and fear, as well as political discourse. Today humor, satire, interpretation, bias, entertainment, journalism, and activism blend together in increasingly active media practices. The contemporary social and media climate, in the United States at least, is largely defined by the movement towards convergence that is fundamentally changing the way in which we think about politics and everyday life (Jenkins 2006). The success of YouTube, the increasing use of Photoshop and advanced video editing programs by lay users, the rise of the blogosphere, and the omnipresence of recording devices have made "alternative" and "amateur" media as ubiquitous and politically relevant as the corporate media, and they are now far easier to place in the public sphere. The unstable relationship between mainstream and alternative media producers, distributors, and consumers is a crucial part of the increasingly fragmented, contested, and cacophonous world of post-9/11 politics, and makes it more difficult for public figures to manage their brand images, for the news industry to effectively manage information flows (i.e., through the "gatekeeping" and "agenda setting" functions of news), or for special interests to mask or hide their machinations.

Significantly, convergence culture does not just rely on something being newsworthy; instead, it relies on the intersections between power and pleasure that are the focus of cultural studies. Humor, satire, and irony are important concepts through which we can understand the post-9/11 world because their popularity in the public sphere is directly connected to their ability to impact audiences. The Sarah Palin parodies by Tina Fey warrant attention not only because they were a fascinating method through which to critique a seemingly untouchable political figure, but because the parodies reached tens of millions more viewers online than they did via the original television broadcast. The news stories generated by their popularity reached tens of millions more, and suddenly the image of a powerhouse candidate was inseparable from the image of her as a ridiculous, ignorant, cynical media construction—at least in the minds of many viewers.

This movement towards convergence is not politically choosy, however. A video on YouTube or a blog post can expose a racist comment by a senator during a campaign (e.g., the George Allen "Macaca" controversy) or a trip to a lesbian bondage nightclub sponsored by the Republican National Committee. Citizens scanning the airwaves and posting clips online can also expose similarities between two supposedly unlike politicians (e.g., *The Daily Show*'s montages comparing Bush administration and Obama administration rhetoric) or differences between a politician's contemporary rhetoric and past rhetoric, and nonprofit or clandestine Web sites like Wikileaks can reveal cover-ups like prisoner abuse in Iraq or a massacre of Afghani civilians by U.S. and NATO forces. However, while convergence media often speaks to power, it does not always speak honestly. It has also provided in some ways an ideal venue and format for so-called "astroturf" movements, and reactionary activists rely heavily on it to spread misinformation, organize protests, and in many cases air extremist messages.

On television there is also ample evidence that the shift to a convergence culture is not an unequivocally progressive one, as the rise of Glenn Beck demonstrates. Yet, as the powerful parody of Glenn Beck's incoherent rage and unhinged mannerisms in the March 18, 2010, episode of *The Daily Show* demonstrates, neither is it unequivocally reactionary. And, as the chapters in this volume suggest, it is precisely this ambivalence that marks the increasingly socially active overall landscape of humor, irony, and satire in the post-9/11 United States. In fact, the theories through which scholars explain these tools suggest that ambivalence is integral to their nature and thus nearly inescapable, even at the level of the individual text.

When we look back on the moments in media that characterize the past decade, therefore, it is not 9/11 alone that we remember, nor is it the staged moments of the Bush administration, either as a president in front of a "Mission Accomplished" banner or as a controversial political attack ad questioning a veteran's right to the medals he earned in Vietnam. It is also the moment when Jon Stewart broke the back of CNN's *Crossfire* by appearing on the show, the moment Stephen Colbert spoke at the White House Correspondents' Dinner, the moment Dave Chappelle inhabited George W. Bush in his sketch "Black Bush," and in the subsequent media viruses each of those moments engendered. What is so important about humor, irony, and satire for an understanding of post-9/11 politics, therefore, is that they show us the moments of instability, of potential change, and of pleasure that have transformed the U.S. political climate. They put on display for consideration our culture's sites of power, regimentation, and contestation—or, in other words, the very symbolic order that holds political structures in place. The annihilation of the World Trade Center towers and the enormous holes in the Pentagon and a rural Pennsylvania landscape created a space for reflection as unprecedented moments of crisis in which America might have been open to radical redefinitions of its political, social, and economic foundations. Some of that space was filled with vital comedic critique, but elsewhere humor recuperated hegemonic practices.

THE POLITICS OF HUMOR, IRONY, AND SATIRE

Humor scholars traditionally begin their analyses with a review of three dominant theories of how humor works to produce a social effect or an experience of mirth (Apte 1992; Berger 1995; Davis 1993; Martin 2007). In *incongruity theory*, humor results from the unexpected but appropriate juxtaposition of two or more frames of interpretation usually not associated with one another (e.g., a word play or an altered drawing). *Superiority theory*, by contrast, suggests that people laugh at those they find to be inferior to themselves (whether that is a person, a race, a class, or even a place or experience), and in *catharsis theory* humor comes from a momentary eruption of relief of psychological and/or social tension (e.g., laughing during a funeral or at a faux pas). These three approaches to understanding humor can also complement or lead to one another, and many forms of contemporary humor rely upon all three strategies to arouse audiences to laughter (Davis 1993, 7). In times of political instability, however, the question is not so much *how* humor works, but rather what it *accomplishes* in the social world—or, more precisely, what people accomplish through humorous performances. As Paul Lewis argues in *Cracking Up* (2006), "humor can help us cope with problems or deny them, inform or misinform, express our most loving and most hateful feelings, embrace and attack, draw us to other people who share our values or fallaciously convince us that they do when they don't" (7). Since much of humor's rhetorical power lies in its ability to delight others and move them to action (or inaction) through pleasing forms, its implications for undermining or supporting a political system should not be underestimated.

James English (1994) posits that "humor and laughter have no politics—that is to say, they have no automatic hegemonic or oppositional trajectory, no global connection with practices of either domination or subversion" (17). Humor is "never innocent," however, because it is grounded in "an assertion of group against group . . . a form of symbolic violence." Because of "the inescapable heterogeneity of society" in which multiplicity and desire lead to "the ceaseless conflict of social life," laughter functions as a way to negotiate the dangers and pitfalls of community (9). Thus, while late-night comedians may consider themselves "equal opportunity offenders"—because they are supposedly as likely to mock a Republican as a Democrat, feminist as antifeminist, or racist as antiracist—this does not in any way make their practices neutral.

Humor is thus a highly complex rhetorical, social, and political tool. Moreover, we can never be quite certain *who* is laughing, *how* they're laughing, or *why* they're laughing (if indeed they are; just because you get the joke doesn't mean you think it's funny). In an illustrative example of how this political ambivalence functions, a "humorous" cartoon that surfaced eleven weeks prior to the 2008 presidential election both spurred outrage in the U.S. and testified to a fundamental difficulty with dismissing (potentially) humorous or ironic texts as harmless. With a title that was ultimately more polysemic than its creator may have intended, "The Politics of Fear," which appeared on the cover of the July 21, 2008, issue of *The New Yorker* magazine, featured Democratic presidential candidate Barack Obama clad in a turban, robe, and sandals, "fist-bumping" his wife, Michelle, who is depicted with an Afro, combat boots, and AK-47 assault rifle thrown over her shoulder (see figure I.2). Standing in the Oval Office, the couple smiles coyly as a portrait of Osama bin Laden hangs on the wall above a fireplace, in which the American flag burns. "The Politics of Fear," according to its Canadian-born and Connecticut-based artist, Barry Blitt, was intended to illustrate "the idea that the Obamas are branded as unpatriotic [let alone as terrorists] in certain sectors is preposterous" (brackets in original, as quoted in Pitney 2008). In a country that is decidedly neither postracial nor postethnic, however, the meaning and appropriate response to Blitt's cartoon are complex. It is obvious in this case (and, we argue, in most cases) that attempts to use humor to respond to racially or politically charged imagery often result in fallout that is, in Michael Pickering and Sharon Lockyer's (2009) terms, "beyond a joke."

It isn't as if some people won't find "The Politics of Fear" funny. In fact, many people that saw Blitt's image probably did find it funny. If we consider it in terms of incongruity theory, the cartoon certainly brings together elements that supporters of Barack Obama would find silly, absurd, or hyperbolic in combination. Casting two centrists as Black Power militants or as Islamic terrorists is absurd, and it does indeed point out several different irrational assertions by those who did not support Obama (e.g., the "fist bump" between Barack and Michelle being called a "terrorist fist jab" by Fox News commentator E. D. Hill). Superiority theory could similarly cast those who don't support Obama as paranoid, racist, cynical, or fear-mongering. However, it could *also* explain how those on the political right could find the image funny. If one did *not* consider the elements to be incongruous, bringing them together could just as easily become a caricature that exposes the "truth." As catharsis, the image is also politically ambiguous. It could provide a release in which audiences feel relieved that we do live in a "postracial" society (e.g., "thank God we're past all that!"). However, other audiences could feel catharsis because the stereotypes and irrational fears they have hidden can now be openly discussed through the cover, without implicating themselves as believers.

This political ambiguity extends through a fourth theory of humor. In "ambivalence theory," humor is generated when an audience finds a text to be both attractive and repulsive; that pairing builds tension, which is

I.2 Cover image for the July 21, 2008, issue of *The New Yorker* by Barry Blitt, entitled "The Politics of Fear."

I.3 Iconic images of Che Guevara and Martin Luther King, Jr., on which Sheperd Fairey's paintings drew.

I.4 Image of Barack Obama on the cover of *Time*; edited image of Obama as the Joker; and repurposed Joker image for a protest poster.

released through laughter. As several commentators have noted, Barack Obama's appeal (and his ability to rouse incredible anger) lies in part in his own contested, multiple, and amorphous image. This image is at once a mobilization of racist rhetoric and history, as David Ehrenstein argued in his 2007 "Obama the 'Magic Negro'" article, and a construction of a sophisticated "lifestyle brand," as Naomi Klein (2010) has suggested. It is significant that "The Politics of Fear" is not too far from either right-wing or left-wing portrayals of Obama. In figure I.3, we have the famous Shepard Fairey poster derived from popular imagery of Dr. Martin Luther King, Jr., and Che Guevara (two figures who were far more progressive than Obama himself). In figure I.4, we have the infamous Obama-as-Joker image initially adapted from a *Time* magazine cover by bored college student Firas Alkhateeb and later decontextualized for use in right-wing protests.

It wasn't through humor, however, that *The New Yorker* and other commentators chose to defend the cover; instead its defenders looked to irony. Blitt told *The Huffington Post*'s Nico Pitney (2007) that he assumed "depicting the concept would show it as the fear-mongering ridiculousness that it is." Blitt's ironic intentions were insufficient to win widespread support, however, even from politically like-minded people. As a Pew Research Center study found (2008), among those who saw Blitt's cover (51 percent), 70 percent of Democrats thought it was "offensive," compared to 41 percent of Republicans. Overall reactions in the mainstream media to Blitt's cartoon were strong, but some, including Democratic strategist James Carville and journalists for *USA Today* and the *San Francisco Chronicle*, dismissed the significance of the cartoon and instructed rattled audiences to "lighten up" (Mooney 2008; "Satire" 2008; Meyer 2008). On *The Daily Show,* Jon Stewart made an explicit connection between "The Politics of Fear" cover and twelve editorial cartoons, most of which depicted the Islamic prophet Muhammad, that were published in the Danish newspaper *Jyllands-Posten* on September 30, 2005, triggering an international controversy. Addressing the Obama staff and its statement that Blitt's cartoon was "tasteless and offensive," Stewart said, "Really? You know what your response should've been? It's very easy here, let me put the statement out for you: Barack Obama is in no way upset about the cartoon that depicts him as a Muslim extremist. Because you know who gets upset about cartoons? Muslim extremists! Of which Barack Obama is not. It's just a fucking cartoon!"

Others (including graphic artist Art Spiegelman and the publisher of *The New Yorker*, David Remnick) defended the cartoon as forcing a dialogue. Steve Brodner argued in *The Nation*, for instance, that this "outrage of the day" was a false one, but it still functioned to put the "truth about Obama" on the table (as cited in vanden Heuvel 2008). Still others (including CNN's Wolf Blitzer and Carol Costello) lamented that people—other people— would miss the cover's satirical intent and that, by implication, their inability to grasp it would have political consequences. A recurring theme in such concerns was that there was a "sophisticated" audience of *New Yorker* readers who "get it" and a strangely coded audience who does not, one defined in geographic (southern or midwestern) or negative terms like "non-*New Yorker*" or "not sophisticated."

Each of these defenses is flawed: Jon Stewart's comment ignores the institutional and structural issues that made the *Jyllands-Posten* controversy so vitriolic, as well as overlooks America's long history of circulating demeaning cartoons of African Americans; Art Spiegleman, David Remnick, and Steve Brodner seem blissfully secure in their view that irony will educate by exposing a debate (as if this particular debate were not already overexposed); and the elitism inherent in the last argument is, we think, self-explanatory. Each defense overlooks or at least downplays larger relations of power, even as they rest on a similar foundation: that irony is a way to mobilize or intervene in political discourse because it relies on a multiplicity of available meanings.

This view of irony is largely in concert with dominant theories of irony in a cultural context. Fittingly, the only thing that irony theorists seem to agree on is that there is no set definition of irony, no set way to tell if something *is* in fact ironic, and no clear path to understanding its potential impact beyond the fact that irony is, by definition, ambivalent. The establishment of irony as a tool of political discourse goes all the way back to Plato's narratives of Socrates. In Socratic irony, individuals are brought to an understanding of an event through extensive questioning, in which their point of view is slowly expanded to include (and be more sympathetic to) the speaker's own. It is, therefore, grounded in the idea that individuals have different interpretations of the world, and that those interpretations are malleable (this is the basis for arguments like Brodner's).

Later discussions of irony preserve this basis, more or less. In rhetorician Wayne Booth's *A Rhetoric of Irony* (1974), he attempts to codify irony for the purposes of persuasion, but has difficulty doing so because of the slippery nature of discourse. The assumed superiority on the part of the ironist indicates that there is a certain amount of desire and pleasure inherent in the act of using irony, but it also comes with a pedagogical or community aim. Thus, texts like "The Politics of Fear" might indeed be *intended* to bring new topics to the table, inform the uninformed, or suggest that we "get over" our allegedly antiquated hang-ups (like discrimination, oppression, or exploitation) and instead embrace, for example, a postracial ideology. However, often such texts just as strongly alienate, anger, or further oppress or exploit those for whom or to whom they claim to speak.

That discursive tension, that dangerous aesthetic, is what Linda Hutcheon (1994) calls "irony's edge," in which "the 'scene' of irony involves relations of power based in relations of communication" and "unavoidably involves touchy issues such as exclusion and inclusion, intervention and evasion" (2). Perhaps more importantly, irony always "plays between meanings, in a space that is always affectively charged, that always has a critical edge" (105). There is "nothing *intrinsically* subversive about ironic skepticism," she argues, and in fact irony has often been "used to reinforce rather than to question established attitudes" (emphasis in original, 10). However, because it is often a part of "tension-filled environments" (12), irony functions to "complexify" rather than to "simplify" discourse (13). Irony is therefore a potentially useful tool by which one can open up new ways of speaking about an issue, even though the possibility of it being offensive and foreclosing discourse is always present. This foreclosure was certainly present with "The Politics of Fear," though one had to look beyond both mainstream and progressive media outlets to see such perspectives. As Anthony Asadullah Samad argues in the *Chicago Defender*, one of the nation's oldest Black newspapers:

> In the most extreme demonstration of xenophobia meets Negro-phobia, every anti-white, anti-patriotic and anti-Christian cue that could be used, was used. The message, the Obamas could be America's worst nightmare, Black radical, unpatriotic Muslims, living in the White House. The cover reminded us that America will do anything to Black people and will do anything to retain political power.... And some people think that was humorous.... I don't know many people that would laugh at having themselves portrayed as the things the nation hates the most, in a time of war, where fear of being attacked is the highest. But then, this is a country that used to laugh at lynching too—and still tries to tell lynching jokes from time to time. (2008, 14)

Samad's article draws attention to how various discursive communities evaluate the appropriateness of subjecting some issues to humorous treatment, and it complicates an assumption about what it means to "get it" that underlies both popular understandings of jokes, irony, and satire, as well as much scholarly work on satirical texts that take up issues of race, ethnicity, and/or politics.

Some of the best-known studies on satirical media use quantitative data to explore the phenomenon by which some audience members "miss" the irony of a given text (e.g., Vidmar and Rokeach 1974; LaMarre et al. 2009). Although these studies occupy an important place in the field, especially as they draw attention to the significance of selective perception and assumption bias to interpretive practices, they also run the risk of reinscribing the myth of the "correct" reading (almost without exception what we imagine to be the author's intended meaning). If we buy into the logic of there being only two alternatives—getting it or not—whereby one is correct and one (or more) is incorrect, it becomes all too easy to fixate on who "gets it" and who does not. Even cultural studies scholars, who are, in theory, well aware of textual polysemy, tend to privilege our own readings over others. Privileging our readings because we believe they are sophisticated entails running the risk of tuning out alternative readings we may not have considered, however. To dismiss any reading other than our own as "incorrect" is in many cases to shut down larger discussions, or at least to deny the fact that someone can "get" irony (or an ironic intention) without finding the text or performance funny or appropriate.

In an interesting (albeit relatively unknown) twist to "The Politics of Fear" controversy, while many white commentators worried that "unsophisticated," "rural," "non-*New Yorker*" readers would miss the cartoon's satirical intent, many African American commentators expressed substantial concern about the self-proclaimed sophisticated community of *New Yorker* contributors and readers, and, in particular, that community's ability to, in a different sense, "get it." In several African American newspapers as well as blogs devoted to issues of race and popular culture, Blitt's cartoon was not celebrated for satirizing conservative paranoia, or generating a discussion. And in a variety of media outlets, many nonwhite journalists, comedians, and artists in fact took *The New Yorker* and its liberal audience to task for being "clueless" and "arrogant" about the nature of racism and historical representation. As Thea Lim (2008), who labeled the cover "quintessential hipster racism," argued on the blog Racialicious, "At the heart of much satire and all bad satire is something snarky and holier-than-thou, the belief that when someone (allegedly) enlightened articulates the exact same thing as someone unenlightened, it's different." Although mainstream and progressive media commentators on "The Politics of Fear" cartoon often sought to distinguish themselves from other readers, we might ask how great the difference is between racism and ironic racism. Such questions warrant serious consideration and discussion. As Paul Lewis thoughtfully argues in chapter 12 of this volume, readings and judgments of humor and irony are related to the interpretive communities of which one is a member. He demonstrates the need for a heightened awareness of humor's ambivalent politics, especially as jokes, cartoons, and videos are exchanged across national, ethnic, and religious lines.

Cartoons such as "The Politics of Fear," in which discourse about a presidential election runs headlong into a maelstrom of social change, histories of opposition, racial and ethnic representation, and a polarized (and increasingly extremist) political climate, are thus indicative of the tension and stakes in post-9/11 politics. The Danish cartoons of the Prophet Muhammad and ensuing controversy resulted in more than one hundred deaths and protests of millions of people; as both the anger over *The New Yorker* cover and the *Jyllands-Posten* cartoons show, the past decade has been marked by deep conflicts over war, surveillance, abuse of power, and widespread cynicism and dishonesty among government and business interests, all of which manifest continually in a convergence culture of information, speed, and entertainment. Examining this time period through the lens of humor and irony might seem strange, or even grotesque, when compared to other scholarly works on 9/11 and its aftermath. We argue, however, that this lens in fact places post-9/11 politics in a new focus, away from assumptions of cultural determination or stasis and towards a vision of our time as one of change, internal conflict, and a burgeoning movement of opposition.

CONSTRUCTING (AND DECONSTRUCTING) "9/11" AS DISCOURSE

The earliest scholarly responses to 9/11 and post-9/11 politics (before the term was widely used) came largely from European philosophers. Their perspectives are understandably diverse, but to a large degree they share the assumption that 9/11 marks a radical shift of some sort, or that it is a "trauma" of national as well as personal proportions. This evaluation is interesting both because it might be the only claim on which these philosophers would agree, and because it mirrors popular accounts of 9/11 as a "national tragedy" on par with Pearl Harbor. As we leave aside the accuracy or political/social charge of the connection between 9/11 and trauma, which is dealt with more extensively in chapter 5, it is important that we recognize 9/11 as not necessarily a moment that changed the world, but perhaps more a moment in which changes that were already occurring manifested spectacularly.

The first coordinated scholarly response to the attacks was published by Verso for 9/11's one-year anniversary, and represented three of the most important contemporary European philosophers: Jean Baudrillard, Paul Virilio, and Slavoj Žižek. Baudrillard's *The Spirit of Terrorism* argues that the attacks were an "absolute event," brought upon the towers by the arrogance of the neo-imperial powers of globalization and late capitalism. He suggests that what distinguishes the attacks from earlier acts of terrorism is in fact their masterful mobilization of the strategies and techniques of the systems they attempted to destroy: "money and stock-market speculation, computer technology and aeronautics, spectacle and the media networks" (2002, 19). Moreover, he argues that the terrorists "won" precisely for the reasons the Bush administration claimed; the attacks questioned the "whole ideology of freedom, of free circulation, and so on, on which the Western world prided itself, and on which it drew to exert its hold over the rest of the world" (32).

Baudrillard has been roundly critiqued, most notably by Bruno Latour (2004), for his arguments being too Manichean in their logic, and by Wolin (2004) and Merrin (2004) for daring to suggest that the United States might have courted disaster with the hubris of its cultural and economic imperialism. The other two books in the series, Virilio's *Ground Zero* (2002) and Žižek's *Welcome to the Desert of the Real!* (2002), to some degree repeat Baudrillard's arguments despite the fact that the three philosophers have radically different perspectives on the world. Virilio's piece is more about his dystopic vision of contemporary social systems than 9/11 itself, although he culminates his discussion of that vision with 9/11 as, again, a demonstration of a cultural limit event—this time of "total war" in which we see the "rise of a global covert state" (82). Rather than blaming the United States per se, Virilio blames what he calls "progress" and understands as an increasingly pornographic vision of day-to-day life, filled with exploitation and horror.

Žižek, by contrast, argues that the attacks of September 11 can only be understood within the framework of simulation, as Hollywood films and the various dramas in U.S. television have already explained to us what events like this are, what they mean, and so on. This was not a new concept, of course, as many commentators on (and victims of) the bombings related their experience to movies like *Independence Day* (1996), *The Matrix* (1999), and *The Siege* (1998), and films like *Spiderman* (2002) and *Collateral Damage* (2002) were changed or delayed due to the attacks. Although, as Jamie Warner argues in chapter 4, *The Onion*'s response to the attacks includes a similar argument about accepting responsibility for the underlying causes of the attacks, in *The Onion* it was accompanied by discussions of other perspectives on the attacks. This points out the difficulty with Žižek's argument. Although he argues that the United States in some fashion simply received a sort of misdirected fantasy fulfillment in the attacks, and that the United States largely succeeded in making itself the victim of unprovoked sadism, rather than an aggressor fighting a rebellion or participant in a broader war, he fails to acknowledge that the symbolic events of 9/11 were copresent with the "real" events of 9/11, and certainly by the "real" events that followed the attacks.

This exclusive focus on the attacks and the "trauma" that "they" caused "us" was somewhat tempered as commentators had more time to think. Susan Sontag's *Regarding the Pain of Others* (2003) is expressly against the division of "us" and "them," and strongly critiques the mainstream claim of 9/11's exceptionalism (35–37). Moreover, she suggests that responses to 9/11 as both "victim" and "aggressor" are problematically reminiscent of the scopophilia that we find in responses to lynchings, torture, fistfights, pornography, and of course war (40–41). The beginning of the "shock and awe" campaign in Iraq, the censoring of flag-draped coffins returning from the war, and (as Paul Lewis [2006] argues) the photos of torture taken by U.S. military prison guards at Abu Ghraib have certainly made her argument more persuasive.

Others have directly addressed the multiplicity and fragmentation in U.S. public discourse after the attacks. Judith Butler's (2004) work *Precarious Life* connects the events surrounding 9/11 to other social issues: the misused privilege of the postindustrial world, confrontations between those who claim victimization in order to achieve political ends and those who contest those ends, and the desire to act out trauma and pain through violence and recrimination rather than through the communal interdependence of mourning and acceptance. Similarly, the interviews in *Philosophy in a Time of Terror* (conducted with Jacques Derrida and Jurgen Habermas by Giovanna Borradori [2004]) represent a shift away from an uncritical acceptance of 9/11 as traumatic, since its corresponding status as an exceptional "limit event" forecloses discussion of its politics and its political use. Instead, they suggest that we rethink life itself as sacred beyond the boundaries and concepts of "state," "nation," or ideology in order to more fully understand and critique how it is so often used in the service of hegemonic power.

Jenny Edkins's (2003) *Trauma and the Memory of Politics*, Wendy Brown's (2006) *Regulating Aversion*, and Susan Faludi's (2007) *The Terror Dream* all also seek to problematize the explicit (and implicit) connections made by neoconservative, neoliberal, and hawkish interests between the "trauma" of 9/11 and the goals and actions of the nation. Attention to post-9/11 politics rather than the events of 9/11 themselves is a hallmark of these works, especially as the war in Iraq loomed in 2003 and escalated for the next five years. Edkins argues that after 9/11 "trauma time" (the feelings of shock, pain, and grief felt by many after the attacks) "collided with the time of the state, the time of capitalism," allowing the state to "take charge" of psychological responses to the attacks

(233). In *Regulating Aversion*, Brown focuses on how the discourse of "tolerance" served to make people unable to understand or react to 9/11. She argues that the use of tolerance discourse to pacify the population allowed for crisis to be immediately co-opted into the state system of propaganda and used to, first, increase commerce, second, displace fear and grief into uncritical anger, and third, mobilize that anger into nationalism aimed at eliminating (not tolerating) those who are not tolerant of us (e.g., "hate our freedom") (103). In Faludi's *The Terror Dream*, she connects this process to a history of misogyny and the use of women to justify oppressive military or cultural policy, and like Butler and Brown encourages us to search for community outside the "virile illusion" of American power (296).

Several scholars of 9/11 take an approach similar to the authors in this volume: they examine the processes of cultural production that produced the climate of post-9/11 politics themselves. In David Simpson's *9/11: The Culture of Commemoration* (2006), he examines the "culture of commemoration" that flattened post-9/11 discourse into a series of justifications and rationalizations for all sorts of things, from war to censorship to reactionary domestic policy ("if we don't do this, the terrorists win"). Similarly, Dana Heller's edited volume *The Selling of 9/11* (2005) provides a broad look at the ways in which anxiety, fear, grief, and anger were turned to the service of capitalism, as well as how genuine political interest was displaced into consumption (both of images and of products). Common to both works is their refusal to conceive of 9/11 as an event, and their desire to instead frame 9/11 as a constructed element of discourse that connected the physical event to broader trends in domestic and geopolitics, in capitalism, and in media.

Jeffrey Jones's analysis in *Entertaining Politics* (2009) continues that process, documenting a shift in media, policy, and politics in which the three tend to not only blur, but also to create feedback and disturbances during those processes of convergence. He points to television news and satire in particular, as do several of the chapters in this volume, to suggest that news parody functions to destabilize the ideological ground of the dominant and subvert the control of information by mainstream news media. Other works, like the edited volume *Satire TV* (Gray, Jones, and Thompson 2009) foreground humor, irony, or satire as evidence of a fundamentally progressive shift towards audiences that become increasingly (self-) critical and informed as they consume satirical media. Paul Lewis's *Cracking Up* (2006), which he updates in chapter 12 of this volume, charts humor in post-9/11 politics as a binary between the utopian rhetoric of "healing" humor and the dystopian rhetoric of "killing" or sadistic humor. He convincingly argues that post-9/11 politics are often framed in terms of allowing unacceptable discourse because it is "just a joke" (e.g., the *Jyllands-Posten* cartoons of the Prophet Muhammad) or conversely in terms of laughable situations that should be taken seriously (e.g., the torture of Iraqi prisoners at Abu Ghraib prison). In *Popular Culture and the Future of Politics* (2009), Ted Gournelos argues that popular culture can often contain, mystify, and mythologize reactionary or conservative ideologies, from war to racism to homophobia. However, he also suggests that we are seeing a shift in popular culture in which digital technology allows for more expanded, sustained, and immediate explorations, critiques, and destabilizations of that same rhetoric, turning from an "opiate of the masses" to a discursive arena that can mobilize or give voice to oppositional politics (as we saw with Tina Fey's parodies of Sarah Palin). He does not, however, suggest that most media do this, or that even programs we consider to be oppositional (e.g., *South Park, The Boondocks*, or *The Daily Show*) are always so, or that (as Paul Lewis argues about humor and Linda Hutcheon argues about irony) oppositional discourse is even always progressive.

RETHINKING POST-9/11 POLITICS

A Decade of Dark Humor: How Comedy, Irony, and Satire Shaped Post-9/11 America is a volume dedicated to the multifaceted ambivalence of oppositional voices. Its authors concentrate on the ways in which specific cultural and media productions (from stand-up comedy to television to political cartoons) often function to destabilize and reinforce the status quo at the same time. This trend has accelerated in recent years, as industrial processes of media convergence, social processes of active protest, and political processes of what often seem the acts of an insane (or at least absurd) system have come into repeated conflict with one another. The election of Barack Obama, the rise of the Tea Party movement, and the battle over health care are all manifestations of a changing political climate based in media processes that have become extremely sophisticated (as well as extremely decentralized) in the past decade, and demonstrate the lasting impact not of the attacks of September 11, 2001, but of the discourse they made possible.

Part 1 of the volume, "First Responders," addresses the instability of political discourse after 9/11 and the attempts by humorists to deal with the events and jingoistic responses to them. It begins with David Gurney's overview of late-night comedy programs, which discusses the reasons why the format largely failed to address the complexity of 9/11, either at all or with humor. In the second chapter, noted humor scholar Giselinde Kuipers looks at alternative narrative forms, particularly Internet-based jokes circulated through e-mail, to explain the various ways in which people (as individuals and groups) came to terms with the attacks and ensuing hawkish rhetoric. In chapter 3 Lanita Jacobs explains how, even in the immediate aftermath of the 9/11 attacks, many African American stand-up comedians evinced an ambivalent patriotism; they were sympathetic to the victims of 9/11, but their jokes called into question the clarity of the "us vs. them" distinction that white America largely embraced after 9/11. In her discussion of *The Onion*'s brilliant response to the attacks and their immediate aftermath in chapter 4, Jamie Warner argues that irony can serve to destabilize dominant binaries and frameworks of public or media events before (and even after) the mainstream media and political parties have cemented them. By mobilizing the discourse of "legitimate" news and turning it against the rapid machine of Bush administration spin, Warner argues that *The Onion* was a valuable voice of dissent that stands as a rare success story in a time of manufactured consent.

Part 1 thus lays the groundwork for understanding competing 9/11 discourses. In revisiting the victories and failures of humorists in the weeks and months following September 11, 2001, we can better understand the ways these "first responders" challenged official framing of the events. Such a review also allows us to understand the rise of what are now known as "post-9/11 politics"—including the Iraq War, the ascendancy of aggressive media pundits, the "culture wars," the 9/11 Commission Report, and the 9/11 Truth Movement—and popular culture's ongoing attempts to not only provide catharsis but alternative counterhegemonic narratives and frameworks of understanding those politics.

In part 2, "Enter the 'War on Terror,'" we begin with Ted Gournelos, who argues that, against the grain of dominant understandings and explanations of 9/11 as a "traumatic" event, we should understand it as a violation of everyday life that was quickly co-opted into a cynical project to cement the attacks as a nationalist landmark. Through a discussion of Art Spiegelman's use of irony in *In the Shadow of No Towers* (2004), Gournelos suggests we rethink how the concept of "trauma" in post-9/11 and prewar discourse largely turned the events into an ephemeral consumer product that might best be approached through the lens of an ironic community that destabilizes the ethos and pathos of that product. In chapter 6, David Holloway uses a variety of post-9/11 texts, in particular Michael Moore's controversial documentary *Fahrenheit 9/11* (2004) and Matt Stone and Trey

Parker's puppet film *Team America: World Police* (2004), to explore the state of republicanism—commitments to citizenship, participatory democracy, and civic virtue—and the ratcheting up of the "culture wars" in popular culture in light of the war in Iraq. He charts an increasing lack of conceptual complexity in politics as such, and describes the importance of humorous political discourse to both furthering and stemming the tide of this process. Similarly, Viveca Greene examines irony as a mode of critique in chapter 7, reworking the theories of unstable and stable irony first detailed by Wayne Booth (1974), and arguing that irony has the greatest potential to transform politics when it makes its ideological commitments apparent. Comparing a *South Park* episode that aired on the eve of the war in Iraq to Stephen Colbert's appearance as the White House Correspondents' Dinner keynote in 2006, Greene contends that directed gestures of stable irony offer the more radical challenges to the power structures that have arisen in the wake of 9/11. Lastly, in chapter 8 Michael Truscello provocatively illustrates how 9/11 skeptic movements tried (and largely failed) to use humor to question the mainstream account of the events, while the movement's opponents were more successfully able to use strategies of ridicule to discredit the movements, silencing any voice outside the official narrative.

The contributors to the last section of *A Decade of Dark Humor*, "Rethinking Post-9/11 Politics," draw on the uncertainty of popular culture uses of irony, humor, and satire to provide us with alternative readings of 9/11. In chapter 9, "Laughing Doves: U.S. Antiwar Satire from Niagara to Fallujah," Aaron Winter provides a valuable historical frame for political discourse in the public sphere, and argues that satirists navigate between the "twin accusations of triviality and treason." In chapter 10 David Monje contributes to the discussion through his analysis of the leftist political cartoons of Jeff Danziger, who, like the satirists Winter examines, often challenged dominant discourses by both inhabiting and operating outside them. Gavin Benke further draws on that duality through a historical look at the humor surrounding an almost-forgotten event: the 2001 Enron scandal. Here Benke argues that early critiques of big business served not only to undermine capitalist interest, but also their champions in the Bush administration. However, he argues that the rhetoric of 9/11 and the Iraq War finally silenced such critiques, leaving them curiously out of place and empty when reborn in the very different world of 2004. Finally, our concluding chapter by Paul Lewis brings to a close (and compellingly expands) the potential extensions of humor and irony in the contemporary political climate. Lewis offers the Danish *Jyllands-Posten* Prophet Muhammad cartoons and Jeff

Dunham's "Achmed, the Dead Terrorist" as case studies to discuss: (1) what internationally powerful mass humor scandals/stories suggest about new directions for empirical humor research, and (2) the need for a new kind of approach to humor studies in the digital age.

A Decade of Dark Humor closes with a coda in the form of an afterword by noted popular culture scholar Arthur Asa Berger, who addresses the importance of humor in cultural studies and its place in pedagogy, cultural domination, and dissent. He argues, as do we, that there is no "final word" on how popular culture can challenge and reinscribe dominant ideologies and discourses, but rather can be used to foment discussion between fields about one of the most important events in our nation's history. The volume, like humor, irony, and satire themselves, seeks to open more questions than it closes, to point out more areas of incongruity than areas of clarity or consensus, and to suggest that instead of understanding 9/11 and America's reaction solely through the dominant frames of fear, anger, and sadness, we look at how those frames can be broadened, opened, fragmented, or broken through a raised eyebrow, a quirked smile, and sometimes even an uncontrollable laugh.

NOTES

1. See Baym (2005; 2007), Gournelos (2009), Jones (2009), and Achter (2008) for a discussion of this process in post-9/11 popular culture and news media.

WORKS CITED

Achter, Paul. 2008. Comedy in Unfunny Times: News Parody and Carnival After 9/11. *Critical Studies in Media Communication* 25 (3): 274–303.

Allis, Sam. 2001. Irony's Death Greatly Exaggerated: The Onion, Peeling Away Layers of Gravity, Pursues a Serious Mission of Poking Fun. *The Boston Globe*, September 29.

Apte, Mahadav L. 1993. Humor. In *Folklore, Cultural Performances, and Popular Entertainments*, edited by R. Bauman. New York: Oxford University Press.

Asadullah Samad, Anthony. 2008. Political Satire Is Part of Popular Culture. *Chicago Defender*, 13, 1.

Baudrillard, Jean. 2002. *The Spirit of Terrorism: And Requiem for the Twin Towers*. New York: W.W. Norton and Company.

Baym, Geoffrey. 2005. *The Daily Show*: Discursive Integration and the Reinvention of Political Journalism. *Political Communication* 22 (3): 259–276.

———. 2007. Representation and Politics of Play: Stephen Colbert's *Better Know a District*. *Political Communication* 24 (4): 359–376.

Beers, David. 2001. Irony is dead! Long live irony! As jingoists call for a New Sincerity, we need irony—the serious kind—more than ever. *Salon.com*, http://archive.salon.com/mwt/feature/2001/09/.25/irony_lives /.

Berger, Arthur Asa. 1995. *Blind Men and Elephants: Perspectives on Humor*. New Brunswick: Transaction Publishers.

Booth, Wayne. 1974. *A Rhetoric of Irony*. Chicago: University of Chicago Press.

Borradori, Giovanna. 2004. *Philosophy in a Time of Terror: Dialogues with Jurgen Habermas and Jacques Derrida*. Chicago: University of Chicago Press.

Boskin, Joseph. 1990. American Political Humor: Touchables and Taboos. *International Political Science Review* 11 (4): 473–482.

Brown, Wendy. 2006. *Regulating Aversion: Tolerance in the Age of Identity and Empire*. Princeton: Princeton University Press.

Butler, Judith. 2006. *Precarious Life: The Power of Mourning and Violence*. New York: Verso.

Colebrook, Claire. 2004. *Irony*. New York: Routledge.

Davis, Murray. 1993. *What's So Funny? The Comic Conception of Culture and Society*. Chicago: University of Chicago Press.

Democrats Highly Critical of New Yorker Cover, Republicans Say It Was Okay. 2008. *The Pew Research Center for the People and the Press, News Interest Index*, http://people-press.org/report/439/obama-new-yorker-cover.

Dettmar, Kevin. 2006. "Authentically Ironic": Neoconservatism and the Backlash. *Journal of the Midwest Modern Language Association* 39 (1): 134–144.

Edkins, Jenny. 2003. *Trauma and the Memory of Politics*. Cambridge: Cambridge University Press.

Ehrenstein, David. 2007. Obama the 'Magic Negro'. *latimes.com*, http://www.latimes.com/news/opinion/commentary/la-oe-ehrenstein19mar19,0,3391015.story.

English, James. 1994. *Comic Transactions: Literature, Humor and the Politics of Community in Twentieth Century Britain*. Ithaca: Cornell University Press.

Faludi, Susan. 2007. *The Terror Dream: Fear and Fantasy in Post-9/11 America*. New York: Metropolitan Books.

Fukuyama, Francis. 1989. The End of History. *National Interest* 16: 3–18.

Gournelos, Ted. 2009. *Popular Culture and the Future of Politics: Cultural Studies and the Tao of South Park*. Lanham: Lexington Books.

Gray, Jonathan, Ethan Thompson, and Jeffrey Jones, eds. 2009. *Satire TV: Comedy and Politics in a Post-Network Era*. New York: New York University Press.

Heller, Dana, ed. 2005. *The Selling of 9/11: How a National Tragedy Became a Commodity*. New York: Palgrave MacMillan.

Hibbs, Thomas. 2001. Meaning in Terror. *National Review*, October 4.

Hutcheon, Linda. 1994. *Irony's Edge: The Theory and Politics of Irony*. New York: Routledge.

Jenkins, Henry. 2006. *Convergence Culture*. New York: New York University Press.

Jones, Jeffrey. 2009. *Entertaining Politics*. Lanham: Rowman and Littlefield Publishers.

Klein, Naomi. 2010. How Corporate Branding Took Over the White House. *Alternet.org* (January 18), http://www.alternet.org/story/145218/.

LaMarre, Heather L., Kristen D. Landreville, and Michael A. Beam. 2009. The Irony of Satire. *International Journal of Press/Politics* 14 (2): 212–231.

Latour, Bruno. 2004. Why Has Critique Run Out of Steam?: From Matters of Fact to Matters of Concern. *Critical Inquiry* 30 (2): 238–39.

Lim, Thea. 2008. The Delusion of Hatred Immunity. In *Racialicious.*

Martin, Rod A. 2007. *The Psychology of Humor: An Integrative Approach.* Burlington, MA: Elsevier Academic Press.

Merrin, William. 2004. *Baudrillard and the Media: A Critical Introduction.* London: Polity.

Meyer, Tom. 2008. It's Satire, Folks . . . Lighten Up. *San Francisco Chronicle,* July 15.

Mooney, Alex. 2008. New Yorker editor defends controversial Obama cover. CNN (July 14), http://edition.cnn.com/2008/POLITICS/07/14/obama.cover/.

Pickering, Michael, and Sharon Lockyer, eds. 2005. *Beyond a Joke: The Limits of Humor.* New York: Palgrave Macmillan.

Pitney, Nico. 2008. Barry Blitt Defends His New Yorker Cover Art Of Obama. In *Huffington Post.*

Rosenblatt, Roger. 2001. The Age of Irony Comes to an End. *Time,* September 24.

Seidman, Robert. 2008. Saturday Night Live Nielsen Ratings Up Almost 50% Vs. Same Time Last Year. TVByTheNumbers.com (28 September), http://tvbythenumbers.com/2008/09/14/saturday-night-live-scores-its-highest-season-premiere-overnight-ratings-since-2001/5101.

———. 2008. Saturday Night Live Scores Its Highest-Rated Season Premiere Since 2001. TVByTheNumbers.com (14 September), http://tvbythenumbers.com/2008/09/14/saturday-night-live-scores-its-highest-season-premiere-overnight-ratings-since-2001/5101.

Simpson, David. 2006. *9/11: The Culture of Commemoration.* Chicago: University of Chicago Press.

Somaiya, Ravi. 2008. The Entire Media Have Gained from a National Obsession. *The Guardian,* November 3.

Sontag, Susan. 2004. *Regarding the Pain of Others.* New York: Picador.

vanden Heuvel, Katrina. 2008. The New Yorker Cartoon Controversy. *The Nation,* http://live.thenation.com/doc/20080721/kvh3.

Vidmar, Neil, and Milton Rokeach. 1979. Archie Bunker's Bigotry: A Study in Selective Perception and Exposure. In *All in the Family: A Critical Appraisal,* edited by Richard Adler. Santa Barbara, CA: Praeger Publishing.

Virilio, Paul. 2002. *Ground Zero.* New York: W.W. Norton and Company.

Wolin, Richard. 2004. *The Seduction of Unreason: The Intellectual Romance With Fascism from Nietzsche to Postmodernism.* Princeton, NJ: Princeton University Press.

Žižek, Slavoj. 2002. *Welcome to the Desert of the Real!: Five Essays on September 11 and Related Dates.* New York: W.W. Norton and Company.

PART ONE First Responders

CHAPTER ONE

EVERYTHING CHANGES FOREVER (TEMPORARILY)

Late-Night Television Comedy after 9/11

—David Gurney

Stand-up comedians are among the most visible practitioners of the comedic arts in contemporary American culture. Small communities have long had their own humorists to lampoon local people and topics, and in the contemporary mass mediated public sphere, successful stand-up comics do this for an audience of national and, in some cases, transnational scale. Although many critics and scholars dismiss comedians as either politically insignificant or as opportunists exploiting social idiosyncrasies for cheap laughs, many of these humorists serve at least two critical public functions: first, they comment upon and reveal potential failings or hypocrisies of American society, especially those perpetrated by individuals in positions of political and/or economic power; second, and less overtly, they function as supplemental gatekeepers and framers in the agenda-setting work of the media.[1] This work has become particularly important in post-9/11 media and politics. As traditional news outlets have in many cases failed to represent and inform, late-night comedy shows have become favored locations for political debate and announcements.[2]

By choosing to satirize particular stories and events from the already parsed field of news media, comedians play a crucial role in determining which news items become more widespread topics of conversation. Stand-up comedians are not confined to further delimiting the range of topics under public discussion though; with a playful and irreverent approach, they can also introduce alternative perspectives on a given topic. The most significant purveyors of this discursive work are late-night television hosts.

Late-night television has been an important site of topical comedy for the past fifty-plus years, but in the immediate pre- and postmillennial era the political nature of this comedy has become much more pronounced. Television broadcasted between roughly 11:30 p.m. and 1:30 a.m. (EST) is now one of the best cultural forums in which to learn the issues and events at the forefront of the collective (i.e., mainstream) American mind. David Letterman, Jay Leno, Conan O'Brien, Jon Stewart, Bill Maher, and their late-night brethren have become high-profile critical commentators, using humor to show the public that the major events and players of the day are not beyond reproach, and that, in fact, the foibles of the powerful are in dire need of the exposure and critique that a cutting joke can bring. Their near-daily responsibilities force them into necessary topicality, which makes them part of the leading edge of social commentators who contextualize news events. Their responses are thus key to understanding the ebb and flow of public sentiment and the role of humor in the immediate aftermath of the events of 9/11.

This chapter will sketch roughly the contours of the discursive formation constituted by American broadcasting's late-night talk show comedians prior to, during, and just following the 9/11 attacks. After outlining the general parameters of their comedic practices, I will set a context for consideration of their varied, though largely unified, reactions to the events and the call to approach news topics more "seriously." Finally, a meditation on the long-term (non)effects of the 9/11 attacks on late-night talk show humor will provide some insight into just how adaptable and resilient this form of mediated political comedy is. Ultimately, I argue that while late-night television comedy has become a more pluralistic space in which potentially divisive opinions are, under some conditions, allowed to enter broader public discourse, because of that possibility external forces are more primed than ever to police that space.

COMEDIANS ON TELEVISION

American comedy of the late twentieth and early twenty-first centuries has been dominated by stand-up comedians—whether on the club stage, as television hosts, or as the stars of sitcoms.

As Joanne Gilbert (2004) points out, by identifying themselves as entertainers pursuing humorous ends, stand-up comics open up a space of "play" and are given license to be pointedly critical towards society with significantly reduced risks for repercussions. In this play space, the comedian creates a tacit social contract with her/his audience that implies the stakes are not the same as in earnest discourse. Jerry Palmer describes this necessary condition for the audience as "comic insulation":

It is precisely because [comedy] is absurd, more implausible than plausible, that we "don't take it seriously," that we have the emotional certainty that all will be well immediately after. In other words, it is not a question of us feeling free to laugh at something that might otherwise be nasty because we are "emotionally insulated" from it by some mechanism that is separate from what we laugh at: it is the very mechanism of humor itself that insulates us. (1988, 56)

Such insulation means that normally taboo topics can be, and usually are, fodder for the comedian's gristmill. Although Palmer is outlining the expectation generated upon the basis of a singular comedic bit, the comedian can take advantage of these expectations and speak in ways that may be more plausible than implausible—more sensible than absurd—with the audience still retaining a degree of insulation.

For the stand-up comic, the result of building an audience's emotional insulation by making taboo topics into jokes is used to construct a measure of immunity against serious backlash. As part of this economy of comedy, the comic's own personal identity is often a starting point for humor; by using her/his persona as a target, the stand-up "seems to know no fear of humiliation and thus appears to be dangerously outside the boundaries of social control . . . he indicates to the audience that he is a psychological daredevil capable of saying things that most of them would not consider saying in public" (Marc 1997, 15). It is by emphasizing their own personal traits such as body type, gender, race, or ethnicity that stand-ups situate themselves in subjugated positions within the culture. In Gilbert's estimation, "a comic's marginality and performance context grants him or her the authority to subvert the status quo; in this way, deviance from social norms and dominant cultural traits serves as a license for social criticism" (2004, 18). Jewish comics Milton Berle and Sid Caesar and famously overweight comic Jackie Gleason are among the numerous television stars who built their early careers as stand-ups operating from such marginal positions.

Although many television comedians stay away from political subject matter, there have always been a few who use the medium to voice dissent. Through the 1950s, '60s, and '70s, the primetime variety format enjoyed significant popularity and offered a platform for many stand-up comics to ply their trade.[3] In this context, Tom and Dick Smothers were highly visible progenitors of contemporary late-night comedy's mixture of sociopolitical commentary and comedy. Through their variety program *The Smothers Brothers Comedy Hour* (1967–69), they and their guests offered slyly critical and comically coded opinions of government policies during the Vietnam War. Following many disagreements with CBS censors over material considered too politically provocative, CBS pulled the plug on the comedy duo; however, for over two years, their program gave voice to the frustrations of a segment of American counterculture that was struggling to be heard in the mainstream (Bodroghkozy 1997).

In American television's earliest days, late-night comedy programming was defined by the talk show, the most enduring and successful example being *The Tonight Show* (1954–present). Usually scheduled after nightly news broadcasts, these programs typically feature an opening monologue, with the comedian host offering a number of jokes and comic observations about the day's news and events. The emergence of the second late-night comedy format came in sketch-based programs like *Saturday Night Live* (1975–present), which continues to provide a space for stand-up comedians to achieve name recognition while parodying various television conventions. One constant point of parody has been *Saturday Night Live's* "Weekend Update" segment, which directly mimics the format of the nightly news. Like the talk show host's monologue, it offers humorous commentary on current events, but by parodically taking on the conventions of news programming it also becomes a site for critical commentary on the modes in which those events are selected and reported. In the early 1990s Bill Maher's *Politically Incorrect* blended these approaches.

BILL MAHER AND THE GENESIS OF
A HYBRID TELEVISION FORMAT

Maher began his career as a comic in the New York club scene of the late 1970s, positioning him well to benefit from the subsequent comedy-club boom of the 1980s. Maher's early routines emphasized his background as the son of an Irish Catholic father and Jewish mother, placing him within a distinct and uncommon hybrid minority group. This condition helped him gain the immunity necessary for his politically charged brand of humor.[4] Following the success of several comedy specials on HBO, its fledgling sister network, Comedy Central, gave Maher the opportunity to develop a series.[5] Struggling to draw consistent ratings, Comedy Central offered little more than syndicated reruns of programming originating on broadcast channels and was in desperate search of original content that would help define its brand (Dempsey 1994). Growing from Maher's propensity for political humor, he and his small production staff developed a hybrid program called *Politically Incorrect* that premiered in 1993.[6]

Like "Weekend Update," *Politically Incorrect* took a preexisting form of television news as its starting point, but rather than working off the standard news broadcast, it drew from (and parodied) political panel discussion programs like *The McLaughlin Group* (1982–present) and *Washington Week in Review* (1967–present), bringing an invited panel of guests to sit with Maher and discuss various political or social topics that he presented to them. However, *The McLaughlin Group* most often features guests with direct ties to the political or news communities, whereas Maher's parodic take on the format mixed typical news panelists with a wider range of guests, including fellow comedians, actors, and other celebrities.[7] The regular inclusion of comedians with established news pundits and politicians of course made the show marketable for Comedy Central, but it also served to open up the panel discussion as a play space with a level of comic immunity similar to a stand-up comic's monologue. As the title of the program suggests, the resulting discussions were often provocative, with the guests not intimately tied to the political establishment being allowed to voice more marginal viewpoints, suggestions, and questions to traditional political figures. Maher set both the tone and topics for each episode in a brief monologue, and in so doing, retained a connection to his role as a late-night comedy host and established the identity of the show as primarily entertainment rather than as news.

Politically Incorrect quickly became a flagship program for Comedy Central and was expanded from airing one night per week, to having reruns throughout the week, to finally, in its second year, airing new episodes Monday through Thursday. Near the end of its third year on the cable network, Maher struck a deal to bring the program to ABC's late-night schedule. On ABC, the program retained its basic structure, allowing Maher's panels to continue pushing the boundaries of discourse on a variety of topics, but by airing at 12:05 a.m. (EST) immediately following the news program *Nightline*, this move from cable to broadcast television shifted the demographic and institutional dynamics of the program (Stanley 1997). Though little actually changed in form, style, and tone, its bigger audience and more visible corporate relationships significantly increased the cultural, economic, and symbolic capital of the program.

Yet, audience presumptions regarding *Politically Incorrect* and other programs like the more recent *The Daily Show* (1996–present) that wed news topicality and formats with comedic intentions are fraught with contradictions. The level of immunity granted to comedians and comedy conflicts with expectations for formats that have a close, albeit mainly parodic, relationship with news programming. When exaggerated opinions safely expressed within a comedian's monologue begin to interact with more accepted, hegemonic positions in a deliberative mode, typical strategies of audience decoding are challenged. To recall Palmer's formulation, the audience may feel less insulated by comedic tonality if the plausible/implausible balance of comic discourse is weighted more towards plausible when it includes, even parodically, earnest political opinion and punditry

The inconsistency of Maher's own words expresses this tension during an interview in *Rolling Stone* two years into *Politically Incorrect*'s run on ABC. At one point, to counter a claim that the show is a model for democracy, Maher insists that "*Politically Incorrect* is proudly part of the problem and not the solution. But, God, we're just an entertainment show. I'm a comedian." Then later, in response to whether or not the show is good for America he states, "Yeah. I think if America could get back to wit, it would be a better country" (Wild 1999). The two statements highlight Maher's ambivalence over comedy's relationship to democracy, as well as demonstrate the conflicted space Maher and his ilk occupy: wanting to expand discursive bounds but still retain comic immunity, contemporary late-night comedy continually negotiates the desire to be taken seriously with the defense of "just kidding." The move to ABC put *Politically Incorrect* in even closer proximity to the serious news—especially as it followed *Nightline*—and thus the show became more closely associated with (and constrained by) the expectations associated with network news. Despite its precarious mix of comedy and news, for its first seven seasons *Politically Incorrect* was largely able to maintain its status as both a play space and political forum; however, in the wake of a major change in social climate, this balance was put into serious peril.

THE POST-9/11 FIELD

The events of 9/11 had an instantaneous impact on American culture on every level, and nowhere was the impact more immediately or publicly evident than on television. Narrowcasting had already splintered the cultural forum of precable television, making it more analogous to a library or warehouse than an active sphere of collective debate (Newcomb 2005, 110); nevertheless, "for a moment the nation returned to something very much like the old three-network system" (Spigel 2004, 257). Television's return to a more unified mediated public sphere was a significant experiential shift for the average American. As Lynn Spigel describes the televisual aftermath:

> The everydayness of television itself was suddenly disrupted by news of something completely "alien" to the usual patterns of domestic TV viewing. The nonstop commercial-free coverage, which lasted for a full week on major broadcast networks and cable news networks, contributed to a sense of estrangement from ordinary life, not simply because of the unexpected nature of the attack itself but also because television's normal routines—its everyday schedule and ritualized flow—had been disordered. (2004, 237)

This disruption of flow was nearly impossible for television viewers to avoid, and it caused many political and cultural commentators to openly question if things could go back to how they were before the attacks, especially with regard to the operations of irony and humor. News reports across the entire spectrum of broadcast and cable networks were especially harmonious, falling into lockstep as America came to grips with the tragedy. The agenda of national unity and support for the victims was pervasive and left virtually unquestioned.[8]

Comedians faced a particular challenge in this new climate. As the conditions for comedy are generally predicated on the ability of a humorist to enter a low- or no-stakes play space with an audience, the turn towards a very strictly defined, nearly jingoistic agenda of seriousness put the ability to create such conditions into jeopardy. As television programming began to return some of its nonnews shows to the lineup, there was much consternation over how comedy could possibly operate in a time of intensified seriousness and monofocus.

Among those programs making an early return to the airwaves was *Politically Incorrect*. Diverting from his usual cheeky monologue, Maher opened the show by stating, "Tonight, I've invited three of the most thoughtful people I know to help me talk about and, hopefully, make some sense of the horror of last week" (*Politically Incorrect* Transcript 9/17/2001). After brief introductions for Arianna Huffington, Dinesh D'Souza, and Dr. Alan Meenan, all recurring guests of the show, Maher explained that the fourth chair would be left vacant in memoriam of Barbara Olson, a conservative CNN commentator who died in American Airlines Flight 77, the plane that had hit the Pentagon. She had been on her way from Washington to Los

Angeles in order to appear on Maher's program scheduled for the night of September 11, 2001. Though the rest of his opening comments bore a sober tone, Maher used it to make the point that this was not a moment to shut down the critical dialogue that was the modus operandi of the show: "I do not relinquish, nor should any of you, the right to criticize, even as we support, our government" (*Politically Incorrect* Transcript 9/17/2001).

The program progressed by first broaching the topic of the culpability of religious fundamentalists, one of Maher's personal favorite targets irrespective of the attacks. Following a commercial break, Maher directed the group to talk about political correctness by echoing the sentiment of his opening remark that frank, open dialogue is a necessity at all times in a democracy. In this segment D'Souza spoke out about the term "cowards" being used to describe the hijackers who carried out the 9/11 attacks.

> D'SOUZA: Bill, there's another piece of political correctness I want to mention. And, although I think Bush has been doing a great job, one of the themes we hear constantly is that the people who did this are cowards.
>
> MAHER: Not true.
>
> D'SOUZA: Not true. Look at what they did. First of all, you have a whole bunch of guys who are willing to give their life. None of 'em backed out. All of them slammed themselves into pieces of concrete.
>
> MAHER: Exactly.
>
> D'SOUZA: These are warriors. And we have to realize that the principles of our way of life are in conflict with people in the world. And so—I mean, I'm all for understanding the sociological causes of this, but we should not blame the victim. Americans shouldn't blame themselves because other people want to bomb them.
>
> MAHER: But also, we should—we have been the cowards lobbing cruise missiles from 2,000 miles away. That's cowardly. Staying in the airplane when it hits the building, say what you want about it, it's not cowardly. You're right. (*Politically Incorrect* Transcript 9/17/2001)

These comments elicited no negative reaction from the panelists or the studio audience; in fact, the final segment turned out to be the most jovial of the program.

Initial newspaper coverage of the show couched it in terms of its reappearance along with other late-night comedy programs like *Late Show with David Letterman*, and mentioned how all the shows were taking a more serious tone.[9] Letterman had in fact dispensed with his usual monologue altogether; instead, while seated at his desk, he spoke earnestly about his uncertainty over whether he "should be doing a show" (qtd. in Carlin 2001). Following his conversation with a tearful Dan Rather, Letterman's only real joking took place with his final guest, fellow New York entertainer/talk show host Regis Philbin. There, the stakes were kept exceedingly low, with Letterman teasing Philbin about whether the events would bring Philbin's former cohost Kathie Lee Gifford back to their morning talk show. Similar to Letterman, the other late-night comedians, including Craig Kilborn, Jay Leno, and Conan O'Brien, all played it safe—serious and reflective, if not mournful—for their first episodes back.

Probing a bit further, one sees that the turn to "seriousness" in late-night comedy was more a turn to limitations on how the events of 9/11 could be discussed in popular venues. Letterman and the others, including Maher, still cracked wise about everyday, banal matters of celebrity culture (e.g., Philbin and Gifford), but any discussion of 9/11 was limited to two primary avenues of discourse. One avenue was the acknowledgment and celebration of the courageousness of the rescue workers and public officials who helped at the plane crash scenes, particularly the World Trade Center. The other was the call for viewers to recognize the commonality between themselves and their fellow Americans, and to unite to show that such attacks wouldn't shake Americans' commitments to the nation. This narrow agenda of national unity and strength was set by the constant news coverage of the preceding week, especially that of network news.[10] While Maher mostly played by these tacit rules, his exchange with D'Souza attempted to challenge the narrow framing of the 9/11 attacks. Despite such challenges being a predefined component of his public persona, the post-9/11 field had significantly shifted the ideological climate in which he was operating.

The real uproar over Maher, at least as discussed in the media, began via talk radio. Dan Patrick, a conservative talk radio host for Houston's KSEV who was later elected to the Texas State Senate, expressed his outrage over the D'Souza-Maher exchange, and in the following day's issue of *The Houston Chronicle* it was reported that "Patrick urged listeners to call KTRK [Houston's ABC affiliate] and urge the station to stop carrying the 'irresponsible' program." Patrick railed, "When you call our men in the armed forces cowards and our military policy cowardly, and when you call these hijackers 'warriors,' that should not be tolerated." Whether it was directly related to Patrick's pleading or not, parcel service FedEx acted by ordering that its ads be removed from airing during *Politically Incorrect*, citing "complaints from around the country, including Houston" (McDaniel 2001). Shortly after, it was reported that retailer Sears was making a similar move (Lazare 2001).

Maher made no reference to the comments or the unfolding situation on the September 18 episode (likely because no sponsor had pulled out by the time of taping), but in his monologue he did note that he had "received a lot of messages today about the show we did last night, most of them positive" (*Politically Incorrect* Transcript 9/18/2001). By the next night, the situation had progressed, and Maher felt he had to acknowledge it. What was particularly at issue, as evidenced in Patrick's reaction, was that many interpreted Maher's comments as criticism of military personnel. In a time where media messaging had become so narrowly defined in steadfast support for troops and rescue workers, such an interpretation threatened *Politically Incorrect*'s bottom line—the willingness of ABC's paying sponsors to align with its messages. At the end of his monologue he attempted to clarify his comment:

> In no way was I ever intending, because I never think this way, to say that the men and women who defend our nation in uniform are anything but courageous and valiant . . . my criticism was for the politicians mostly, who, fearing public opinion, have not allowed the military to do the job which they are absolutely ready, willing and able to do. And now that they can, I have no doubt they will do what they have always done and get the job done. (*Politically Incorrect* Transcript 9/19/2001)

His argument was for a more critical evaluation of the politically powerful and their methods of conducting military action, and thus for challenging the rigidity of the media's framing. Yet the homogeneity of the dominant message remained strong; several ABC affiliates pulled the program the following day as talk about its questionable content increased in volume (though notably, KTRK did not follow suit).

Thus began a series of explanations in which Maher attempted to repair his reputation and that of his show, always stopping just short of a full capitulation by asserting the importance of allowing for dissenting opinions to be heard. The stakes (for Maher and his staff at least) were made glaringly clear in Maher's comment on his September 20 program, during which he conjectured that it "truly may be one of the last times I have to talk to my audience" (*Politically Incorrect* Transcript 9/20/2001). His subsequent appearances on *The O'Reilly Factor* and *The Tonight Show* were made in hopes of fomenting support. The following week Maher reappeared on those ABC affiliates that chose to continue airing his program. Tom Smothers appeared as a panelist who both symbolically and rhetorically offered, in addition to his personal support, a historical perspective on Maher's comments: "When things get tough, there's always these people who wanna stop the very concepts of what we're about, which is free expression, and it's always in a righteous, national, sick sense of the word. And when I look at you, Bill, and what you're going through this past week, I have such compassion for you" (*Politically Incorrect* Transcript 9/24/2001). Going on to compare the situation directly to his own in the late 1960s, Smothers argued that Maher had been patriotic, not un-American, in his willingness to expand the parameters of post-9/11 media discourse.

At a time when both politicians and shocked Americans were scrambling somewhat ineffectively to direct their negative energy at a (nonexistent) finite enemy nation, any potential targets for criticism were seized upon quickly. Given the jingoistic climate and newfound power of twenty-four-hour news networks, very few mass media personalities, newscasters, comedians, or other public figures were making statements that questioned U.S. foreign policy. Even when defending Maher's comments as "downright American," an editor for *Business Week* could not help but cut him down based on *The Tonight Show* apology, stating that "[Maher] was nothing more than a little man without the courage of his convictions" (Scotti 2001). Jonah Goldberg of *National Review* expressed a similar perspective. Despite having been a guest of the program a number of times and agreeing that the comments were "not entirely wrong," Goldberg joined the chorus of those wishing the program a speedy demise "because it's inappropriate, dated and boring just like the title of the show" (2001). Even among those who thought the reasons for Maher's persecution were unjust, some commentators seemed all too happy to have something tangible to attack and deride.

Reactions to Maher's comments of September 17 were not limited to journalists. In a September 26 press conference, White House spokesman Ari Fleischer was asked if he had anything to say in response to Maher. After admitting that he had not seen the airing or read the actual transcript of Maher's comments, he nevertheless asserted that "[i]t's a terrible thing to say, and it's unfortunate. There are reminders to all Americans that they need to watch what they say, watch what they do. And this is not a time for remarks like that. There never is" (qtd. in Johnson 2001). This hyperbolically stern condemnation of something of which he had no firsthand knowledge illustrates how the actual comments had already become rather immaterial within the broader discursive field. The boundaries of acceptable discourse were tightened and vehemently policed post-9/11, and even the intimation of transgression became unacceptable. As is clear from the press secretary's "watch what they say, watch what they do" comment, Fleischer and the Bush administration saw such restrictions as universally applicable. Maher had become a symbol of the potential return to a critical comedy that might upset the narrowly established agenda of news commentators and political pundits, and posing such a threat was unacceptable for those with a public platform and indefensible for those without one.

A few public voices from across the political spectrum did attempt support, both of Maher's basic right to express an opinion and of the veracity of his statements. Independent progressive columnist Huffington, who was present on the panel on September 17, wrote a blog post defending Maher and impelling her readers to contact Sears, FedEx, and ABC to express their support for *Politically Incorrect* (2001). She also pointed out that "Dan Patrick from Houston who started this tempest in a teapot...called the show to suggest himself as a guest" in order to decry the hypocrisy of Patrick calling his listeners to boycott the program while simultaneously negotiating to have himself booked as a guest. Rush Limbaugh, a conservative talk radio host, somewhat unexpectedly supported Maher as well, stating on his program, "This was, in my mind, one of the few things Bill Maher has ever said that's correct. In a way, he was right" (qtd. in Kovacs 2001). And, without naming Maher or D'Souza directly, Susan Sontag also backed their position in a piece for the September 24 issue of *The New Yorker*. In her piece, Sontag asserts that "[i]f the word 'cowardly' is to be used, it might be more aptly applied to those who kill from beyond the range of retaliation, high in the sky, than to those willing to die themselves in order to kill others" (Sontag 2001, 32). Her comment directly echoes Maher's statement, and she received her own share of flak for it.[11]

By early October, the ABC affiliates that had dropped *Politically Incorrect* brought it back onto their schedules (Greppi 2001), but the incident had not died.[12] Maher commented in an interview that "[a]fter this whole thing, I'm not expecting to be [on ABC] after my contract runs out in 2002—if we make it that long" (qtd. in Kovacs 2001). While no immediate announcements were made, Maher's prediction was prescient; on May 14, 2002, ABC announced that it would not renew *Politically Incorrect*, opting instead to replace it with "a more traditional late-night show" hosted by comedian Jimmy Kimmel who was at that time best known as "one of the hosts of the raunchy [*The*] *Man Show*" (Carter 2002).[13] *The Toronto Star* (May 15, 2002) reported that "ABC chairman Lloyd Braun said Maher's controversial comments had nothing to do with the decision to replace him," but in talking to the *St. Petersburg Times* (May 15, 2002), Maher confirmed that he felt the decision was directly linked to the controversy. While ratings actually improved slightly following the debacle (Rutenberg 2001), Maher never regained Sears or FedEx, two of the more notable corporate sponsors for the program, which makes it seem likely that ABC would have wanted a less potentially controversial show in the time slot. The final episode aired on June 28, 2002.

Regardless of why the show was not renewed, however, Maher's comments, the ensuing controversy, and the ultimate cancellation of *Politically Incorrect* serve as a fascinating and disturbing case history of televisual comic immunity breaking down in a time of heightened sensitivity. As it had for the Smothers Brothers in the 1960s, the tacit social contract of comedians to create play spaces with their audiences, already complicated through Maher's hybridization of comedy and news formats, broke down after 9/11. Maher's efforts to broaden the agenda or challenge the rather unvarying message about the attacks and the mounting U.S. response were deemed unacceptable. Other comedians, at least when operating in the mass media, began with seriousness and then incrementally and cautiously moved back toward satirical jabs at the political establishment.[14] Though Maher's comments themselves were not "jokes," they were unquestionably spoken by Maher the comedian, and in a context that was developed to maintain discursive immunity and allow a wide array of viewpoints to be enunciated. That his ability to maintain a space of open dialogue was undercut largely by the decontextualized commentary of an isolated radio host demonstrates just how fragile comedians' discursive licenses are in the public sphere. However, shortly after the cancellation of *Politically Incorrect* and as the restrictions on discourse imposed after 9/11 began to subside, Maher found a new and quite similar platform from which to practice his brand of humorous infotainment.

LATE-NIGHT COMEDY'S FATE POST-9/11

News arrived at the end of 2002 that Maher would be reentering television (Collins 2002). Moving back to the channel that had originally given him the most freedom in a mass media platform, Maher began his HBO series *Real Time with Bill Maher* (2003–present) on July 25, 2003, just over a year after his final *Politically Incorrect* taping. Moving from a nightly airing during the week to a single episode on Fridays, his new program has retained much of the basic structure of *Politically Incorrect*, with a panel discussion at the core of the show. A significant addition has been Maher's closing segment that he calls "New Rules," in which he outlines a number of cultural phenomena that he would like to see changed by imposing "new rules" on them. Of particular interest in the segment is the "new rule" that political rhetoric should become more flexible, and that dissenting opinions must be allowed into the conversation. It seems appropriate that one so affected by a change in what was allowable discursively would try to wield the same power (albeit through comedy) against those whom he sees to be discursive aggressors. Unfettered by concerns over advertising, and directed at an audience that pays directly for his program, *Real Time* appears to be a more forgiving pulpit for Maher's style of comic subversion.

In a constantly changing mediascape, Maher's trajectory may be indicative of how the stand-up comedian wishing to maintain a politically critical edge will need to operate, and how the social contract of comedy may carry different weights depending upon the position from which s/he speaks. The program politicized the late-night television comedy arena in an innovative fashion, hybridizing comedy and news in a manner perpetuated by *The Daily Show* and *The Colbert Report*. In so doing, Maher set the tone for an increasing presence of political figures and discussion even in the antecedent late-night formats of talk shows and sketch programs. In expanding the critical potential of television comedy, he experienced the acute pressure on public voices when discursive boundaries contract in the wake of events like those of 9/11. Comedians can normally count on the immunity necessary to critique newsmakers and even challenge the news media's response to current events, but at times traumatic events and the public response to them can be used to shut the window on the play space comedians seek to create. Yet, as the continued presence of political topics and discussion on late-night television comedy programming and Maher's own soft landing at HBO illustrate, the window need not remain closed for very long.

NOTES

1. For an early take on agenda-setting, see Maxwell McCombs and Donald Shaw's influential piece (1972). For more contemporary approaches that include second-level affective agenda-setting, see McCombs's later work (McCombs et al. 1997) as well as Renita Coleman and Stephen Banning (2006).

2. Jeffrey P. Jones (2009) offers a detailed account of this recent shift in the political charge of television comedy and the part it now plays in mediated epistemologies of the political.

3. In the early 2000s, television broadcasting has recycled the variety format to some degree through the rise of reality competition programming. However, these are notably different in their almost exclusive focus on undiscovered, "amateur" performers to the exclusion of the more transmedially tested rosters that populated earlier variety programming.

4. A review of an early HBO comedy special (Passalacqua 1989) recounts jokes regarding Maher's heritage and political views. For more on Bill Maher's biography, see Gregory Cerio and John Griffiths (1995) or Maher's official Web site at www.billmaher.com.

5. At that moment, Time Warner owned HBO and shared ownership of Comedy Central, splitting it with Viacom. Between the time of series development and airing, HBO sold its interest to Viacom. Though the series still initially aired on Comedy Central, HBO Downtown Productions controlled production.

6. For a thorough account of *Politically Incorrect*'s genesis, airing, and general impact on televised political comedy, see Jeffrey P. Jones (2009).

7. The inaugural episode of *Politically Incorrect* broadcast on July 25, 1993, featured an eclectic grouping typical of the entire series run. It included two comedians, Larry Miller and Jerry Seinfeld, radio personality Robin Quivers, and political strategist Ed Rollins (Beller 1993).

8. One notable exception were the comments made by evangelist leaders Jerry Falwell and Pat Robertson on Robertson's syndicated program *The 700 Club*, where they ascribed blame for the attacks to politically progressive activists (pro-choice advocates, feminists, etc.) who were angering God with their attack on Christian moral values (Harris 2001).

9. See articles by Peter Ames Carlin (2001), Eric Deggans (2001), and Bill Keveney (2001) for examples of early coverage of the return of late-night comedy broadcasts. It is quite possible that none of these reporters even viewed the program, thus explaining why the Maher comment is not mentioned. Of course, any of them might also have heard the comment and considered it to be unworthy of mention. *The Denver Post* did note that "*Politically Incorrect* will be a delicate balancing act this week" (Ostrow 2001).

10. This alignment and uniformity of media response is well detailed in Lynn Spigel's take on the televisual aftermath of 9/11 (2004).

11. Still, just months later Sontag published *Regarding the Pain of Others* (2003), a book that paid special attention to the way images can be used to sell war and was well received.

12. As Greppi (2001) reports, the three Citadel-owned affiliates in the Midwest made it a condition of their reacceptance of Maher to have him tape apologies directed at each specific station.

13. Having failed in an attempt to hire David Letterman to replace Maher, there is more than a little irony in ABC's replacement, Kimmel, being most known for his own politically incorrect show, albeit one more focused on reembracing sexism than voicing unpopular political views.

14. It is worthy of note that on September 29, 2001, at the Friars Club Roast of Hugh Hefner, comedian Gilbert Gottfried attempted to incorporate a direct 9/11 joke, remarking that he "wanted to catch a plane but I couldn't get a direct flight because they had to stop at the Empire State Building first" (qtd. in Tatangelo 2006). That the joke was met with shocked silence and an audience member shouting "too soon" is recounted in the film *The Aristocrats*,

as Gottfried recovered by telling the extremely sexually subversive joke "The Aristocrats" for the audience.

WORKS CITED

Beller, Miles. 1993. *Politically incorrect. The Hollywood Reporter*, July 23.

Bodroghkozy, Aniko. 1997. *The Smothers Brothers comedy hour* and the youth rebellion. In *The revolution wasn't televised: Sixties television and social conflict*, eds. Lynn Spigel and Michael Curtin, 200–19. New York: Routledge.

Carlin, Peter Ames. 2001. Letterman back with some tears, a few laughs. *The Oregonian* (Portland), Living, September 18.

Carter, Bill. 2002. ABC to end *Politically Incorrect. The New York Times*, C, May 14.

Cerio, Gregory, and John Griffiths. 1995. Maher the merrier. *People*, July 24, 147–48.

Coleman, Renita, and Stephen Banning. 2006. Network TV news' affective framing of the presidential candidates: Evidence for a second-level agenda-setting effect through visual framing. *Journalism and Mass Communication Quarterly* 83: 313–28.

Collins, Scott. 2002. Maher up late for HBO talker. *The Hollywood Reporter*, November 20.

Deggans, Eric. 2001. TV networks grapple with two challenges. *St. Petersburg Times*, City & State, September 18.

Dempsey, John. 1994. Cable channel seeks a 'Beavis'-style boost: Comedy central aims for firstrun future. *Variety*, February 14, 27.

Gilbert, Joanne R. 2004. *Performing marginality: Humor, gender, and cultural critique*. Detroit: Wayne State University Press.

Goldberg, Jonah. 2001. Maher's final half hour. *National Review Online*, September 28.

Greppi, Michele. 2001. The insider. *Electronic Media*, October 8, 12.

Harris, John F. 2001. God gave U.S. 'what we deserve', Falwell says. *The Washington Post*, Style, September 14.

Huffington, Arianna. 2001. Land of the free? *Arianna Online*, September 24. http://ariannaonline.huffingtonpost.com/columns/column.php?id=153.

Jenkins, Henry. 1992. *What made pistachio nuts?: Early sound comedy and the vaudeville aesthetic*. New York: Columbia University Press.

Johnson, Peter. 2001. Public affairs officers pressed into service as TV cameramen in NYC. *USA Today*, Life, September 27.

Jones, Jeffrey P. 2009. *Entertaining politics: Satiric television and civic engagement*. 2nd ed. New York: Rowman & Littlefield.

Keveney, Bill. 2001. Late-night TV shows return, toned down. *USA Today*, Life, September 18.

Kovacs, Joe. 2001. Rush Limbaugh: Bill Maher "was right." *WorldNetDaily*, November 9. http://www.wnd.com/news/article.asp?ARTICLE_ID=25267.

Lazare, Lewis. 2001. Sears pulls *Incorrect* ads. *Chicago Sun-Times*, September 20.

Marc, David. 1997. *Comic visions: Television comedy & American culture*. 2nd ed. Oxford: Blackwell Publishers.

McCombs, Maxwell E., and Donald L. Shaw. 1972. The agenda-setting function of mass media. *Public Opinion Quarterly* 36: 176–87.

McCombs, Maxwell E., Juan P. Llamas, Esteban Lopez-Escobar, and Frederico Rey. 1997. Candidate images in Spanish elections: Second-level agenda-setting effects. *Journalism & Mass Communication Quarterly* 74: 703–16.

McDaniel, Mike. 2001. *Politically Incorrect* comes under fire for comments about terrorists. *The Houston Chronicle*, September 19.

Murray, Susan. 2005. *Hitch your antenna to the stars: Early television and broadcast stardom.* New York: Routledge.

Newcomb, Horace. 2005. Studying television: Same questions, different contexts. *Cinema Journal* 45 (1): 107–11.

Ostrow, Joanne. 2001. Entertainment can help a nation in crisis calm frazzled nerves. *The Denver Post*, F, September 18.

Palmer, Jerry. 1988. *The logic of the absurd: On film and television comedy.* London: British Film Institute.

Passalacqua, Connie. 1989. *One night stand* has its moments on HBO. *St. Petersburg Times*, April 2.

Politically Incorrect transcript 9/17/2001. 2001. http://web.archive.org/web/20010925191411 /http://abc.go.com/primetime/politicallyincorrect/transcripts/transcript_20010917.html.

Politically Incorrect transcript 9/18/2001. 2001. http://web.archive.org/web/20010925191411 /http://abc.go.com/primetime/politicallyincorrect/transcripts/transcript_20010918.html.

Politically Incorrect transcript 9/19/2001. 2001. http://web.archive.org/web/20010927183431 /http://abc.go.com/primetime/politicallyincorrect/transcripts/transcript_20010919.html.

Politically Incorrect transcript 9/20/2001. 2001. http://web.archive.org/web/20010927183431 /http://abc.go.com/primetime/politicallyincorrect/transcripts/transcript_20010920.html.

Rutenberg, Jim. 2001. Bill Maher still secure in ABC slot, at least now. *The New York Times*, C, October 8.

Scotti, Ciro. 2001. *Politically Incorrect* is downright American. *Business Week Online*, September 26. http://www.businessweek.com/bwdaily/dnflash/sep2001/nf20010926_1917 .htm.

Sontag, Susan. 2001. The talk of the town. *The New Yorker*, September 24, 32.

———. 2003. *Regarding the pain of others.* New York: Farrar, Straus and Giroux.

Spigel, Lynn. 2004. Entertainment wars: Television culture after 9/11. *American Quarterly* 56 (2): 235–70.

Stanley, T.L. 1997. Bill Maher meets the bleeper: *Politically Incorrect* tries to keep its edge in move from cable to ABC. *Mediaweek*, January 6.

Tatangelo, Wade. 2006. Gilbert Gottfried: From *aladdin* to *aristocrats*. *Bradenton Herald*, November 16. http://www.bradenton.com/mld/bradenton/entertainment/music/16013634 .htm.

Wild, David. 1999. Checking in with Bill Maher. *Rolling Stone*, April 15: 57–59.

CHAPTER TWO

"WHERE WAS KING KONG WHEN WE NEEDED HIM?"

Public Discourse, Digital Disaster Jokes,
and the Functions of Laughter after 9/11[1]

—Giselinde Kuipers

When I arrived in the United States on September 12, 2002, exactly one year
and one day after the attack on the World Trade Center, to study American
humor, many people told me that I had come too late. "September 11 was the
death of comedy," people would tell me. "After 9/11, Americans have stopped
laughing." Most Americans felt that after these events, humor and laughter
had become inappropriate. A year later, the nation's sense of humor still had
not recovered completely. Humor about 9/11, as the attacks on the World
Trade Center and the Pentagon had become known, was considered offensive by most people.

However, Americans still laughed after 9/11. They even laughed at the
events of 9/11—albeit somewhat bitterly. The events of September 11 gave
an impetus to a new genre: cut-and-paste Internet jokes that were shared
and spread around the world through e-mail, Usenet newsgroups,[2] and
Web sites. This chapter looks at the way the events of 9/11 affected American humor. It discusses the temporary moratorium on humor in the United
States, as well as the jokes that did emerge, both in the United States and
outside, in the wake of 9/11. I will discern three different ways in which these
events affected American humor: first, the suspension of humor; second,
the call for humor as a means to cope with the events of 9/11; and finally,
and most extensively, the jokes that did emerge about these events, notwith-
standing the public discourse about the inappropriateness of such humor.
The chapter will focus specifically on the new genre of Internet jokes about
these events. I will argue that these jokes cannot be understood as a means
of coping with grief and suffering. Rather, they are a comment on the serious and mournful tone of public discourse and media culture surrounding

the events of 9/11, and a way for jokesters, for a variety of reasons, to separate themselves from that obligatory response.

HUMOR AND DISASTER

The attack on the World Trade Center is the typical event that gives rise to disaster jokes: highly covered by the media, much talked about, tragic but undeniably sensational. The explosion of space shuttle *Challenger*, the Oklahoma City bombing, the tsunami of Christmas 2004, and the deaths of Princess Diana or Michael Jackson are examples of other events that became the focus of disaster jokes.[3] The first jokes about 9/11 emerged almost immediately after the attacks. Bill Ellis (2001) reports finding the earliest American jokes about the attacks on September 12, 2001. I collected the first jokes on Dutch Web sites on September 13, 2001.

The basis of humor always is some kind of humorous incongruity or "script incompatibility" (Attardo and Raskin 1991). This incongruity can be between real and unreal (absurd humor), between taboo and nontaboo (sexual humor, toilet humor, aggressive humor), or between the gruesome and the innocent, banal, or cheerful (sick humor). Although this incongruity can be exclusively linguistic, the easiest way of achieving such an incongruity is by some sort of transgression. Thus, inappropriate references to sexuality, hostility, and degradation are common ingredients of humor (Zillman 2000).

Disaster jokes are usually sick jokes, based on an incongruity between the gruesome and the innocuous. The basis mechanism of these jokes is a "humorous clash" (Kuipers 2002): in the joke, the disaster is linked in a humorous way with a topic that is felt to be incompatible with such a serious event. This incompatibility can go two ways. In some cases, the joke combines the disaster with a reference to something shocking or taboo. In these cases, the humorous clash results from confronting the disaster with "forbidden" references popular in many jokes, such as sex, religion, aggression, or ethnicity. However, in most cases, disaster jokes focus on topics rather less common in jokes: innocent or innocuous themes like advertising, children's games, or fairy tales. The effect of this mixture of an extremely serious topic with such unserious themes may cause outrage and amusement: disaster jokes, like other sick jokes, derive much of their appeal from their inappropriateness (Oring 1987). That many people do not like them only adds to their attraction.

The most common explanation holds that disaster jokes are a means of coping with unpleasant experiences. Morrow describes the jokes about the explosion of the space shuttle *Challenger* in 1986 as part of a process similar to coping with a crippling disease: "the M.S. patient passes through stages of anger, acceptance, and acceptation, the same stages that many of us who have been hurt by the *Challenger* catastrophe must pass through" (Morrow 1987, 182). Likewise, Dundes states, "The available evidence strongly suggests that sick joke cycles constitute a kind of collective mental hygienic defense mechanism that allows people to cope with the most dire of disasters" (Dundes 1987, 73).

Indeed, humor can be used to cope with trauma by distancing oneself from the unpleasant experience and building community and solidarity with others (Martin 2007). However, humor can have many different functions, and there is little evidence that disaster humor primarily functions to alleviate trauma. An obvious problem with this explanation for disaster jokes is that many people who in no way can be said to suffer personally from the disaster appreciate them. Christie Davies describes how the death of Diana, for instance, gave rise to a worldwide cycle of jokes (1999). One can wonder whether the jokers around the world really were struggling to accept her death. Similarly, it seems likely that people in the Netherlands— where I collected many jokes about 9/11—were not as shocked about these events as Americans, or New Yorkers. Even within the United States, emotional responses were quite varied.[4]

The worldwide popularity of 9/11 jokes indicates that coping might not be the prime function of these jokes. Especially for those more distant from the event, such jokes might provide very different pleasures. In the literature on disaster jokes, as often happens in the study of humor, humor is reduced to one specific psychological function that all humor is supposed to have: if humor *can* be used to cope with trauma, vent aggression, or express superiority—then all humor does so, in all circumstances, for all people. I will argue here that different types of humor have different functions, ranging from coping with trauma to expressing hostility (cf. Kuipers 2008; Lewis 2006; Martin 2007). Moreover, the same joke might have different functions for different people.

Another problem with the coping explanation is that it tries to explain the existence of the jokes without looking at the jokes themselves. Sick jokes about Teletubbies jumping off the World Trade Center (see figure 2.1) may add to people's suffering rather than relieve it. In my view, a close look at the content of the jokes is needed before one can explain their existence. A final

2.1 "Oh-Oh!" The Teletubbies in the World Trade Center.

objection to this approach is that it cannot account for historical change. Although it is hard to trace the history of jokes, disaster jokes are probably a fairly recent genre (Davies 1998, 142–49), but suffering and disaster are as old as humanity.

A different approach to the meaning of disaster jokes is the analysis of the *Challenger* jokes by Elliott Oring (1987), who suggests that the rise of these jokes is connected with the coverage of disasters in the mass media. The media attempt to prescribe audience's reactions, forcing feelings of grief and mourning upon them, openly discussing and showing what is usually considered "unspeakable" suffering. The estrangement this causes is augmented by the "sandwiching" of tragedy between commerce and entertainment in the media. Oring suggests that these jokes are a "rebellion" against this "discourse about disaster" (Oring 1987, 276). He provides several examples of jokes that clearly refer to media coverage. For instance, many jokes about the explosion of the *Challenger* contain references to television commercials.

Oring's approach seems more apt to explain the global joking about 9/11 than the coping explanation. Since the explosion of the (first) space shuttle, the impact of mass media has increased significantly. New digital media have joined the traditional media and enabled an even more rapid global circulation of texts, sounds, and images in a global media culture. September 11 was unprecedented in many ways, but it also was a media event on a grander scale than ever before; all around the world, people watched the event, in real time, creating a worldwide public discourse about 9/11. However, the effects of these images were not the same around the world. Moreover, the discourse surrounding the terrorist attacks, which provided the context for the images and the jokes, differed immensely around the world. As a result, the same images have evoked different emotions in different people—grief and shock, but also less empathic emotions: fascination, gloating, or even outright triumph. Explaining the appreciation of such disaster jokes with one specific emotion, such as coping with grief, seems unhelpful for such global genres.

AMERICAN HUMOR AFTER 9/11

After the events of September 11, 2001, American humor and comedy were suspended for some time. Late-night comedy shows went off the air, the satirical magazine *The Onion* did not appear for two weeks, and *The New Yorker* magazine appeared with a black cover and without its famous cartoons. The general sentiment was that humor was inappropriate and laughter was impossible in times of such shock and grief. When humorists resumed their work about a week after the attacks, their tone was uncharacteristically serious. Comedian David Letterman made an emotional speech expressing his doubts whether he could go on making a humorous show. The (little) humor in this speech was gentle and quite unlike Letterman's usual acerbic wit.

Watching all of this, I wasn't sure that I should be doing a television show, because for twenty years we've been in the city, making fun of everything, making fun of the city, making fun of my hair, making fun of Paul ... well ... So, to come to this circumstance that is so desperately sad, I don't trust my judgment in matters like this. There is only one requirement for any of us, and that is to be courageous, because courage, as you might know, defines all other human behavior. And I believe, because I've done a little of this myself, pretending to be courageous is just as good as the real thing.[5]

Other talk show hosts like Jay Leno, Conan O'Brien, and Jon Stewart also started with emotional, solemn speeches instead of their usual humorous monologues.

Jon Stewart, the host of the Comedy Central news show parody *The Daily Show*, was the last to resume his show. He directly addressed the (im)possibility of humor in his opening monologue.

> Good evening and welcome to *The Daily Show*. We are back. This is our first show since the tragedy in New York City . . . I'm sorry to do this to you. It's another entertainment show beginning with an overwrought speech of a shaken host. TV is nothing, if not redundant. So, I apologize for that. It's something that unfortunately, we do for ourselves so that we can drain whatever abscess is in our hearts and move onto the business of making you laugh, which we really haven't been able to do very effectively lately. Everyone's checked in already, I know we're late. I'm sure we're getting in right under the wire before the cast of *Survivor* offers their insight into what to do in these situations.
>
> They said to get back to work. There were no jobs available for a man in the fetal position under his desk crying, which I would have gladly taken. So I came back here. Tonight's show is obviously not a regular show. We looked through the vaults, we found some clips that we thought might make you smile, which is really what's necessary, I think, right about now. (Stewart 2001)

Although Stewart expressed the notion that the grief about 9/11 left no room for humor, he also addressed another theme that became dominant in American public discourse in the months after 9/11: the need for humor in dark times. The belief in the healing power of humor, which is central to American thinking about humor, was invoked often in the period after 9/11.

Several weeks after September 11, a public discussion emerged "when it will be all right to laugh again." The urgency of this question is visible, for instance, in the fact that it was Mayor Giuliani himself who gave New Yorkers permission to laugh again. On October 10, 2001, a charity event featuring many New York comedians was covered by the *Los Angeles Times* under the heading "NY Finds It Can Laugh Again." Mayor Giuliani opened the night, saying, "I'm here to give you permission to laugh. If you don't, I'll have you arrested" (quoted in Lieberman 2001). That a humor charity was organized to commemorate the events illustrates the American belief in the importance of humor in times of grief. The feeling that humor can have beneficial effects is very widespread in the United States.[6] However, similar to Oring's observation about public discourse regarding the *Challenger* explosion, the attacks themselves were off-limits to comedy. Although the meeting was intended to raise funds for the WTC disaster, most comedians did not joke about the attacks.

During my research on American humor in 2002–2003 (Kuipers 2006), many people mentioned "the first thing that made them laugh again" after September 11. Besides the speeches by Stewart and Letterman, two "humor landmarks" were mentioned many times. The first was a piece in *The Onion* of a fictitious press conference:

> "I tried to put it in the simplest possible terms for you people, so you'd get it straight, because I thought it was pretty important," said God, called Yahweh and Allah respectively in the Judaic and Muslim traditions. "I guess I figured I'd left no real room for confusion after putting it in a four-word sentence with one-syllable words, on the tablets I gave to Moses. How much more clear can I get?
>
> "But somehow, it all gets twisted around and, next thing you know, somebody's spouting off some nonsense about, 'God says I have to kill this guy, God wants me to kill that guy, it's God's will,'" God continued. "It's *not* God's will, all right? News flash: God's will equals 'Don't murder people.'... Why would you think I'd want anything else? Humans don't need religion or God as an excuse to kill each other—you've been doing that without any help from Me since you were freaking apes!" God said. "The whole point of believing in God is to have a higher standard of behavior. How obvious can you get?" (*The Onion* 2001b)

The other "humor landmark" was the "New Yorkistan" cover of *The New Yorker* of December 10, 2001: a map of New York showing different parts of the city named Bronxistan, Central Parkistan, or, after the lifestyles of its inhabitants, Al Zheimers, Perturbia, Hiphopabad, and Pashmina.

These examples show that humorous references to 9/11 and the ensuing war in Afghanistan became possible in the public sphere. However, they were of a specific sort of humor: benign, nonhostile, solidarity-building humor, stressing solidarity between New Yorkers (in *The New Yorker*) and even religions (in *The Onion*). This humor very likely served as healing humor, a coping strategy for America.

THE DIGITAL DISASTER JOKES ABOUT 9/11

American or Global: The Spread of the Jokes

Despite the public humor moratorium, people started joking about 9/11 almost immediately after the attacks (Ellis 2001). I have collected approximately 850 jokes about 9/11, bin Laden, and the war in Afghanistan on Dutch and American-based Web sites. The Dutch materials, consisting of 398 different visual jokes collected between October and November 2001, were analyzed in detail in "Media Culture and Internet Disaster Jokes" (Kuipers 2002). About 450 jokes (visual and verbal) were collected on American-based sites between October 2001 and March 2002. At the time of writing the revised version of this piece (February 2010), most visual jokes were not available on the Internet anymore. Many verbal jokes can still be found in the Usenet archives on groups.google.com.[7]

The humorous pictures on Dutch and American sites were very similar. In my estimation, some 85 percent of the visual jokes found on the Dutch sites were also present on the American sites. These jokes involved pictures and short movies. I also found a number of "kill Osama" computer games, but I am not completely sure whether they should be counted as humor. In the Netherlands, I found virtually no verbal jokes, whereas I found many on American sites. Thus, the visual jokes seem to be much more global than the verbal ones—probably because images are less dependent on language. In general, the visual jokes were as blandly global as most of the Internet: the language was English, without any clear references to their origin. It is likely that most of the images were created in the United States, as it is the largest national community on the Internet, and because Americans clearly were most concerned with 9/11, but it is hard to tell. Judging from the patriotism or the references to exclusively American brands (e.g., Target, WalMart), some were definitely made by Americans.

The American-based sites yielded more or less the same visual jokes as the Dutch sites, with two exceptions. First, in the American collection, the proportion of jokes that were patriotic or directly hostile was larger. The Dutch collection contained mostly jokes that were more like traditional sick disaster jokes. Moreover, on the Dutch sites, I found some jokes that clearly originated in the Netherlands; they were either in Dutch

2.2 Osama Bin Laden and Saddam Hussein.

2.3 "Somebody's in Big Trouble!"

2.4 "Are You Sure You Want to Delete Both Towers?"

2.5 Taliwars.

2.6 "What will happen if the Taliban wins?"

What will happen if the Taliban wins?

or referred to Dutch inside knowledge (references to Dutch advertisements or celebrities). On the whole, the technique and content of these
jokes were similar to the international ones. Other peripheral countries
had their own jokes. I encountered Swedish, Spanish, and Belgian jokes.
Thus, these jokes show the interaction between a global joke culture and
local cultures: American pictures conquer the world, and other cultures
invent their own variety for "domestic" use. This means that we cannot
really speak of American (or Dutch or European) culture when it comes
to these jokes. On the Internet, a global popular culture has emerged that
transcends national boundaries. However, this Internet culture has its
basis in American culture, and as will become clear in this article, most of
its references are also American.

Themes and Techniques

Like most popular forms, these visual disaster jokes have a limited number
of recurring themes. The main themes in these jokes center on Osama bin
Laden as the evil perpetrator (see figure 2.2) and as the enemy who has
to be crushed and degraded (see figure 2.3). Bin Laden is by far the most
prominent figure in these jokes. Another category concerns jokes about the
attacks themselves (see figure 2.4). More common than the jokes about the
WTC were jokes about the war in Afghanistan and the Taliban. Obviously,
these were made several weeks after the attacks, after the start of the war
in Afghanistan on October 7, 2001, when "it was all right to laugh again."
These jokes are often rather hostile. I also found a number of jokes about
Bush, sometimes together with other American or Western politicians such
as Cheney, Powell, or Tony Blair (see figure 2.5). Finally, there were a number
of jokes about Muslims and Islam, including a well- known series featuring
the "Islamization" of New York (see figure 2.6). On the basis of the main
humorous technique, the jokes can be divided into two broad categories:
humor based on a clash of incongruous domains, and jokes containing
more aggressive and/or degrading references.

Sick Jokes: The Humorous Clash

Most of the visual jokes were based on a "humorous clash," a clash of incongruous domains similar to verbal disaster jokes: a reference to bin Laden,
the war in Afghanistan, or the attack on the World Trade Center, combined
with a reference to something that is relatively innocent or banal. In the 9/11
joke repertoire, most of these innocent or banal references came from three
specific domains: commercials, popular culture, and computers.

Most common were jokes referring to the attacks, combined with commercials and advertisements—advertisements with bin Laden's picture pasted into it, well-known slogans ("Just do it") added to pictures of the attack on the WTC, or pastiches of the packages of goods with bin Laden's name or face on them. Also popular were references to popular culture, varying from *Sesame Street*'s Bert flying a plane into the WTC to variations on pop song titles, lyrics, and CD covers. This technique was not limited to visual jokes; sometime in October 2001, a Taliban version of "The Banana Song" started circulating on the Internet. A much smaller category consisted of jokes referring to computer culture: flight simulator games, pictures of the WTC with the Microsoft window asking, "Are you sure you want to delete both towers?" Other domains that were used featured weather forecasts, children's culture ("Talitubbies," a pun on Teletubbies and Taliban), tourism and travel ("Greetings from New Palestine"; "Bin Laden Travel: The Fastest Way to the Heart of Manhattan"). All are domains that are very much part of everyday life, very remote from the extraordinary events of September 11, and prominent in contemporary visual culture.

What these pictorial jokes do is best described as playing with genres: they combine news events with the generic conventions of the computer game, the postcard, the karaoke video, the advertisement, or the CD cover. The basic mechanism resembles verbal disaster jokes: a clash of domains, one of which is felt to be incompatible with the serious nature of a disaster. However, where the oral joke is a genre in itself, the Internet joke has no generic conventions of its own (yet); by definition, it borrows from other genres. As can be seen from the many incongruous domains used in these jokes, the new medium offers a whole new repertoire of pictorial and linguistic conventions to play with.

These humorous clash jokes are deliberately amoral. They do not contain any empathy, nor do they make any statement. There is no sign of the shock and grief that was present in the public discourse about 9/11, and the jokes do not show much respect for the victims. In addition, these jokes do not really take a stand against the villain or in favor of the hero; bin Laden is portrayed as a video game villain, but he is also shown as Superman and as travel agent, and the American government is shown as the A-team—all of which suggest a more detached look than most people could manage and felt was appropriate in the weeks after 9/11.

Oring's interpretation of these jokes as a form of rebellion seems apt here. Much of the fun probably lies in the irreverence of these jokes, in the deliberate disregard of the serious, moral, emotional, emphatically unhumorous discourse about the terrorist attacks. However, this fun may contain a comment on culture and the media. The Internet jokes in the next category are similarly irreverent and amoral, but some do contain a statement. The humor in these jokes is based on aggressive and degrading references, and not all of these references are entirely amoral, neutral, and detached.

Aggressive Jokes: Patriotism, Hostility, and Degradation

A significant number of the jokes contained elements that can be described as hostile, degrading, or patriotic. This type was more popular in the United States than in the Netherlands. These jokes have a similar collage form, and they also contain many references to popular culture. What sets these jokes apart from the earlier humorous clash jokes is their general aggressive tone.

These aggressive references vary from playful pastiches on war movies to unmistakable bellicosity. In some cases, the pictures are best understood as play with genres that contain a lot of violence, such as computer games or action movies (see figure 2.7). However, a fair number of these jokes contained an aggressive statement, such as pictures of bin Laden being hanged, gutted, raped, or beheaded (see figure 2.8). The hostility in these jokes was usually aimed at bin Laden, sometimes at Afghanistan or the Taliban, and in some cases, at the American government. Only very rarely was the aggression aimed at Muslims in general; this makes this genre stand out from oral jokes, which thrive on references to generic ethnic and religious stereotypes. A rare example of anti-Muslim sentiment can be found in figure 2.9, which shows a plane crashing on the holy site of the Muslims in Mecca.

The aggression and degradation were mostly expressed visually, rather than in words. Ample use was made of signs and symbols denoting war and aggression, again showing how strongly these jokes are embedded in visual culture. Some pictures denoted direct physical aggression, such as the picture of bin Laden's severed head eaten by an American eagle. Others contained symbols of modern warfare: mushroom clouds and fighter planes. Not all of these jokes were equally explicit; many jokes were pictures of bin Laden with the concentric circles of a shooting target.

American national symbols were recurrent themes in these jokes. These were usually visual as well—stars and stripes, the American eagle, Uncle Sam, and, more commercially, McDonald's golden arch. Many of these patriotic pictures were quite vengeful. Sometimes these were rather humorous, as in figure 2.10, which was one of the best-known of these pictures. This version has a Dutch caption, reading "Architects reveal design for new WTC." In some cases, these patriotic pictures were no less than a declaration of war:

2.7 Bin Laden man.

2.8 "Liberty."

2.9 "Don't get mad, get even."

2.10 New design for the World Trade Center.

2.11 Eagle crying.

2.12 Bin Laden and camel.

"Dear Mr. bin Laden, now that you have taken the time to get to know Boeing's fine line of commercial aircraft, we would like to get you acquainted with Boeing's other fine products." These patriotic pictures stood out from the rest because some of them were rather serious, with pictures of flags waving and eagles crying above the World Trade Center (see figure 2.11). However, I found them on pages that were clearly marked as "humor," so I assume that people seemed to feel that they fit in.

The degrading pictures, on the other hand, were clearly humorous. These degrading pictures had mainly to do with traditional shameful categories: sex, gender, feces. Several pictures showed bin Laden engaged in sex with animals, or with Bush, Saddam Hussein, or anonymous males. Homosexual themes were very prevalent in these pictures. Accusations of homosexuality are a common form of (humorous) insult and degradation among men, especially common in the military and competitive sports. Hence, the suggestion of homosexuality has clear undertones of hostility and bellicosity.

Other images showed bin Laden's photo at the bottom of a toilet, or a dog defecating on his picture. The few degrading pictures that did not refer to bin Laden himself were concerned with his mother or his birth, or concerned Afghan women ("Miss Afghanistan"), who were pictured as fat, hairy, or both. Finally, a fair number of pictures portrayed bin Laden either as an animal or congregating with animals such as pigs, monkeys, goats, and other "degrading" animals (see figure 2.12).

However, simple debasement is usually not funny in itself. A good joke has to have some kind of incongruity or clash of domains. There is a whole series of jokes, for instance, where the annihilation of Afghanistan is suggested in a humorous way: the map of the Middle East showing Afghanistan as nothing but scorched earth, or replaced by "Lake America" or "Lake Victory"; and a picture of the American flag planted on the barren landscape of the moon, with a caption "Planting the Flag in Afghanistan." Another technique is the "simile": bin Laden among pigs, bin Laden toilet paper, bin Laden diapers. In the cleverer jokes, the incongruity was enhanced by a text accompanying the degrading picture. One of the porn pictures of Bush being penetrated by bin Laden came with the text, "Make love not war" (interestingly, here is it President Bush who is portrayed as being degraded by bin Laden—a reversion of typical roles in these images).

Although oral disaster jokes, like the humorous clash jokes, may play with aggressive genres and references (as in the *Star Wars* poster; see figure 2.5), they usually are not as openly degrading as these jokes. This difference may be related to the nature of the events. Unlike other disasters, this was not an accident, but an act of violence with a clearly defined evil perpetrator. In addition, most disasters don't culminate in war; and war gives, of course, rise to aggression. In this respect, these jokes may be more like war jokes than disaster jokes. This may also suggest that they fulfill yet another function than either coping or rebellion: the venting of aggression and the creation of solidarity by targeting someone outside the group.

However, another reason for the prominence of aggressive symbolism in these visual jokes may simply be the prominence of warlike rhetoric in (American) media, and political discourse about the events. Just as disaster jokes were interpreted by Oring as a reaction to the "discourse on disaster," the bellicose jokes may be a comment on the discourse on war. Content analysis does not do complete justice to the ambiguity of humor. Depending on the context and the intention of the person creating or sending the picture, such jokes may express hostility, or a mockery of this hostility.

The technique underlying these jokes is again genre play. These jokes made use of visual symbolism well known from other genres. For degradation, they used (gay) pornographic pictures, but many other popular genres were parodied in these jokes as well, such as comics (bin Laden in Superman outfit flying into the WTC; see figure 2.7), television series (the A-Team defeating bin Laden), and movie posters ("Afghanic Park"; the *Home Alone* poster showing Bush assaulted by bin Laden). The most prominent genre was cinema: pictures of fighter planes in Afghanistan and the explosion of the WTC were transformed into movie stills by adding captions or actors. One joke nicely sums up the mood of these jokes: King Kong in his famous Empire State Building pose on the WTC, swatting planes like flies. The caption says, "Where was King Kong when we needed him?" (see figure 2.13). These jokes seem to present the events of 9/11 as an event of popular media culture—a media culture that is mostly American.

DISASTER JOKES, MEDIA CULTURE, AND PUBLIC DISCOURSE

The relationship with a predominantly American visual culture is visible in the jokes themselves; all of the Internet jokes use existing visual material. In some cases, text was added to an existing picture: a caption to a cartoon, or a headline to a news photograph. In the majority of the jokes, a picture was literally assembled from elements of other pictures.

The procedure by which these pictures are created is best described with the term collage (Giddens 1991, 26 ff.) or bricolage (Lévi-Strauss 1962). The

2.13   "Where was King Kong when we needed him?"

creators of these jokes use pictures, words, sentences, and slogans from many sources to assemble their jokes; they paste the face of one person onto the other's body, the slogan of one brand onto another picture. All of the pictures collected are in some way composed of disparate elements. Even the simplest variety, adding a phrase to an existing picture, effectively creates a new picture with a new message. Often, this procedure changes the genre: news photograph to advertisement, military promotional material to computer game. A good example of such a genre shift is a picture of bin Laden making a speech, subtitled with karaoke lyrics to the Abba song "Supertrooper" (see figure 2.14). Manipulation of the pictures provides even more opportunities for genre play than adding words; it can turn news items into commercials, war into weather forecasts, human tragedy into a comic strip, terrorism into an action movie. In these Internet jokes, the collage technique was used deliberately and self-consciously. The creators of these pictures have not tried to disguise the fact that the jokes are pasted together. On the contrary, they seem to want the collage to show.

2.14 Supertrooper.

Through this collage technique, these jokes are constantly parodying, mimicking, and recycling items from American popular culture. These jokes are strongly embedded in the visual culture of commercials, movies, television, computer games, and programs, and the various entertainments of modern popular culture. Oring shows how traditional disaster jokes often use commercials; Internet jokes use genres from all domains of popular culture. This takes us back to Oring's thesis: that the analysis of the pictures clearly shows their relation with the media discourse—news, commercials, and many other genres—in both old and new media. Even in the aggressive jokes, the aggression is often visualized with imagery from popular culture.

Why do the anonymous creators of these jokes use images and phrases from popular and commercial culture? Oring's analysis provides a good starting point here. Indeed, these pictures reflect the sandwiching of the images of terrorism and war between commercials, comedies, and games. And the discourse of the media, as well as the coverage, is as intrusive as Oring describes in the case of the *Challenger*. Not just the United States, but the whole world was drawn into a discourse of shock and fear, then grief and mourning, and finally, bellicosity and patriotism. This media discourse causes conflicting emotions in media users; they are drawn into feelings for people they do not know, and they are confronted with constant talk of things usually considered "unspeakable." These mixed emotions are complicated even more by the (slightly guilty) fascination experienced by many people in the audience. The ambivalence, alienation, and annoyance this causes may well be vented in humor.

Moreover, this discourse explicitly states that humor was inappropriate—and we have seen that doing the inappropriate is the basis of most humor. These visual jokes defy the moral discourse of the media, provide the pleasure of boundary transgression, and block feelings of involvement. In this respect, they are completely different from the healing humor that was present in the American public domain. These jokes do not build community or stress solidarity, but set the jokers apart from public discourse, and presumably, mainstream sentiments.

However, the clash and alienation caused by media presentation of disasters cannot explain the strong connection with popular culture. In my view, the reason for these references to popular culture is that the media coverage of disasters is itself like popular culture. It is "just like a movie," many people said when they saw the explosion and collapse of the WTC. As Ellis observes, "I am . . . struck by how many people found the video footage of the real Trade Center disaster strikingly similar to the special effects in popular action movies like the *Die Hard* Series" (2002, 5). This was parodied in *The Onion*—specializing in irreverent humor—in the first issue after September 11: "American Life Turns into Bad Jerry Bruckheimer Movie":

NEW YORK—In the two weeks since terrorists crashed hijacked planes into the World Trade Center and Pentagon, American life has come to resemble a bad Jerry Bruckheimer–produced action/disaster movie, shellshocked citizens reported Tuesday. "Terrorist hijackings, buildings blowing up, thousands of people dying—these are all things I'm accustomed to seeing," said Dan Monahan, 32, who witnessed the fiery destruction of the Twin Towers firsthand from the window of his second-story apartment in Park Slope, Brooklyn. "I've seen them all before—we all have—on TV and in movies. In movies like *Armageddon*, it seemed silly and escapist. But this, this doesn't have any scenes where Bruce Willis saves the planet and quips a one-liner as he blows the bad guy up." (*The Onion* 2001a)

Many people watching television on September 11 remarked how "unreal" it all seemed—yet so familiar: images of wars and exploding skyscrapers are part and parcel of popular culture. Internet jokes referring to action movies such as *Die Hard* (set in a New York skyscraper assaulted by terrorists) explicitly articulate the similarity between images from popular culture and these events. Media users have been "trained" to respond to messages and images in a specific way. Grief and tears are usually restricted to the genre of drama, explosions to the action movie, burning skyscrapers to the disaster movie. When disaster strikes, what are supposed to be "fictional" events enter into "the news."

This gives another clue to the importance of genre play in Internet jokes: disaster jokes occur when genre boundaries become fuzzy. Disaster jokes, verbal and digital, put disasters back where they are usually seen: in fiction and popular culture. This explains the prominence of movie posters, characters from children's programs, and other references to fictional genres from popular culture. It also explains the symbolism in many of the aggressive jokes; this was the visual language of pop culture aggression of comic strips, computer games, and war movies.

These disaster jokes can be interpreted as a play on reality and fictionality of events. Modern mass media constantly address people's emotions and understanding, and their skill in dealing with disparate and unrelated pieces of information at the same time. This collage effect forces the audience to constantly keep in mind the boundaries between different items and genres in the media. Most of all, it forces them to keep in mind the boundaries between fact and fiction, commerce and the stuff in between commercials. The main signaling device in dealing with this collage effect is genre.

The ability to play with something is the highest proof of one's grasp of the matter. These jokes play with many elements of media culture, but especially with genre, in a highly sophisticated way. Thus, these visual jokes are not just a comment on the discourse of disaster; they are a more general reflection on and of the structure of modern media. Never does the collage effect become as clear—the policing of genre boundaries as complicated—as in the case of disasters. Emotion, news, commerce, games, fun, popular culture, and human suffering are then more entangled then ever. Internet jokes can be interpreted as a joking attempt to put these disasters back to where they usually are, where we feel they belong, and where we want them to stay: into the fictional, pleasurable domain of (American) popular culture.

CONCLUSION

The humorous responses to 9/11 underscore a more fundamental point about humor and related nonserious forms of communications such as irony or satire: humor can never be reduced to one single function, meaning, or purpose. As I have argued here, some of the humorous responses to 9/11 were examples of "coping humor," such as the responses in the late-night comedy shows. But most disaster jokes speak to very different pleasures. They are closer to the "killing jokes" described by Paul Lewis (2006): a cruel form of humor that became increasingly popular in America in the past decades, and that Lewis relates to fundamental anxieties in American culture. In his book *Cracking Up*, Lewis shows that humor is a deeply ambiguous form of communication that can express many moods and emotions. The events of September 11, which aroused so many different emotions in people around the world, highlight the variety of moods that can be voiced through nonserious communication.

Even the same joke can have different meanings and functions for different people. This became very clear to me when I showed the "Where was King Kong" picture to people during my interviews with American about their sense of humor (see Kuipers 2006). Some people experienced this image as a pleasantly absurd reflection on 9/11. Other people appreciated it for its bluntness, as a form of sick humor. However, during my interviews, in the spring of 2003, most people were still slightly offended by the image, and not very amused—at least not in the context of a formal interview. Certainly, the majority did not feel it alleviated their horror or grief in any way. Clearly, if one single picture can arouse so many different responses, humor can never be said to have one single function (cf. Martin 2007). In itself, humor is neither a force of good, nor a force of evil.

Disaster jokes like the King Kong joke are best understood as a collective reaction to a phenomenon that is, to a large extent, experienced collectively through the media. The images of the terrorist attacks and the ensuing events confronted people around the world with conflicting emotions; they showed, from up close, the suffering of others. These images were shown in the same media that also teach people around the world to react to such images, through the ubiquitous images of fictitious suffering in the American-dominated global media culture (cf. Davies 2003). The images, as well as the comments, summoned our involvement, but to many people, this may have remained confusing, distant, unreal, and fictional. In such mediated disasters, the boundaries between news, popular culture, and fiction become blurred. The terrorist attacks of September 11, 2001, were mediated into a collective experience on a larger scale than ever before—not just America, but worldwide. To many people, this caused an even greater alienation and ambivalence than disasters closer to home. Again, for most people who saw these images, New York was not experienced in reality, but had been experienced more vividly as a place in the movies.

These disaster jokes speak to these mixed feelings of ambivalence, alienation, unrealness, and rebelliousness about the media culture and public discourse about 9/11, rather than to the emotions of shock, grief, and disbelief that people also felt after September 11. To be sure, humor can definitely help in troubled times, but mostly after the first shock has subsided, as we saw in the description of the humor moratorium in the first few weeks after 9/11. The WTC jokes, however, started at exactly the same time as the humor moratorium, when humor was felt to be most inappropriate. In addition, the completely amoral tone of these jokes does not seem very healing. The open hostility of some of these jokes also does not seem to support the notion that the main function of these 9/11 jokes is to cope with trauma.

The global spread of these jokes speaks against the coping explanation of the jokes as well; if grief were the main factor, these jokes would have been most popular in New York. Instead, I have found that many New Yorkers still are not very responsive to these jokes, and the farther away from New York people are, the more sympathetic they are. This seems to be slightly different in the case of the aggressive jokes, which resonate with hostile feelings that are more widespread in the United States than outside. Given the global spread of these jokes and the very different contexts in which these jokes are appreciated, it seems unlikely that these jokes all express one single emotion or opinion about the events of 9/11, whether it be grief or hostility. The experiences of people around the world are too different and too varied to allow them to feel the same about one event. However, what people around the world do share is their knowledge of American media culture. It is this collective knowledge, and collective experience, that is reflected in these jokes.

Disaster jokes may very well be a comment on the public discourse about disaster. However, they are also a rebellion against the official discourse about humor: that humor is inappropriate in times of disaster and that some topics are too serious to be joked about. Any such attempt to forbid humor tends to evoke it, and many disaster jokes may simply be attractive because they are so inappropriate. Besides being a reaction to official discourse about disaster and the meaning of humor, disaster jokes about the events of September 11 are a comment on the moral and emotional language of the American media culture as a whole—of which both the discourse on disaster and the humor discourse are a part. The mostly visual language of this media culture has shaped the experiences, emotions, and expectations of people around the world. It is small wonder that people around the world responded to these images with other images. And what these images show is mostly this: that the images of the attacks had spoken to their media-trained emotions, but betrayed their media-trained expectations, because in the America they knew from the movies, King Kong would have been there when we needed him.

NOTES

1. This is an updated version of a paper that was published in *The Journal of American Culture* Volume 23, Number 1, in a special issue on responses to 9/11 edited by Jane Caputi. Copyright March 2005 by John Wiley & Sons. Reprinted by permission of John Wiley & Sons via the Copyright Clearance Center.

This article was written during a research stay at the University of Pennsylvania funded by grant S50–453 from the Netherlands Organization for Scientific Research (NWO) and the Amsterdam School for Communication Research. It is reprinted I want to thank Jeroen de Kloet, Christie Davies, Jane Caputi, and the anonymous reviewers for *The Journal of American Culture* for their comments on the original version, and Viveca Greene and Ted Gournelos for their kind, and flattering, request to reprint it.

2. Usenet newsgroups are a now almost obsolete application of the Internet where people post public messages. The archives are still available on groups.google.com.

3. For discussions of other sick jokes cycles, see Davies (1999, 2003); Dundes (1987); Goodwin (2001); Morrow (1987); and Oring (1987).

4. Discussions of the variations in American responses to 9/11 can be found in Huddy, Khatib, and Capelos (2002); Pyszczynski, Solomon, and Greenberg (2003); and Schildkraut (2002).

5. Cited in the "crooked timber" Web forum: http://www.crookedtimber.org/archives/#00##0492.html (consulted January 13, 2004, currently unavailable).

6. Influential examples of American proponents of healing humor are Norman Cousins (1991); Allen Klein (1989); and Paul McGhee (1996).

7. Images were originally retrieved from two Dutch sites: http://www.members. rott .chello.nl/maalst1/ (accessed November 19, 2001) and http:// www.home.student.uva.nl/ thomas.roes/wtc/index.html (accessed November 4, 2001). Neither site is currently available. Most of those jokes, and many others, I later found on two U.S.–based sites such as Daniel Kurtzman's political humor site, http://politicalhumor.about.com/ and http://www.lifeisajoke .com. A large number of verbal 9/11 jokes are available in the archives of Usenet newsgroups such as rec.humor.funny and alt.tasteless.jokes, which can be accessed through http://groups .google.com. A good scholarly overview of the entire cycle can be found in Ellis (2003). Most visual 9/11 jokes cannot be found on the Internet anymore. I would be happy to share my extensive collection with anyone interested.

WORKS CITED

Attardo, Salvatore, and Victor Raskin. 1991. "Script Theory Revis(it)ed: Joke Similarity and
    Joke Representation Model." *HUMOR: International Journal of Humor Studies* 4: 293–347.
Cousins, Norman. 1991. *Anatomy of an Illness as Perceived by the Patient.* New York: Bantam.

Davies, Christie. 1998. *Jokes and Their Relation to Society*. Berlin/New York: Mouton de Gruyter.

———. 1999. "Jokes about the Death of Diana, Princess of Wales." In *The Mourning for Diana*, ed. Tony Walter, 253–268. Oxford: Berg.

———. 2003. "Jokes That Follow Mass-Mediated Disasters in a Global Electronic Age." In *Of Corpse: Death and Humor in Folklore and Popular Culture*, ed. Peter Narváez, 15–34. Logan: Utah State UP.

Dundes, Alan. 1987. "At Ease, Disease—AIDS Jokes as Sick Humor." *American Behavioural Scientist* 30.3: 72–81.

Ellis, Bill. 2001. "A Model for Collecting and Interpreting World Trade Center Disaster Jokes." *New Directions in Folklore* 5. http://www.temple.edu/english/isllc/newfolk/journal_archive .html (last consulted February 16, 2010).

———. 2002. "Making a Big Apple Crumble: The Role of Humor in Constructing a Global Response to Disaster." *New Directions in Folklore* 5. http://www.temple.edu/english/isllc /newfolk/journal_archive.html (last consulted February 10, 2010).

Giddens, Anthony. 1991. *Modernity and Self-Identity: Self and Society in the Late Modern Age*. Cambridge: Polity.

Goodwin, Joseph. 2001. "A Supplemental Update to 'Unprintable Reactions to All the News That's Fit to Print: Topical Humor and the Media.'" *New Directions in Folklore* 5. http:// www.temple.edu/english/isllc/newfolk/journal_archive.html (last consulted February 16, 2010).

Huddy, Leonie, Nadia Khatib, and Theresa Capelos. 2002. "Reactions to the Terrorist Attacks of September 11, 2001 [in the United States]." *Public Opinion Quarterly* 66.3: 18–51.

Klein, Allen. 1989. *The Healing Power of Humor: Techniques for Getting Though Loss, Setbacks, Upsets, Disappointments, Difficulties, Trials, Tribulations, and All That*. New York: J. P. Tarcher.

Kuipers, Giselinde. 2002. "Media Culture and Internet Disaster Jokes: Bin Laden and the Attack on the World Trade Center." *European Journal of Cultural Studies* 5: 451–71.

———. 2006. *Good Humor, Bad Taste: A Sociology of the Joke*. Berlin/New York: Mouton de Gruyter.

———. 2008. "The Sociology of Humor." In *The Primer of Humor Research*, V. Raskin, ed., 365–402. New York/Berlin: Mouton de Gruyter.

Lévi-Strauss, Claude. 1962. La pensée sauvage. Paris: Plon.

Lewis, Paul. 2006. *Cracking Up: American Humor in a Time of Conflict*. Chicago: University of Chicago Press.

Lieberman, Paul. 2001. "N.Y. Finds It Can Laugh Again: Mayor Giuliani Kicks Off a Comedy Fund-Raiser at Carnegie Hall Featuring Jerry Seinfeld, Bill Cosby and Other Stars." *Los Angeles Times*, October 9, 2001: A19.

Martin, Rod. 2007. *The Psychology of Humor: An Integrative Approach*. Burlington: Elsevier.

McGhee, Paul E. 1996. *Health Healing and Amuse System: Humor as Survival Training*. Dubuque: Kendall/Hunt.

Morrow, P. 1987. "Those Sick Challenger Jokes." *Journal of Popular Culture* 20.4: 175–84.

Oring, Elliott. 1987. "Jokes and the Discourse on Disaster—The Challenger Shuttle Explosion and Its Joke Cycle." *Journal of American Folklore* 100: 276–86.

Pyszczynski, Tom, Sheldon Solomon, and Jeff Greenberg. 2003. *In the Wake of 9/11: The Psychology of Terror*. Washington: American Psychological Association.

Schildkraut, Deborah. 2002. "The More Things Change . . . American Identity and Mass and Elite Responses to 9/11." *Political Psychology* 23: 511–35.

Stewart, Jon. 2001. "September 11: A Reaction." Comedy Central. 2001. http://www .comedycentral.com/tvshows/thedailyshowwithjonstewart/dailyshowsept11.html (consulted January 13, 2004, not available anymore).

The Onion. 2001a. "American Life Turns into Bad Jerry Bruckheimer Movie." *The Onion.* September 26, 2001. http://www.theonion.com/ onion3734 (last consulted January 5, 2004, not available anymore).

The Onion. 2001b. "God Angrily Clarifies 'Don't Kill' Rule." *The Onion.* September 26, 2001. http://www.theonion.com/onion3734/god_ clarifies_dont_kill.html (last consulted January 5, 2004, not available anymore).

Zillman, Dolf. 2000. "Humor and Comedy." In *Media Entertainment: The Psychology of Its Appeal,* ed. Dolf Zillman and Peter Vorderer, 37–58. Mahwah: Erlbaum.

CHAPTER THREE

"THE ARAB IS THE NEW NIGGER"

African American Comics Confront the Irony & Tragedy of 9/11[1]

—Lanita Jacobs

> "Black people, we have been delivered. Finally, we got
> a new nigger. The Middle Easterner is the new nigger."
> —Comedian Ian Edwards

> *"Finally."*
> —(African American audience member)

Undeniably, the events of September 11 stunned and momentarily silenced many American comics, including some of the nation's most popular humorists. As Jay Leno and David Letterman expressed their personal grief onscreen, Los Angeles–based African American comics and their largely Black and Brown audiences had somehow found the will to laugh. *How did they find humor in the wake of such wide-scale tragedy and loss?*

These questions consumed me in the weeks following the terrorist attacks, transforming a long-held casual interest in Black stand-up comedy into an impassioned preoccupation. In October 2001, I immersed myself in urban comedy shows and competitions in and beyond the Los Angeles area. I also spoke with comedians, club owners, promoters, and club-goers to gain deeper insights into 9/11-related humor and audience laughter (or silence) in response. In time, I amassed a wealth of jokes highlighting such topics as the war on terrorism, patriotism, racial profiling, and President Bush.

Significantly, many of these jokes belie popular claims that America has become more unified and its citizens more patriotic as a result of the national tragedy. While certainly sympathetic to the victims of the 9/11 attacks, including one of their own (comic David Williams, a.k.a "Dogface"), many comics maintained an unabashedly critical stance toward American foreign policy, presidential rhetoric, and frenzied flag-waving. Their jokes evoke an ambivalent patriotism—indeed, a pervasive Du Boisian "double consciousness" still felt by many African Americans. In merging observations of everyday culture with the political, these jokes offer important, racially nuanced perspectives on what it means to be an American in the aftermath of the terrorist attacks.

RACE AND 9/11 JOKES

Race proved to be a prevalent theme in many jokes about September 11. Shang Forbes, a comic and poet, vehemently opposed President Bush's post-9/11 war rhetoric and what he viewed as the nation's heightened and reactionary patriotism. In a typical rant, he asked a Hollywood Improv crowd, "Why were there no flags being displayed before 9/11? Where was the patriotism? . . . Look at the flag—*it was made in China!*" He ended his set by alluding to the then pending police brutality case in Inglewood, California, involving Donovan Jackson: "They [critics] always say [stereotypic southern accent], 'Don't make fun of the flag you fucking . . . nigger boy. It's America!' Well [then] stop slapping [Black] teenage heads against the hood of motherfucking police cars!" Other comics voiced similar opinions, while also providing pseudopatriotic rejoinders. "Earthquake," a particularly gifted comic, mused, "Many people wonder why I'm not tripping after the terrorist attacks in New York and D.C. I'm a niggah—I've been dealing with [White] terrorists all my life! *Still*, I'm glad the White man came over to Africa and got *me!*" The tenor of these and other jokes, and audience reactions to them, reveal how race continues to qualify the experiences of African Americans in the United States. Race proved to be a pervasive undercurrent in other jokes as well, including those that cynically hailed the arrival of a "new nigger."

THE ARAB AS THE NEW NIGGER

The Arab or Middle Easterner as the "new nigger" theme echoed like a riff in many urban comedy rooms. Comic/actor Don "D. C." Curry remarked at the Ha Ha Café, "It's a good time to be Black. If you ain't got no towel wrapped around your head, your ass is in the game!" Glenn B. speculated that "good things come out of bad things," since racists now deflect their hatred from Blacks to people of Middle Eastern descent. At the Comedy Store, he reported meeting a skinhead in the post office who sought to reassure him by saying, "We don't hate you. We hate the Arabs." Similarly, "A. C." acknowledged that, while the national tragedy was "messed up," it had fortuitous consequences as well. He told a crowd at Mixed Nuts, "I haven't been a nigger for a month! Everyone's like, 'Hey, brother!'"

Comics who celebrated waning antagonism toward African Americans also alluded to more recent embittered histories between Blacks and newly (dis)favored groups. Tony Rock evoked contentious relations between African American passengers and Middle Eastern cab drivers in New York City when he quipped, "It's a good time to be Black. Afghanis are the new niggers. Cab drivers pick me up and let *me* drive!" Similarly, New York native Frantz Cassius invoked a history of conflict between Blacks and the New York Police Department when he joked, "There's one good thing that came from the terrorist attacks. For a good while, the police left Black people alone. [Recently] the police stopped me. I had some weed in my hand and some cocaine in the trunk. They asked me if I'd seen anything out of the ordinary. I told them [puffs an imaginary blunt], 'I just saw two Arabs walking down the street, and they looked suspicious. You may want to go check 'em out.'"

In this exaggerated plot, Cassius turns the notorious DWB, or "Driving While Black," phenomenon on its head—in the face of a perceived Arab threat, driving over the speed limit while smoking marijuana becomes an excusable offense after September 11. His joke also acts as a veiled critique by underscoring African Americans' newfound "rights" consequent to Arab Americans' waning civil liberties. But the story behind the joke may be more compelling than the punch line. In an interview, Cassius revealed that his joke was inspired by an actual interaction with a New York police officer just days after the terrorist attacks. Accustomed to aggressive police action during routine traffic stops, Cassius was surprised when the officer simply admonished him to stop speeding and released him without issuing a ticket. Cassius explained the irony of his good fortune, noting, "Now, the focus is on something bigger than the Black man—someone who's *really* after White people, and not some imaginary enemy."

In a similar play on the "Arab as new nigger" premise, comic/actor Ralph Harris alleged that first-class passengers now gladly welcome rap artists into their exclusive cabin space. Using hyperstandard diction, he impersonated a passenger issuing a rather unorthodox request: "Excuse me, stewardess? That gentleman who walked by with the gold chains and baggy jeans—do you think he could have a seat next to me? You can just take it off my tab." This joke sardonically expounds on the ways racist stereotypes about Blacks have evolved since the terrorist attacks. In Harris's world, the harrowing events of 9/11 did not necessarily absolve Black men of the stigma of being dangerous so much as it temporarily recast them as potential allies in America's new war on terrorism.

Comic Courtney Gee expands the "Arab as new nigger" premise by framing the September 11 tragedy as a great equalizer. At the Ha Ha Café, he joked that everyone, including the most privileged and unquestionably American (i.e., White men), are subject to heightened scrutiny under new airport security laws: "[Now] White men . . . get to be suspects too. They get to see what it feels like." Gee then performed his interpretation of an angry White male passenger at an airport security checkpoint: "What?! Take off my shoes? What the fuck for?! I don't own a 7-Eleven or have a fucking dot on my head!" Here, Gee exploits multiple stereotypes to highlight the seeming dissolution of racial profiling in the wake of 9/11. Collectively, he and other comics depict a new day wherein non–African Americans—e.g., Whites, Pakistanis, Indians, and particularly Arab Americans—are vulnerable to indiscriminate searches and police harassment. Read as political commentaries, these and other jokes also suggest that, despite such generalized vulnerability, not all Americans experience equal footing with regard to their civil liberties.

RACIAL DIFFERENCE AND 9/11

Racial difference was another prevalent theme in jokes about September 11. In countless Black–White–other comparisons, comics coaxed humor out of stereotypes and defined Blackness and Whiteness in oppositional and highly generalized terms. Often, comics portrayed "ghetto" sensibilities, cunning, and urban combat skills as authenticating descriptors of Black culture and identity. Comics also qualified their frequent use of the slur "nigger," distinguishing it from their colloquial use of the term "niggah" as an in-group and affinity marker. For example, comic/actor Chris Spencer echoed the general consensus when he discouraged Whites from using the word in any context. Spencer added, "[Plus] when we [African Americans] say it, it's 'nigg*ah*' not 'nigg*er*.' Avoid the '-er' [suffix] if you want to stay out of the 'E.R.' [emergency room]." In 9/11-related humor set within the trope of racial difference, comics often used "niggah" to reference African Americans as a whole and valorize streetwise—essentially "real"—Black folks who would sneer at the threat of a box cutter.

For example, Earthquake repeatedly roused diverse audiences to hysterics when he mused that Osama bin Laden must be highly persuasive to have convinced the terrorists to sacrifice their lives. At the Comedy Store, he joked: "'Sama bin Laden is a hell of a motivator. He [lives] in caves while others blow shit up. Ain't no niggahs gon' go along with that. If I worked for him it would be a whole 'nother story. He'd be like, 'Go do that [stage a suicide bombing]!' I'd be like, 'Where you gon' be?!' Hell, I know a pimp when I see one!"

Other comics invoked racial difference to vouch for the valor of African Americans in the face of terrorist threats. For example, many comics expressed a common suspicion that if Blacks had been on the doomed flights, or if the terrorists had merely opted for Southwest Airlines (a low-cost airline), the terrorist attacks might not have happened. Michael Colyar speculated, "There must not have been a lot of brothers in first class the day that the planes were hijacked. I'm sorry, but you can't hijack no niggahs with a knife!" Comic "Scruncho" bluntly proffered: "God bless all those who died on September 11, but I gotta be real. If it had been at least three *real* niggahs on the plane, It-Wouldn't-Be-No-War-Right-Now!" Scruncho has performed this routine at multiple venues, garnering thunderous applause nearly every time.

Other jokes offered surprising, if not controversial, elaborations on this theme. While hosting the Comedy Store's legendary Phat Tuesday show, comedian Geoff Brown jested, "God rest the souls of those who died. But them must've been some passive Whites on the plane. What happened to those nigger-killing, Indian-land-stealing White folks? Where's the Aryan when you need him? . . . We needed some big niggahs to guard the plane. They would've made the terrorists change their minds." Brown fearlessly flirts with the forbidden by daring to question how the victims aboard the two fateful flights allowed themselves to be overtaken. His provocative query further pushes the envelope by highlighting America's complicity in a contentious history of slavery and conquest; arguably, this tactical maneuver of revisiting tragic histories within the United States complicates an "America-as-victim-*only*" response to 9/11.

AUDIENCE RESPONSES TO 9/11 HUMOR

However, not all jokes about September 11 managed to provoke laughter. One amateur comedienne met silence before a predominantly Black crowd when she jested that the tendency of African Americans to run first and ask questions later had contributed to the death of Blacks on the upper floors of the World Trade Center. Additionally, some jokes, which were otherwise successful in predominantly Black rooms, generated controversy when performed in wider venues. This was especially true of 9/11 humor marking a racial divide in the ethnic group(s) targeted by terrorists and the perceived impact of September 11 on Black versus White Americans. For example, comic and actress Thea Vidale provoked a surge of protest letters after an appearance on National Public Radio's *Tavis Smiley Show* when she quipped:

> White people, I love you dearly. I do. But Osama bin Laden—he ain't mad at us, he mad at y'all. Y'all got a problem . . . I don't know what you did to him, made him mad, but y'all got a problem . . . America was shocked 'cause it's not so much that we got bombed; it's *where* they bombed us. They bombed us at the World Trade Center. That's the World Bank in this country! You know 'cause if it had . . . been bombed in Compton . . . or Harlem, they would've been saying [upbeat reporter voice], '. . . Osama bin Laden has bombed Compton, California, and Harlem, New York. *Next*, Jim with sports.'

Many listeners found her comments to be distasteful, divisive, and anti-White, compelling Smiley to devote a subsequent segment to respond to listener comments.

The controversy surrounding Vidale's joke is itself a commentary about the way audiences police the boundaries of tragic humor. Understood against the broader spectrum of Black stand-up comedy after 9/11, it also raises questions about how race can constrain or facilitate laughter at such comedy. It's worth mentioning, for example, that the sentiments expressed by Vidale were not only echoed by other comics, but were also overwhelmingly endorsed by predominantly Black and Brown audiences throughout Los Angeles.

For example, comic/actor Arie Spears presented what Black audiences found to be a plausible and humorous theory about why poor Black communities were not targeted in the terrorist attacks. He quipped, "A lot of people don't know it, but the safest place to be right now is the ghetto. Osama and them not worried about niggahs. Can you imagine al Qaeda trying to convince bin Laden to bomb Black people. They'd be like, 'Osama, we have found a target!' Osama would be like [highly agitated], 'What is this Compton?! Look, I don't have time for this . . .'" In Spears's comedic reality, the reason why Blacks are spared from greater casualties is not because of their cunning or combat skills. Rather, the fate of Compton and other poor minority enclaves is predicated on the their marginal status in the United States, and hence, their negligible currency as American targets in the terrorists' imaginations. Spears's and Vidale's jokes are similar in this regard. Spears's impersonation of a weary bin Laden exposes his devaluation of the ghetto as a strategic American target, much like Vidale's parody of an impassive American news reporter reveals the media's disregard of a potential terrorist strike (and, presumably, other tragedies) in the ghetto. Both underscore the relative status of African Americans within and beyond America.

Many comics also emphasized the disproportionate impact that September 11 seemed to have on White versus Black Americans. Several comics coyly asked Black audiences to indicate, by show of hands, their lingering trauma after the terrorist attacks. Audiences responded, in line, with more chuckles than raised hands. Chris Spencer, host of the Laugh Factory's Chocolate Sunday show, also observed, "It's a damn war going on and Black folks are the only ones going out [and] having a good time!" Comic Loni Love similarly joked that she was angry with the terrorists for interrupting her hair appointment, but even more perturbed with White Americans for not preventing the September 11 attacks. With hands on her hips, she chided, "White people?! Why y'all let this happen?!" Dave Chappelle also won laughs after wearily informing a crowd at the Hollywood Improv, "White folks done got us into some problems *again.*"

AN AMBIVALENT PATRIOTISM

Why do these jokes work in comedy clubs, and why are predominantly minority audiences able to laugh at them? African American humor, from slavery to present, has proven to be a balm in times of trouble, as well as an indirect means of confronting racial injustice. As a genre characterized by expressive "lies," poignant "truths," and lively call-and-response, Black stand-up comedy has also offered a formalized and communal mechanism for commenting on daily and monumental tragedies, often in contrast to mainstream accounts. Laughter and applause from African American audiences can thus serve to endorse comics who are perceived to "speak truth to power" about the war on terrorism and other political matters. For many minority audiences, 9/11 jokes "work" as political commentaries that resist pro-war rhetoric and implicate a larger shared history of racial marginalization. These jokes also work because they invoke problems of race in

America, particularly comics' ongoing struggles against violations of their civil liberties. As actor/comic Evan Lionel solemnly notes, these recurring domestic struggles complicate expressions of loyalty to America, even in the face of war:

> We all love this country but a lot of folks think that Blacks don't support the war on terrorism. That's bullshit. It's just hard for me to get behind the war on terrorism over there when we haven't done it here. Can we stop off in Alabama and hunt the terrorists there before [we go to] Afghanistan?! ... People say, "Well, if you don't like it then go back to Africa." What African tribe I'm-a go back to?! Plus, Black people helped build this country! ... I love America.

On October 28, 2001, political columnist Jonetta Rose Barras wrote in the *Washington Post* that African American responses to 9/11 encompass sadness, fear, and grief, as well as doubts concerning the meaning of the American flag and how far civil liberties extend in times of crisis (A6, A19). The laughter I observed arguably reflects more than the ideological idiosyncrasies of African American comics and their audiences. Instead, the nature of 9/11 humor reflects a widely shared ambivalence among African Americans concerning the nation's response to the attacks and their collective identity as Americans at this critical historical moment.

The "Arab as new nigger" premise is itself a telling exemplar of the paradoxical impact of September 11 on the lives of many African Americans. As noted earlier, many comics adopted this premise as a sardonic celebration of their newfound privileges resulting from the curtailment of Arab American freedoms. In other jokes, comics invoked this premise, directly or indirectly, to critique America's diminished attention to racism, poverty, and other social ills plaguing African American communities following September 11. Some comics, including Don "D.C." Curry and Brandon Bowlin, acknowledged the plight of Arab Americans in their jokes but nevertheless found the "Arab as new nigger" comparison to be an inappropriate, if not insulting, metaphor to endorse verbatim. Curry's quip provides an interesting case in point (see "The Arab as New Nigger" above). While his joke emphasizes the vulnerable position of Arab Americans in the wake of 9/11, Curry personally takes issue with the "Arab as new nigger" comparison. In his eyes, the metaphor fails to problematize the slur "nigger" and falsely equates the recent hardships experienced by Arab Americans with the chronic struggles faced by African Americans. Still other comedians, such as Ray Chatman, alluded to the tenuousness of the "Arab as new nigger" thesis in light of past and recent high-profile cases (e.g., the O. J. Simpson trial) in which the alleged sins of one Black person serve to stigmatize African Americans as a whole. Referring to the Washington, D.C., sniper case, Chatman recently inspired raucous laughter when he joked: "Hell, if we had placed bets on whether or not the [Washington, D.C.] sniper was Black or White, we would've all lost money! I couldn't believe it was a brother! He [sniper] done set us back *again*! After September 11, we wasn't niggers no more. We had *new* niggers! Now, we niggers again. . . . How you gon' be niggers *again*?!"

In speculating on the new dangers facing African Americans, given the disclosure of the sniper's ethnicity, Chatman's joke challenges the very premise upon which it is based. In essence, he suggests that the post-9/11 framing of the Arab as "new nigger" was a bittersweet outcome at best, since it only afforded African Americans *basic* freedoms as U.S. citizens (e.g., temporary reprieve from indiscriminate racial profiling and police brutality). Moreover, his conclusion—"How you gon' be niggers *again*?!"—is strictly rhetorical, suggesting that African Americans are ever vulnerable to disparaging labels and perceptions.

9/11 HUMOR AS POLITICAL COMMENTARY

Overwhelmingly, the 9/11 jokes I observed in "urban" comedy clubs offer cautionary perspectives about America's war on terrorism and its sociopolitical ramifications. Besides denouncing blanket racial profiling, comics also condemn simplistic and ahistorical accounts of U.S.–Middle East conflict that conveniently absolve America from culpability in past and present tragedies. Moreover, comics carefully consider what America's new war on terrorism will mean for them as African Americans, who, in the words of comic/actor Faizon Love, "only get to be Americans when [the nation] needs something from them." As complex political commentaries, these and other jokes offer important, racially nuanced perspectives on what it means to be an American in the aftermath of the terrorist attacks—perspectives too often lost when our nation rallies in the face of "new" vulnerabilities.

ACKNOWLEDGMENTS

I would like to thank my colleagues Stan Huey Jr. and Marvin Sterling, as well as the USC Norman Lear Celebrity, Politics, and Culture Seminar for their invaluable comments on this manuscript. I also want to thank a host of comics, club owners, promoters, and managers, especially Brandon Bowlin, Don Curry, Jack Assadourian, Bené Benwikere, Kenya Duke, Enss Mitchell, Chris Spencer, Spike Thompson, Leland Wigington, Michael Williams, and Tony and Rhonda Spires, all of whom provided support and inspiration for this manuscript. Financial support for this research was provided by the USC Visual Anthropology Endowment Fund and the James Irvine Center for Scholarly Technology at USC.

NOTES

1. This chapter was initially published under the title "'The Arab Is the New Nigger': African American Comics Confront the Irony and Tragedy of September 11." Reproduced by permission of the American Anthropological Association from *Transforming Anthropology* Volume 14, Issue 1, pp. 60–64, 2006. Not for sale or further reproduction.

CHAPTER FOUR

HUMOR, TERROR, AND DISSENT

The Onion after 9/11[1]

—Jamie Warner

In the emotion-laden days following the terrorist attacks of 9/11, American writers, editors, and pundits wondered out loud what the attacks meant: for our national identity, for democracy, for the world. One unusual strain of this discussion focused on what seemed at first glance to be a peripheral topic: irony, or more specifically, the death of irony. In a *Time* magazine article entitled "The Age of Irony Comes to an End," Roger Rosenblatt declared that, before 9/11

> [n]othing was real. With a giggle and a smirk, our chattering classes—our columnists and pop culture makers—declared that detachment and personal whimsy were the necessary tools for an oh-so-cool life. Who but a slobbering bumpkin would think, "I feel your pain"? The ironists, seeing through everything, made it difficult for anyone to see anything. The consequence of thinking that nothing is real—apart from prancing around in an air of vain stupidity—is that one will not know the difference between a joke and a menace. (2001, 79)

Many agreed. Camille Dodero of the *Boston Phoenix* wondered if "a coddled generation that bathed itself in sarcasm will get serious" (Beers 2001). Peter Kaplan, editor of the *New York Observer*, observed that, for the media industry "irony is on the junk heap now...Irony is the mold that grows on old things" (Kirkpatrick 2001). "Are you looking for something to take seriously?" asked Rosenblatt. "Begin with evil" (2001, 79).

President Bush was one step ahead of Rosenblatt. His administration, the Republican Party, and its supporters immediately, forcefully, and repeatedly invoked an old, yet very useful emotional framework for making sense of the terrorist attack: the dichotomy of Good versus Evil. Many Americans wholeheartedly bought in to this framework, which soon became the accepted paradigm for American foreign policy, lasting well into the invasion and occupation of Iraq. And while this framework for making sense of the attacks helped to unite the country together in our distress and sorrow, it also had profound consequences for dissent. This either/or construction not only had the effect of demonizing the terrorists, but also worked to demonize anyone who questioned either side of the binary or even the construction of the binary itself. In a sea of American flags and "United We Stand" bumper stickers, those who disagreed with or even had questions about the official version of events were guilty by association and directed to keep their opinions to themselves. What started as the official government version of events quickly became the only legitimate version of events.

While the vast majority of news organizations quickly adopted the official frame, one newspaper began a series of cogent critiques of the Bush administration and its newly named War on Terror. In fact, on October 10, 2001, just one month after the terrorist attacks, it ran the following story: "Freedoms Curtailed in Defense Of Liberty":

> WASHINGTON, DC—Responding to the threats facing America's free democratic system, White House officials called upon Americans to stop exercising their democratic freedoms Monday.
>
> Ari Fleischer urged Americans to keep their mouths shut. . . ."Now more than ever, if we want to protect democracy for future generations, it is vital that nobody speak out about the issues of the day.". . .
>
> U.S. Sen. John McCain (R-AZ), who advocated permitting the CIA to engage in various illegal activities during a recent Tonight Show with Jay Leno appearance, stressed the importance of not merely submitting to freedom-curtailment policies, but also blindly agreeing with them.
>
> "Now is not the time for such divisive, destructive things as dialogue and debate," McCain said. "Now is not the time for, 'My opinion is just as valid as yours,' and 'What are my country's leaders doing and why?' and 'I have a question, Mr. President.' Now is the time for one thing and one thing only: The defense of the American democratic ideal."

This is, of course, not your typical newspaper. The article above comes from the satirical newspaper *The Onion: America's Finest News Source* (*The Onion* 2001g). In what follows, I argue that *The Onion* was as a sly critic of the Bush administration and their policies. Specifically, instead of directly criticizing the Bush administration or their dualistic rhetoric, *The Onion* playfully used satire to introduce ambiguity into the powerful dualism of

Good versus Evil, holding it up for ridicule. In order to more carefully examine *The Onion*'s subversive satire, however, it is first necessary to look at the rhetorical context that made overt and direct criticism of the Bush administration in the years after 9/11 difficult.

TAKING EVIL SERIOUSLY: PROPHETIC DUALISM

> "Every nation, in every region, now has a decision to make.
> Either you are with us, or you are with the terrorists."
> —President George W. Bush, September 20, 2001

Using a dichotomous frame like the one President Bush used in the quotation above to describe the attacks of 9/11 has proven over time to be an exceptionally effective symbolic architechtonic. Phillip Wander, in a 1984 article examining the rhetoric of the Eisenhower-Dulles administration during the cold war, calls this type of Manichean binary, the "either/or" dichotomous framing of foreign policy, "prophetic dualism":

> In its perfected form prophetic dualism divides the world into two camps. Between them there is conflict. One side acts in accord with all that is good, decent, and at one with God's will. The other acts in direct opposition. Conflict between them is resolved only through the total victory of one side over the other. Since no guarantee exists that good will triumph, there is no middle ground. Hence neutrality may be treated as a delusion, compromise appeasement, and negotiation a call for surrender. (1984, 342)

Prophetic dualism is ideologically rigid and authoritative, and presents a stark, mutually exclusive choice between two morally soaked alternatives. According to Murray Edelman, frames like prophetic dualism construct an "enemy" defined by inherent characteristics, rather than an "adversary" defined by the current political process (1988, 67). Adversaries may come and go but an enemy is forever.

Because of the very human propensity to define oneself against an evil Other who is fetishized as everything "we" are not, prophetic dualism also seamlessly taps into a virtuous self-definition for those on the "Good" side of the dichotomy: "To support a war against a foreign aggressor who threatens national sovereignty and moral decency is to construct oneself as a member of a nation of innocent heroes" (Edelman 1988, 76). This paradox—being both a hero and an innocent victim simultaneously—makes the Good as impervious to critique as the Evil are to any claim of praiseworthy, or even human, qualities. This framing admits no space for questioning.

✦ ✦ ✦

Setting up a prevailing frame, however, is difficult and requires a system of interrelated communicative networks. Robert Entman describes this process as "cascading activation" (2003a, 418). Just like a cascading waterfall, the rhetoric, ideas, and emotions engendered by the frame flow more easily downhill; those that start at the White House and flow down through political elites and the press to the public unimpeded gather the most strength and speed and thus are the most persuasive. According to Entman, ideas can encounter obstacles at different levels on the way down or even flow back up the heavily stratified system, but, again like a waterfall, this is much more difficult, requiring an impressive counterforce to "pump" the ideas back up through the network (2003a, 419–20).[2]

Drawing on Kenneth Burke's discussion of binaries, Coe et al. argue that repetition is very important to the "establishment" phase of any new interpretive frame (2004, 236). Thus, to establish this frame as the hegemonic interpretation, the Bush administration would need to constantly repeat the terminology of prophetic dualism, which would then be reiterated exponentially as it cascaded down through the echo chamber of political elites, press, and public—and this is exactly what happened. At the top of the cascade, President Bush began to invoke the authoritative, morally soaked dichotomy as the dominant frame the morning after the attacks: "The deliberate and deadly attacks which were carried out yesterday against our country were more than acts of terror, they were acts of war ... This will be a monumental struggle of good versus evil ..." (qtd. in Entman 2002a, 415). And just eight days later, in a speech to a joint session of Congress and televised live, the president spelled out the binary in its starkest, most repeatable terms: "Every nation, in every region, now has a decision to make. Either you are with us, or you are with the terrorists" (Bush 2001). He repeated the dualism often, in instantly recognizable and unambiguous language.[3]

There were very few obstacles and no legitimate competing frames from political elites as prophetic dualism cascaded down to the public in the months following the attacks. The press also obliged, not only by repeating the terms of prophetic dualism in their coverage of events, but also by actively seeking out opportunities to reaffirm that they, too, were on the correct side of the dualism. Coe et al. found that the editorial pages of twenty major U.S. papers continued to repeat and endorse the president's prophetic dualism through March 2003 (2004, 241). Fox News's Irena Briganti put the situation of journalists bluntly: "Given the choice, it's better to be viewed as a foot soldier for Bush than a spokeswoman for al-Qaeda" (Finnegan 2007, xix). Anchor of the CBS Evening News, Dan Rather, also famously expressed his support for the president on *Late Show with David Letterman*: "George Bush is the president . . . Wherever he wants me to line up, just tell me where" (Finnegan 2007, xix). Not all journalists were ready to line up, but few publically expressed their misgivings. In fact, many have argued that the mainstream media completely abdicated its traditional role during this time.[4] Apparently, watchdogs were unnecessary for those who are on God's side.

Not surprisingly, Americans in turn adopted prophetic dualism as their way to make sense of 9/11 and threw their support behind the president. President Bush's approval rating jumped from 51 percent on September 10, 2001, to 86 percent on September 15 and then to the highest recorded approval rating since Gallup started asking this question in the 1940s: 90 percent on September 22, 2001 (Hetherinton and Nelson 2003, 37). The "rally 'round the flag" effect that always occurs after a major foreign policy event is not surprising—after all, this was a violent terrorist attack on American soil—but the resonance and duration of the effect can partially be attributed to the successful establishment of the prophetic dualism frame.

No frame, however widespread and powerful, could have complete adherence; in a democratic society, some dissent is inevitable. However, dualisms in general and prophetic dualism in particular construct a rhetorical milieu designed to stifle critique. Additionally, there is an overtly religious component to prophetic dualism that makes questioning and critique not only unseemly but also immoral. As Wander observed in early cold war rhetoric: "God dampens public debate. How can one argue with God's will when it is clearly expressed?" (1984, 344). While 9/11 did not bring the magnitude of threats and intimidation to critics that accompanied the McCarthyism of the early Eisenhower era (unless one was of Middle Eastern descent), any overt and obvious act of questioning or criticism of the administration provoked an equally overt and obvious reinvigoration of the power of the dualism by someone from the Bush administration. For example, in response to questions about the use of military tribunals, the loss of attorney/client privilege in suspected terrorism cases, and the detention of hundreds of immigrants without warrant, John Ashcroft told the Senate Judiciary Committee in December of 2001: "To those who scare peace-loving people with phantoms of lost liberty, my message is this: Your tactics only aid terrorists, for they erode our national unity and diminish our resolve. They give ammunition to America's enemies and pause to America's friends" (Gullo 2001). The implicit threat in a statement like this was not physical in the sense that the critic would disappear or be jailed or executed for her opinions; the threat existed at the level of meaning. One's freedom was not necessarily in question, but one's loyalty was, and that had ramifications. Within the prophetic dualistic frame, there was no way to legitimately voice dissent.

As an interpretative framework, prophetic dualism remained hegemonic and dissent remained muted until well into the Iraq War when it slowly began to erode along with President Bush's popularity. In what follows, I argue that *The Onion* refused to take prophetic dualism seriously. Specifically, instead of explicitly criticizing the Bush administration or their dualistic rhetoric—something very easily reappropriated and then dismissed within the frame—*The Onion* used satire to plant ambiguity into the carefully drawn and policed dualism of Good versus Evil, thus prompting the reader to reevaluate the frame. By introducing a little levity into the unflinching gravity of prophetic dualism, *The Onion* successfully reframed Bush administration policies for their readers and talked back to the powers that be.

PRANCING AROUND IN AN AIR OF VAIN STUPIDITY: THE CASE OF SATIRE

How can one critique in a situation where any overt and obvious dissent that is not precluded preemptively is automatically reappropriated into a hegemonic interpretive frame which labels it unpatriotic? Satire provides one such method of indirect critique and, contrary to Roger Rosenblatt's suggestion that 9/11 caused irony's death, I argue instead that ironic discourse, this time in the form of satire, was not only alive and well after 9/11 at *The Onion*; it also functioned as one of the few effective forms of critique.

Before I turn to a more detailed discussion of *The Onion*, though, it is first necessary to look briefly at both ironic and satirical discourse. Both are notoriously difficult to define. Irony is by far the larger category and has been the topic of countless scholarly considerations. However, it is an indirect, ambivalent, ambiguous mode of communicating meaning, making it problematic to cleanly define. Donald Muecke offers this basic definition:

"What can be said, putting it very simply, is the art of irony is the art of say-ing something without really saying it." Specifically, according to Muecke, irony must, first, have a "double-layer," meaning that it must be able to be viewed at least two different ways, one literally and one from the point of view of the ironist. Second, there must always be some type of incongruous opposition between the two layers, and, third, there must be an element of "innocence." Either the victim or the reader must be unaware of the other layer, or the ironist must pretend to be unaware of it (1980, 19–20). There is a rupture, a disjuncture, an ambiguity lurking somewhere in the transmis-sion of meaning. I use the term "lurking" purposively here, because irony is often intended to be subtle; one needs hints and clues, by definition contex-tual, that signal to the audience that they should be wary, that there might be more going on in this particular situation than a literal interpretation would have them believe. In a more fluid rhetorical context, irony is often employed merely as clever word play; in a more repressive rhetorical regime, the ambiguity inherent in irony can become a potent weapon.

Satire almost always employs the double-edged nature of irony. In fact, almost all satire is ironic, but not all irony is satirical.[5] For irony to be satirical, it must be, as Northrop Frye observed, "militant" (1957, 223). It has a grievance with someone or something, a predicament to highlight, and, according to George Test, the satirist "exploits the ability of irony to expose, undercut, ridicule and otherwise attack indirectly, playfully, wittily, profoundly, artfully" (1991, 17). Satire is thus well positioned to work within a more repressive rhetorical regime because it can "[embed] a threatening idea in a non-threatening form" (Boyd par. 8). The ambiguity of the dual-layered nature of irony combined with the presence of satire's often playful, laughing yet aggressive and judgmental attitude make it less likely that it will be addressed, or even noticed, by those who are the object of the aggression and judgment.[6] In fact, the ambiguous, double-layered construction of sat-ire always has the ability to retreat back to the literal as need be. Thus, it can operate rather stealthily. Instead of overt criticism of powerful people, satiri-cal pieces can circulate as simply ridiculous literal suggestions—although, hopefully, some will know better.

This last point deserves more explanation. Satire requires an audience that understands the second nonliteral ironic layer of meaning. This creates what Wayne Booth calls a "tight bond," a conspiracy of sorts between the author and the audience that gets the joke (1974, 11). Linda Hutcheon argues that marginalized groups often turn to irony, and by extension, satire, as a counterdiscourse and from that become a "discursive community," one that can then challenge the hegemonic power (1991, 89). The literal layer of discourse is made for the consumption of those in power while the underlayer can be used to problematize that same power. The double-layered construction of all kinds of ironic speech, R. Jay Magill argues, thus refuses to be governed by the powers that be; in fact, it cannot even be governed by what it actually said. As the comedian Stephen Colbert remarked while he was a correspondent on the fake news program *The Daily Show with Jon Stewart*: "I can retreat from any statement I've ever made on *The Daily Show* without anyone impugning my credibility because I've never claimed any. But a pundit has to back up what he says with statistics and some study from the Pew Research Center . . . I don't. And so I can say anything because I'm not asking you to believe that I mean it. I'm just hoping that you'll laugh at what I say. [But that] doesn't mean I don't mean it" (Magill 2007, 5).

As Colbert's remarks demonstrate, irony is "not serious about seriousness" (Magill 2007, 4–5). It does not automatically venerate nature, customs, institutions, traditions, history, or power. Because of this, Magill argues that "ironic insights can provide a muscular counterweight to the dominant culture and politics of an age; it challenges power assumed natural, or more poignantly, that overreaches its authority. Most importantly, the ironic mentality is rooted in a belief that individuals have the legitimacy to challenge those structures of power" (2007, 58).[7]

After 9/11, prophetic dualism became the powerful interpretive frame for much of the United States. In what follows, I argue that *The Onion* refused to be governed by this frame. *The Onion*, as Magill suggests above and as Rosenblatt accused, took neither Good nor Evil very seriously. Specifically, instead of directly criticizing the Bush administration and their dualistic rhetoric, *The Onion* used the multilayered nature of ironic satire to judge and to ridicule the stark dualism of Good versus Evil.

A JOKE OR A MENACE:
THE ONION AS AN AGENT OF SATIRICAL INSURGENCY

First published in 1988 by a group of former University of Wisconsin students and unemployed journalists and now relocated in New York City, *The Onion* is consistently one of the most popular sites on the Web with more than 3 million hits weekly, in addition to 690,000 print newspapers in ten cities. More than 1 million more people listen to *The Onion Radio News* each week, and in 2007 *The Onion* launched the *Onion News Network*, which provides twenty-four-hour video news (*The Onion* 2008).[8] *The Onion's Our Dumb Century* was a *New York Times* best seller and won a Thurber Prize for American Humor. *The New Yorker* has called *The Onion* "the funniest publication in the United States" (*The Onion,* 2008). On NPR's *Weekend Edition Sunday,* reporter John Kalish went even futher, estimating that *The Onion* might be the most widely read humor publication on the planet (Kalish 2003).

The Onion is satirical parody of a newspaper. To achieve the double layer of meaning necessary for irony, *The Onion* must look like a newspaper and it does. It has sections entitled "Video," "Sports," and "World," as well as "Election 08," "Local," and "Nat'l" sections very similar to the online versions of *The New York Times* and *The Washington Post.* There are opinion columns, "American Voices," and "Horoscope" sections. The visual format mirrors a "real" online paper; pictures punctuate the story lines with "serious" captions.

But *The Onion* is not "real" news and this helps create the ambiguity in meaning necessary for irony. While *The Onion* looks like a real news source and relies on real world events, it is replete with technical misrepresentations and false statements. Its stories, features, and columns are fake—lies in the strictest factual sense. They include quotations from imaginary people, imaginary quotations from real people, and make-believe scenarios, settings, and situations. Some stories are quite crude and many contain (and these are real) curses and profanity.

Parodying the sober and seemingly impartial language and layout of a newspaper also gives the content an air of legitimacy, objectivity, and respectability which then allows an automatic contrast with both the judgmental, yet mischievious and funny, satirical content of many of the articles. The journalistic form, says former *Onion* editor in chief Rob Seigel, is "the vessel. . . . It has to look like real journalism to create the comedic tension between what is being said and how it is presented" (Wenner 2002). I would like to argue, however, that *The Onion* is much more than just a joke; it did its small part in attempting to slow the cascading activation of prophetic dualism by (1) playfully calling attention to ambiguities in hegemonic frame itself and (2) highlighting shades of gray in the supposedly mutually exclusive options of Good and Evil. *The Onion* thus invited its audience to critically examine the Bush administration's policies, but in a way not easily reappropriated and dismissed by the hegemonic frame.

The Ambiguous Relationship Between Good and Evil

Cascading activation is most effective when the hegemonic frame originates with the topmost political elites. In this case the Bush administration and their allies frequently repeated the Good/Evil rhetoric of prophetic dualism, which eventually became the hegemonic interpretive frame of 9/11. Later Saddam Hussein was simply added to the Evil side of the dualism, despite a lack of evidence of any collaboration with Osama bin Laden.[9] Because the Bush administration repeated the dualism early and often, many of *The Onion* articles direct their critique here, teasingly alerting its readers to the frame's shortcomings. For example, the same day that Ari Fleischer reminded Americans that they needed to watch what they say (September 26, 2001), *The Onion* ran the following story in its first issue since the 9/11 attacks: "U.S. Vows To Defeat Whoever It Is We're At War With":

> WASHINGTON, DC—In a televised address to the American people Tuesday, a determined President Bush vowed that the U.S. would defeat "whoever exactly it is we're at war with here."...
>
> Bush is acting with the full support of Congress, which on Sept. 14 authorized him to use any necessary force against the undetermined attackers. According to House Speaker Dennis Hastert (R-IL), the congressional move enables the president to declare war, "to the extent that war can realistically be declared on, like, maybe three or four Egyptian guys, an Algerian, and this other guy who kind of looks Lebanese but could be Syrian. Or whoever else it might have been. Because it might not have been them."...
>
> U.S. Sen. John McCain (R-AZ), one of Congress' decorated war veterans, tried to steel the nation for the possibility of a long and confusing conflict.... "Christ," McCain [said], "what if the terrorists' base of operation turns out to be Detroit? Would we declare war on the state of Michigan? I suppose we'd have to." (2001d)

One week later as more information on the attackers became available, *The Onion* responded with "U.S. Urges Bin Laden To Form Nation It Can Attack" (2001f). While both of these stories are based on a factual truth—President Bush did set up the Good/Evil frame before he knew who had attacked the United States and there was some confusion as to how to deal with mobile, stateless terrorists—both of these stories also drew attention to the false confidence and the strategic nature of the Good/Evil dichotomy. President Bush made claims about the mortal soul of the attackers before he even knew who

they were or why they attacked. Either you are with us or with the terrorists, said the president, but who exactly are the terrorists? By wittily setting
up the false scenario, *The Onion* encourages its readers to assess the frame
critically, something prophetic dualism, with its single clear choice between
two starkly drawn alternatives, disallows. As Phillip Wander argued above,
under prophetic dualism neutrality is considered an illusion, compromise
is viewed as appeasement, and negotiation is the same as surrender. Frames
that admit some uncertainty, i.e., framing the attacks as a crime rather than
evil, would not be so vulnerable.

Other stories that invite judgment by confusing the easy "either/or" of the
dualism include "U.S. to Arab World: 'Stop Hating Us Or Suffer The Consequences'" which begins "In a strongly worded ultimatum Tuesday, President Bush warned the Arab world . . . 'You have exactly 10 days to put aside
your deep-rooted resentment and rage toward America and learn to like
us'" (2001j). Here *The Onion* does not come out and directly criticize the
frame, but it uses what Donald Muecke calls "irony by overstatement" (1980,
70–71). *The Onion* story uses the same either/or logic of prophetic dualism,
but in exaggerated form that highlights prophetic dualism as a rhetorical
tactic. Related examples of ironic overstatements that muddy the founda-
tional binary of prophetic dualism are "Bush Seeks U.N. Support For 'U.S.
Does Whatever It Wants' Plan" (2002b) in October of 2002 and the March
2003 article "U.S. Forms Own U.N.":

> "The U.S.U.N. resembles the original in almost every way, right down
> to all the flags outside our headquarters," said Condoleezza Rice, a U.S.
> delegate to the U.S.U.N. "This organization will carry out peacekeeping
> missions all over the world, but, unlike the U.N., these missions will not
> be compromised by the threat of opposition by lesser nations."
>
> In its first act, the U.S.U.N. Security Council unanimously backed a
> resolution to liberate Iraq's people and natural resources from the rule
> of Saddam Hussein. . . .
>
> Added [Vice President and U.S. delegate] Cheney: "I can't tell you
> how much easier it is to achieve consensus when you don't have to
> worry about dissent." (2003d)

In the quotation above, *The Onion* introduces ambiguity into prophetic
dualism's Good/Evil binary by insinuating that we must be the only "Good"
country, hence the need for our own "inter"national body that will let us
do what we, the "Good," need to do. Since it is impossible to define every

single one of the other 187 nations in the United Nations as "Evil", the binary becomes more ambiguous and therefore less sustainable.

The story "U.S. To Fight Terror With Terror" follows a slightly different logic. The starkly drawn Good and Evil cannot by definition use the same tactics:

> "It's vital to remember that these terrorists hate freedom," [Secretary of Defense Donald] Rumsfeld said. "Well, guess what? From now on, we're going to hate it even more...." Elliott Abrams, Special Assistant to the President ... said that the Bush Administration acknowledged the ethical inconsistencies of its opposing-terrorism-through-terrorism stance, but doesn't really care. (2004c)

"Privileged Children of Millionaires Square Off on World Stage" works in a similar fashion (2001i). It also disrupts the dualism by alleging that the dichotomy is not as stark as prophetic dualism would have us believe. Here the article playfully insinuates that Bush's privileged upbringing, family fortune, youthful indiscretions, and later spiritual awakening are very similar to the life of Osama bin Laden, as is the huge economic gulf between both leaders and their soldiers on the ground in Afghanistan. According to *The Onion*, the two leaders have much more in common that the prophetic dualism would allow us to believe.[10]

They Are (Mostly) Evil and We Are (Mostly) Good

The Onion ran another series of stories that honed in on the ambiguities inherent in prophetic dualism, encouraging the readers to evaluate and judge the veracity of the frame. Instead of disputing the dualism directly by disrupting the mutual exclusivity of the dichotomy, these stories call attention to the complexity and diversity within each side of the dualism without necessarily referring to the other. While President Bush consistently defined each side as a monolithic, *The Onion*, instead, chose to emphasize each side's muddiness and complexity, again asking the reader to assess the frame. I will examine the Evil side of the dichotomy first. While fewer in number compared to the stories focusing on the diversity in the Good side of the dichotomy, many of the Evil stories were quite striking—for example, "Bush Sr. Apologizes To Son For Funding Bin Laden In 80s" (2001a), "Vital Info On Iraqi Chemical Weapons Provided By U.S. Company That Made Them" (2003e), and "Bin Laden's Mother Worried Sick" (2006b). All three stories variously highlight possible shades of gray within the Evil side of the dualism. The first two stories highlight an ambiguity at the heart of the construction of "Evil": the fact that we were "friends" with both Osama bin Laden and Saddam Hussein in the past. Does that mean that we routinely did business with Evil when it suited our needs? Does it mean that they were mislabeled by President Reagan and the first President Bush or that it is necessary to support Evil when they fight against those who were even more Evil, in this case, the Soviet Union and Iran? The third draws attention to something prophetic dualism obscures: bin Laden has a mother, one who might be worried about him. Ambiguities abound. The most interesting of these stories, however, occurred in the first issue after 9/11—"Hijackers Surprised To Find Selves In Hell":

JAHANNEM, OUTER DARKNESS—The hijackers who carried out the Sept. 11 attacks on the World Trade Center and Pentagon expressed confusion and surprise Monday to find themselves in the lowest plane of Na'ar, Islam's Hell . . . .

According to Hell sources, the 19 eternally damned terrorists have struggled to understand why they have been subjected to soul-withering, infernal torture ever since their Sept. 11 arrival. . . .

"I was told that these Americans were enemies of the one true religion, and that Heaven would be my reward for my noble sacrifice," said [Abdul Aziz] Alomari, moments before his jaw was sheared away by faceless homunculi. "But now I am forced to suckle from the 16 poisoned leathern teats of Gophahmet, Whore of Betrayal, until I burst from an unwholesome engorgement of curdled bile. This must be some sort of terrible mistake." (2001b)

Prophetic dualism discourages a close examination of either side of the dichotomy. In contrast, the satire of *The Onion* gives a much more complex picture. While *The Onion* clearly thinks that the terrorist acts were terrible enough to warrant eternal punishment by Islam's own standards, words in the story above like "confusion," "surprise," "struggle to understand," and "terrible mistake" present the terrorists as people who were duped by a charismatic leader who lied to them, rather than as uniformly and purposively Evil, as prophetic dualism demands.

The Onion also draws attention to the complexity of the hegemonic side of the dualism: the Good. Under prophetic dualism Good is the opposite of Evil, but it is just as monolithic, and thus, pointing out its striations and blemishes also invites the reader to reassess the power of the dichotomy.

For example, President Bush declared on September 20, 2001, in his address to the nation that "[f]reedom and fear are at war. . . . Freedom and fear, justice and cruelty have always been at war, and we know that God is not neutral between them." Later in the same speech, he added, "They hate our freedoms—our freedom of religion, our freedom of speech, our freedom to vote and assemble and disagree with each other" (2001). The Good in this scenario would obviously be the protectors of freedom and justice, while the Evil would revel in fear and cruelty. *The Onion*, however, reports this a little differently, using pointed satire to call attention to the fact that "freedom" is not an absolute good in this country. For example, in December of 2002, *The Onion* ran the story "Bill of Rights Pared Down to a Manageable Six":

> A Republican initiative that went unopposed by congressional Democrats, the revised Bill of Rights provides citizens with a "more manageable" set of privacy and due-process rights by eliminating four amendments and condensing and/or restructuring five others. The Second Amendment, which protects the right to keep and bear arms, was the only article left unchanged. . . .
>
> "We're not taking away personal rights; we're increasing personal security," [Attorney General] Ashcroft said. "By allowing for greater government control over the particulars of individual liberties, the Bill of Rights will now offer expanded personal freedoms whenever they are deemed appropriate and unobtrusive to the activities necessary to effective operation of the federal government." (2002c)

"U.S. Capitol Cleaning Turns Up Long Lost Constitution" (2003a) also makes the same point (it was behind the couch), as does the story from the beginning of the essay: "Freedoms Curtailed in Defense Of Liberty." All three stories use the ironic technique of overstatement, which is taking an idea or issue that is factually true and then stretching it to its logical extreme. "CIA Chief Admits To Torture After Six-Hour Beating, Electrocution" (2005d) and "American Torturing Jobs Increasingly Outsourced" (2005b) also introduce ambiguity into the monolithic Good through overstatement. According to President Bush above, justice and cruelty are at war. If we torture, on which side of the war do we belong?

The Onion also blurs the Good in more subtle ways. One example of this is "Bush Bravely Leads 3rd Infantry into Battle." President Bush's lack of military experience and privileged background are stressed here, again not with a direct discussion, but by praising the president as willing to risk his life just like the hundreds of servicemen and -women whom he ordered to Iraq, something we know to be untrue:

> "Bush is the real deal, and when he talks about fighting for freedom, he means it," said Pvt. Tom Scharpling, 21. "He'd never ask one of us grunts to take any risks for our country that he wasn't willing to take himself."
>
> According to reports from the front, many of the soldiers were initially suspicious of the president, doubtful that an Ivy Leaguer who once used powerful family connections to avoid service in Vietnam had what it took to face enemy fire head-on. However, Bush—or, as his fellow soldiers nicknamed him in a spirit of battlefield camaraderie, "Big Tex"— quickly overcame the platoon's reluctance to having a "fancy-pants Yalie" in its ranks.
>
> "Bush is the best soldier I've ever had the honor of fighting along-side," said Pvt. Jon Benjamin, 23. "I'd take a bullet for that man, because I know he'd take one for me if he had to." (2003b)

Donald Muecke calls this ironic tactic "praising in order to blame" (1984, 67). One of the most unsettling examples during this time period involved a more subtle variation of this tactic, although this displayed a more serious type of satire than *The Onion* usually employs: "Dead Iraqi Would Have Loved Democracy."

> BAGHDAD, IRAQ—Baghdad resident Taha Sabri, killed Monday in a U.S. air strike on his city, would have loved the eventual liberation of Iraq and establishment of democracy, had he lived to see it, his grieving widow said.
>
> "Taha was a wonderful man, a man of peace," his wife Sawssan said. "I just know he would have been happy to see free elections here in Iraq, had that satellite-guided Tomahawk cruise missile not strayed off course and hit our home."
>
> ... "My husband was no fan of Saddam," Sawssan said. "He felt he was a terrible despot. If the Americans do drive him from power, it will be that much more of a shame that they killed Taha." (2003c)

What does it mean when the Good indiscriminately kills large numbers of innocent people, many more, in fact, than the number of innocent people killed on 9/11? *The Onion*'s satire repeatedly raises these types of questions and invites the reader to judge the veracity of the frame.

Finally, while most of *The Onion*'s articles targeted the originators of the prophetic dualism frame, it also ran stories that underscored the Democratic Party's lack of power in the face of the frame, as well as the confusion of the American people who were waiting for information at the bottom of the cascade. There were fewer of these stories, but they functioned in a similar way and no one was immune from ridicule. Not surprisingly, many of *The Onion*'s stories revolved around the incompetence of the Democrats. Examples include "Democrats Somehow Lose Primaries" (2004e) and "Kerry Makes Whistle-Stop Tour From Deck of Yacht" (2004b), as well as "Democrats Vow Not To Give Up Hopelessness":

> According to Sen. Ted Kennedy (D-MA), Democrats are not willing to sacrifice their core values—indecision, incoherence, and disorganization—for the sake of short-term electoral gain.
> "Don't lose faithlessness, Democrats," Kennedy said. "The next election is ours to lose. To those who say we can't, I say: Remember Michael Dukakis. Remember Al Gore. Remember John Kerry."
> Kennedy said that, even if the Democrats were to regain the upper hand in the midterm elections, they would still need to agree on a platform and chart a legislative agenda—an obstacle he called "insurmountable." (2006a)

These stories do not call attention to the ambiguities within the dominant frame. Instead, they highlight the strength of prophetic dualism. The one group from which one would expect opposition to President Bush's policies was completely reduced to incoherence in the face of the overwhelming power of the frame.

Interestingly, at the bottom of the cascade, American citizens were portrayed in *The Onion* as either overreacting or confused by prophetic dualism. The articles that highlighted overreacting to the threat of another terrorist attack ran along the lines of "Security Beefed Up At Cedar Rapids Public Library" (2001e), "Trick-Or-Treaters Subject to Random Bag Searches" (2005c), and "Woman With Sore Throat Thinks It Might Be Anthrax" (2001h). Examples of stories highlighting confusion were "Not Knowing What Else To Do, Woman Bakes American Flag Cake" (2001c) in the first issue after 9/11 and "Area Man Not Exactly Sure When To Take Down American Flags" in January of 2002:

> Last Thursday, seeking to gauge public opinion, he asked coworker Jim Bowden when he thought the office should take down the flag hanging

by the receptionist's desk. Bowden said it should remain "until the injustice is eradicated around the world and God's peace prevails."

"I had no idea what Jim meant, but I guess now is clearly not the time," Wenger said. (2002a)

The Onion writers appeared to realize that American citizens were at the bottom of the cascade and therefore rhetorically held hostage by the dominance of prophetic dualism, as well as the lack of any legitimate counternarrative. Because of this, *The Onion* reserved most of its scorn for the originators of the frame, the Bush administration.

CONCLUSION
January 25, 2005: "Bush Celebrates Millionth Utterance Of 'Lessons Of Sept. 11'" (2005a)

I have argued that *The Onion* refused to take the morally soaked, starkly drawn dichotomy of prophetic dualism seriously, writing stories that purposefully, albeit playfully, asked the reader to question and then to judge the hegemonic framework. Specifically, instead of overtly critiquing the Bush administration or their dualistic rhetoric, *The Onion* uses the multilayered nature of satire to introduce ambiguity into the seemingly unassailable dualism of Good versus Evil. It did this by mischievously suggesting ambiguous relationships between the starkly drawn and mutually exclusive sides of the dichotomy and by highlighting shades of gray inside both sides of the supposedly monolithic opposites of the dichotomy.

But so what? A satirical newspaper like *The Onion* seems quite insignificant compared to the power of the Bush administration and its supporters. And it was. There is a vast asymmetry between the enormity and strength of prophetic dualism and the snarky, sometimes juvenile satire of *The Onion*. To put it more harshly, *The Onion* did not close Guantanamo Bay, stop the invasion of Iraq, or even prevent President Bush from being elected to serve a second term.

The importance of satires like *The Onion*, however, lies in what Linda Hutcheon calls "discursive communities" (1994, 96–97). Satirical performances such as *The Onion*, Hutcheon would emphasize, both draw on shared cultural knowledge and create new cultural knowledge in their wake, allowing potent counterpublics to form out of the watchful eye of the administration. That is to say, *The Onion* was a kind of safe space for those who wanted to critique both the prophetic dualism frame and the policies the Bush administration was pursuing under cover of the frame. The online format allowed articles to be forwarded and inside jokes shared, and it provided the knowledge that the silenced critics of the administration were not alone in their judgment. There were others who saw what you saw and disagreed with the same things with which you disagreed, and that knowledge allowed for strength, hope, and patience until such a time that overt critique could once again be spoken freely.

NOTES

1. This chapter initially appeared under the title "Tyranny of the Dichotomy: Prophetic Dualism, Irony, and *The Onion*" in the Electronic Journal of Comunication, vol. 18, nos. 2, 3, 4, 2008.

2. For more a more detailed discussion of the cascading activation model, see Entman (2003).

3. For a detailed content analysis of the president's speeches from 2001–2003, see Coe et al. (2004).

4. There is an emerging literature that details the failures of the media to question the Bush administration's version of both 9/11 and the Iraq War. See, for example, Zelizer and Allen (2002), Dadge (2004), Hatchen (2005), Finnegan (2006), Thomas (2006), and Bennett et al. (2007).

5. For example, ironic tropes known as Socratic irony, situational irony, cosmic irony, irony of fate, romantic irony, etc., are not considered satirical. For a detailed description of various scholarly approaches to irony stemming from rhetoric and literary criticism, see Knox (1961), Booth (1974), Muecke (1980), Behler (1990), and Dane (1991).

6. See the first chapter of Test (1991).

7. However, it is important to remember that irony and satire are not inherently subversive or radical.

8. The official *Onion* Web site is www.theonion.com. *The Onion* officially has no bylines; every major article is collaborative. Each week, the writers all submit headlines, from which eighteen are picked for the next issue. All of the writers comment on the writing and editing of each piece.

9. For more discussion of how Saddam Hussein became Evil, see the introduction in Finnegan, op cit., as well as Rich (2006).

10. Douglas Kellner (2004) takes it one step farther, arguing that both the Bush administration and the Islamic Jihadists employ the same type of Manichean absolutist and fundamentalist discourses.

WORKS CITED

Alicastro, Joe. 2007. We Are All Americans Now. *The Daily Nightly*–MSNBC, September 11. http://dailynightly.msnbc.msn.com/archive/2007 /09/11/355294.aspx.

Beers, David. 2001. Irony is dead! Long live irony! As jingoists call for a New Sincerity, we need irony—the serious kind—more than ever. *Salon,* September 25. http://archive.salon .com/mwt/feature/2001/09/.25/irony_lives/.

Behler, Ernst. 1990. *Irony and the Discourse of Modernity.* Seattle: University of Washington Press.

Bennett, W. Lance, Regina G. Lawrence, and Steven Livingston. 2007. *When the Press Fails: Political Power and the News Media from Iraq to Katrina.* Chicago: University of Chicago Press.

Bohlen, Celestine. 2001. THINK TANK; In New War on Terrorism, Words Are Weapons, Too. *The New York Times,* September 28. http://query.nytimes.com/gst/ fullpage.html?res=9B04 EFDA163DF93AA1575AC0A9679C8B63&sec=&spon=&pagewanted=1.

Booth, Wayne. 1974. *A Rhetoric of Irony.* Chicago: University of Chicago Press.

Boyd, Andrew. TRUTH IS A VIRUS: Meme Warfare and the Billionaires for Bush (or Gore). http://www.culturejamming101.com/truthisavirus.html.

Bush, George W. 2001. Address to a Joint Session of Congress and the American People. United States Capitol, Washington, D.C., September 20. http://www.whitehouse.gov/news /releases/2001/09/20010920-8.html.

Carter, Bill, and Felicity Barringer. 2001. A Nation Challenged: Speech and Expression; In Patriotic Time, Dissent is Muted. *The New York Times,* 28 September. http://query.nytimes .com/gst/fullpage.html?res=9B0CE4D91F3AF93BA1575AC0A9679C8B63&scp=2&sq=In+ Patriotic+Times%2C+Dissent+is+Muted&st=nyt.

Coe, Kevin, David Domke, Erica S. Graham, Sue Lockett John, and Victor W. Pickard. 2004. No Shades of Gray: The Binary Discourse of George W. Bush and an Echoing Press. *Journal of Communication* (June): 234–252.

Dadge, David. 2004. *Casualty of War: The Bush Administration's Assault on the Free Press.* Amherst, NY: Prometheus.

Dane, Joseph. 1991. The *Critical Mythology of Irony.* Athens: University of Georgia Press.

Edelman, Murray. 1988. *Constructing the Political Spectacle.* Chicago: University of Chicago Press.

Entman, Robert. 2003a. Cascading Activation: Contesting the White House's Frame After 9/11. *Political Communication* 20: 415–432.

———. 2003b. *Projections of Power: Projections of Power: Framing News, Public Opinion, and U.S. Foreign Policy.* Chicago: University of Chicago Press.

Finnegan, Lisa. 2007. *No Questions Asked: News Coverage Since 9/11.* Westport, CT: Praeger.

Fitch, John, Catherine Helen Palczewski, Jennifer Farrell, and Eric Short. 2006. Disingenuous Controversy: Responses to Ward Churchill's 9/11 Essay. *Argumentation and Advocacy* 42 (Spring): 190–205.

Frye, Northrop. 1957. *Anatomy of Criticism: Four Essays.* Princeton, NJ: Princeton University Press.

Gullo, Karen. 2001. Ashcroft Defends Anti-Terror Tactic. Associated Press. December 6.

Hatchen, William A. 2005. *The Troubles with Journalism: A Critical Look at What's Right and What's Wrong with the Press.* Mahwah, NJ: Lawrence Erlbaum.

Hetherington, Marc J., and Michael Nelson. 2003. Anatomy of a Rally Effect: George W. Bush and the War on Terrorism. *PS: Political Science and Politics:* 37–42.

Hutcheon, Linda. 1994. *Irony's Edge: Theory and Politics of Irony.* New York: Routledge.

Kalish, John. 2003. *Weekend Edition Sunday.* National Public Radio. July 6. http://www.npr .org/features/feature.php?wfId=1321485.

Kellner, Douglas. 2004. 9/11, Spectacles of Terror, and Media Manipulation. *Critical Discourse Studies* 1.1 (April), 41–64.

Kirkpatrick, David. 2001. A Nation Challenged: Pronouncements on Irony Draw a Line in the Sand. *The New York Times*, September 24. http://query.nytimes.com/gst/fullpage.html?res =9400E3D9173AF937A1575AC0A9679C8B63&scp=3&sq=david+kirkpatrick+a+nation+ challenged&st=nyt>.

Knox, Norman. 1961. *The Word "Irony" and Its Context: 1500–1755*. Durham, NC: Duke University Press.

Lindsey, Daryl, and Steve Kettmann. 2001. We Are All Americans. Salon. September 13. http://archive.salon.com/news/feature/2001/09/13/ germany/index.html.

Magill, R. Jay, Jr. 2007. *Chic Ironic Bitterness*. Ann Arbor: University of Michigan Press.

Muecke, D.C. 1980. *The Compass of Irony*. 2nd ed. New York: Methuen.

Rich, Frank. 2006. *The Greatest Story Ever Sold: The Decline and Fall of Truth from 9/11 to Katrina*. New York: Penguin Press.

Rosenblatt, Roger. 2001. The Age of Irony Comes to an End. *Time*. September 24: 79. Academic Search Premier. EBSCO. Marshall University Libraries, Huntington, WV. January 27, 2008. http://search.ebscohost.com/login.aspx?direct=true&db=aph&AN= 5170486&site=ehost-live.

Test, George. 1991. *Satire: Spirit and Art*. Tampa: University of South Florida Press.

The Onion. 2001a. Bush Sr. Apologizes To Son For Funding Bin Laden In '80s. September 26. http://www.theonion.com/content/node/31475.

———. 2001b Hijackers Surprised To Find Selves In Hell. September 26. http://www.theonion .com/content/ node/38673.

———. 2001c. Not Knowing What Else To Do, Woman Bakes American-Flag Cake. September 26. http://www.theonion.com/content/node/28148.

———. 2001d. U.S. Vows To Defeat Whoever It Is We're At War With. September 26. http://www.theonion.com/content/news/u_s_vows_to_defeat _whoever_it_is.

———. 2001e. Security Beefed Up At Cedar Rapids Public Library. October 3. http://www .theonion.com/content/node/28133.

———. 2001f. U.S. Urges Bin Laden To Form Nation It Can Attack. October 3. http://www .theonion.com/content/node/31466.

———. 2001g. Freedoms Curtailed In Defense Of Liberty. October 10. http://www.theonion .com/ content/node/28121.

———. 2001h. Woman With Sore Throat Thinks It Might Be Anthrax. October 17. http://www .theonion.com/content/node/31455.

———. 2001i. Privileged Children Of Millionaires Square Off On World Stage. October 24. http://www.theonion.com/content/node/28092.

———. 2001j. U.S. To Arab World: "Stop Hating Us Or Suffer The Consequences." November 14. http://www.theonion.com/content/node/31395.

———. 2002a. Area Man Not Exactly Sure When To Take Down American Flags. January 16. http://www.theonion.com/content/node/28169.

———. 2002b. Bush Seeks U.N. Support For "U.S. Does Whatever It Wants" Plan. October 2. http://www.theonion.com/content/node/27693.

———. 2002c. Bill of Rights Pared Down To A Manageable Six. December 18. http://www .theonion.com/content/news/bill_of_rights_pared_down.

———. 2003a. U.S. Capitol Cleaning Turns Up Long-Lost Constitution. March 5. http://www
.theonion.com/content/news_briefs/ u_s_capitol_cleaning_turns.

———. 2003b. Bush Bravely Leads 3rd Infantry Into Battle. March 26. http://www.theonion
.com/content/news/bush_bravely_leads_3rd_infantry.

———. 2003c. Dead Iraqi Would Have Loved Democracy. March 26. http://www.theonion
.com/content/news/dead_iraqi_would_have_loved.

———. 2003d. U.S. Forms Own U.N. March 26. http://www.theonion.com/content/
node/27948.

———. 2003e. Vital Info On Iraqi Chemical Weapons Provided By U.S. Company That Made
Them. March 26. http://www.theonion.com/ content/node/31343.

———. 2004a. Democrats Somehow Lose Primaries. February 2. http://www.theonion.com/
content/news/democrats_somehow_lose_primaries.

———. 2004b. Kerry Makes Whistle-Stop Tour From Deck Of Yacht. February 18. http://www
.theonion.com/content/news/kerry_makes_whistle_stop_tour_from.

———. 2004c. U.S. To Fight Terror With Terror. May 19. http://www.theonion.com/content/
node/30570.

———. 2005a. Bush Celebrates Millionth Utterance Of "Lessons Of Sept. 11." January 25.
http://www.theonion.com/content/node/33009.

———. 2005b. American Torturing Jobs Increasingly Outsourced. March 30. http://www
.theonion.com/content/node/33067.

———. 2005c. Trick-Or-Treaters To Be Subject To Random Bag Searches. October 26.
http://www.theonion.com/content/node/41899.

———. 2005d. CIA Chief Admits To Torture After Six-Hour Beating, Electrocution.
December 21. http://www.theonion.com/content/node/43704.

———. 2006a. Democrats Vow Not To Give Up Hopelessness. February 2. http://www
.theonion.com/content/news/democrats_ vow_not_to_give_up.

———. 2006b. Bin Laden's Mother Worried Sick. October 10. http://www.theonion.com/
content/node/53893.

———. 2008. Mediakit 2008. http://mediakit.theonion.com/index.html.

Thomas, Helen. 2006. *Watchdogs of Democracy? The Waning Washington Press Corps and
How It Has Failed the Public*. New York: Scribner.

Wander, Philip. 1984. The Rhetoric of American Foreign Policy. *The Quarterly Journal of
Speech*. 70.4: 339–361.

Wenner, Katherine. 2002. Peeling the Onion. *American Journalism Review*. September 2002.
College Park, MD: Philip Merrill College of Journalism, University of Maryland.
http://www.ajr.org/Article.asp?id=2618.

Zelizer, Barbie, and Stuart Allen, eds. 2002. *Journalism After September 11*. New York:
Routledge.

PART TWO Enter the "War on Terror"

CHAPTER FIVE

LAUGHS, TEARS, AND BREAKFAST CEREALS

Rethinking Trauma and Post-9/11 Politics in
Art Spiegelman's *In the Shadow of No Towers*

—Ted Gournelos

> My project at the time was to try to figure out, when I started, what I actually saw,
> unmediated, and try to not let the media images fully replace what I saw: the bones of
> those towers, that glowing tower, which stays with me, printed on the inside of my eye-
> balls. And most people didn't see it. What was visible on the tv screen was that cloud
> of toxic smoke that replaced those bones . . . So next week I was trying to draw what
> I saw, but then the hijacking got hijacked and very soon the project changed. This is
> part of what made this more published in Europe than America. I did not think this was
> political; I thought this was just a description of what I was living through that month.
> Each one of these monthly pages ran from September '02 to September '03. Each of
> those pages was done like a diary entry, and the first five or six, I didn't think I would
> be around to see it printed. So I wasn't thinking about books, I was thinking about
> ephemera. And I was thinking about putting down what I saw and felt, and what I saw
> and felt had a lot to do, very quickly, with a political machine that had run amok.
> —Art Spiegelman, "Ephemera vs. the Apocalypse"

The discursive shift from the events of September 11, 2001, to the "trauma" of "9/11" to the "war on terror" wasn't easily accomplished, although in retrospect it sometimes appears that seamless. In fact, considering 9/11 *as trauma* wasn't as automatic as we (as humans, as Americans, as students or scholars) often think. However, the two concepts are deeply connected; had it not framed 9/11 as a national trauma, the Bush administration would never have been able to make a steady or seamless case for war, either against Afghanistan or against Iraq. "9/11" itself, as several scholars have noted, is a constructed term that at once mythologizes the attacks of September 11, 2001, and renders them as open and ripe for cultural/historical commemoration, economic commodification, and political exploitation. The movement to the "war on terror" and the mobilization of U.S. nationalism against a perceived threat to our security stems, I argue, form a larger issue in which the American Dream has broken down as a central cultural mythology, leaving, if not a traumatized culture, then at least the *imagery* of a traumatized culture in its wake. As the chapters in part 1 of this volume suggest, there was in fact a deep ambivalence about the role the attacks should play in our culture. The manufacture of post-9/11 imagery and emotional responses, as well as a powerful regime of de facto cultural and political censorship and repression, facilitated a particular (right wing) sociopolitical and geopolitical agenda. Art Spiegelman's *In the Shadow of No Towers* (2004) attempts to destabilize the dominant narrative of this time of transition, questioning the assertion of 9/11 as a national trauma and critiquing the tone and rise of post-9/11 politics. In a complex and monumental assemblage, Spiegelman brings together his September 24, 2001, cover image for *The New Yorker*, his early illustrated responses to the U.S. warmongering and profiteering after the attacks from various (mostly international) papers, visual tropes from his masterpiece *Maus*, elements of retrospective commentary, and reproductions of earlier cartoons from U.S. political history. In so doing he questions many of the assumptions we make about this time of transition, and helps explain how social and political instabilities masked by 9/11 set the stage for both reactionary and progressive political movements.[1]

RETHINKING POST-9/11 TRAUMA, POLITICS, AND POPULAR CULTURE

In an earlier article on images of trauma in Hollywood film, I argued that trauma theory was a good way to understand "how people react to the violations of their hopes, dreams, and worldviews in what often seem irrational ways," and that these images imply a set of "internal inconsistencies, contradictions, and dissonances" endemic to late capitalism (Gournelos 2009, 510). More importantly, perhaps, I argued that trauma as a source of U.S. political discourse did not occur *after* September 11, 2001, although the widespread acceptance of the Department of Homeland Security's color-coded alert system and the Department of Defense's widespread wiretapping scheme certainly seems to reflect a traumatized numbness due to persistent feelings of terror. Instead, I suggested that the sense of trauma many of us noticed after 9/11 had a much longer history and was connected to "conflicting cultural mythologies and the breakdown of signifying chains [which] are traumatic on the levels at which individuals and groups construct and maintain their social spheres," specifically the simultaneous breakdown and (re)assertion of the American Dream through the white suburban ideal (511). In this sense, trauma relates to the violation of the mythologies that construct our everyday realities; for example, the myth of the perfect suburban life, of equitable upward mobility, of the economic security of our social safety nets, and of the eventual rise and success of our offspring. In such a sense, trauma suggests not a response to a traumatic event, but rather the creation of a new, incoherent, and often violent identity to deal with (or avoid dealing with) a weakened social foundation.

As expressions of these violations are rampant in popular culture, from the brutal competitions of reality television to the laughter elicited by horrific torture scenes in television shows like Showtime's *Dexter* (2006–present) or the *Saw* film series (2004, 2005, 2006, 2007, 2008, 2009), it seems more likely to point to these traumas as the root of our post-9/11 social and political malaise rather than the events of 9/11 themselves. If we were so complacent and happy before 9/11 (when "everything changed"), I argued, why did "even happy films like romantic comedies continually rely on the betrayal of family, job, marriage, children, and fantasies, and often share visions of emotional vacancy or instability, hypermasculinity, paranoia, and other reactions to a feminizing, boring, smotheringly normative suburban world almost in spite of their goal to cement or encourage that world" (514)? Isn't it significant, as Paul Lewis also argues in chapter 1 of *Cracking Up* (2006), that this instability often manifests in gleeful destruction or self- destruction (Gournelos 2009, 520–22)? If 9/11 allowed the United States government to successfully channel anxieties over domestic insecurities and ambivalences about economic, social, and political realities towards a (brown) Other or even an (unpatriotic) Self, should we not look at *that* process rather than at the events that gave it/us the excuse?

Beyond the first week or two of uncertainty, in fact, our own responses to the events in many ways do not suggest that 9/11 evoked the traits of eternal repetition, shell shock, or unclaimed experience that trauma theorists usually suggest characterize the impact of psychological trauma, or post-traumatic stress disorder (PTSD). U.S. television turned to the war on Afghanistan ("America Fights Back!"), comedians carefully returned to their jobs, *The New York Times* and other media outlets ran rather exploitative and maudlin retrospectives (e.g., the "Portraits of Grief" series), and we were emphatically told to buy new cars (preferably the increasingly popular and ironically fragile suburban tanks known as sport utility vehicles) and travel to Disneyland. Even Hollywood's self-censorship of films that dealt with terrorist attacks or the twin towers, including *Spiderman* (2002), only indicates a desire to *avoid* evoking any sense of trauma. The rise of exploitative films *after* the narrative of national trauma was created, however, as well as, of course, the popularity of television shows like the conservative *24* (2001–present), make it clear that popular culture was more interested in eliminating challenges to the status quo than any sense of eschewing profit for ethics.

It is the "culture of commemoration," to take David Simpson's (2006) term, and the accompanying general ethos of consumerism that followed 9/11 that should make us wary of too quickly containing, explaining, or writing off social and political reactions to 9/11 as trauma, as well as the strongly mediated relationship even New Yorkers eventually had to the events. As has been remarked in almost all scholarly (and even lay) discussions of the attacks and their immediate aftermath, 9/11 is one of the most media-saturated events in history, and is remarkable as much for the quick consolidation of images into a particular narrative as it is for the sheer volume of coverage. This is not without consequences, of course; as Wyatt Mason argued in his review of *In the Shadow of No Towers*, such "oversaturation can make the unforgettable seem unremarkable. Too many images can turn the horrifyingly strange into something so familiar as to make it all but invisible for its visibility. One can be blinded by literalism" (Mason 2004, 31). We should therefore immediately question the "traumatic" nature of 9/11. For whom was it traumatic? How so, and for how long? Were all traumatic responses similar? Many commentators (perhaps most hilariously David Cross in his 2002 stand-up comedy album *Shut Up You Fucking Baby*) remarked that not all New Yorkers, even those that lived close to the towers, were traumatized by the events. Shocked and frightened, of course, but not necessarily placed in a state of traumatic alienation, fragmentation, and repetition. To suggest that all or even many U.S. citizens were traumatized by the imagery (as, for instance, an indication of pure evil) is even more questionable. Even scholars who strongly claim 9/11 was a traumatic event are often struck by this disconnect between the experience of the attacks, the experience of the discourse that immediately framed/constrained/mediated them, and the responses advocated by the Bush administration. In Kristiaan Versluys's (2006) article on trauma in *No Towers*, for instance, she remarks that "the voice of the direct witness is no match for the Dan Rathers of this world. The media stars have appropriated the event, even while it happened. They have reduced first-hand experience to the level of a news show and cheapened trauma into mere sensationalism. That is, they have immediately expropriated the real owners of the event, those who underwent it personally or watched it from close by" (997). Her point is key, even though it is certainly still questionable whether or not (re)claiming the trauma for those, like Art Spiegelman, who directly witnessed or were impacted by the events is productive or even accurate. Suggesting that any event traumatized an entire nation all too often leads to nationalist rhetoric and the appropriation of the event by the interests of capital, the state, the military, or the culture industry, and this is certainly the case in a country like the United States where the boundaries between those four elements are blurry at best. Indeed, moving from *personal* to *national* trauma disconnects social and political responses from the events themselves, and instead relies only on the mythic construction of the events as traumatic. This construction emphasizes "the danger of trauma and memory discourses supplanting rather than complementing historicization, and the danger of a substantial displacement of narrative historicization by types of association closer to a logic of images than to inherently temporal causality" (Orbán 2007, 60). As the history of the calls to war in the United States should demonstrate, emphasis on "traumatic" events like this, from the sinking of the U.S.S. *Maine* in 1898 to the bombing of Pearl Harbor in 1941, is always questionable and dangerous.

When the idea of 9/11 is disconnected from the physical events and attached more firmly to the *media* event (to borrow Dayan and Katz's [1992] terms), discourse surrounding the "trauma" of 9/11 becomes even more obviously problematic. David Simpson suggests that critics should

> question those who have presented 9/11 as an attack on culture itself, on any meaningful continuity with the past and with a projected future. In the eyes of our enemy, they tell us, 9/11 was intended as a cataclysmic imposition of revelation and apocalypse of eternally present time, on the complacent faith in merely historical and evolutionary temporality that characterizes our secular preference for prudence, profit, and accumulation in the world of trade, a world of self-cultivation measured by the reassuring ticking of a predictable clock ... Michael Ignatieff's "apocalyptic nihilism" partakes of this rhetoric, as does Thomas Friedman's description of 9/11 as a "hole in the fabric of civilization." The attribution of nihilism or nothingness (despite Osama bin Laden's explicit demands for specific changes in U.S. foreign policy) creates a space for speculation and interpretation that is literally inexhaustible.

In the light of this construction of nothing, of inviting emptiness, everything becomes a possible motive ... (6–7)

In other words, positing 9/11 as a national trauma inflicted on "our" culture,
institutions, or way of life is a deliberate process of both obfuscation and
co-optation with very real social and political repercussions. Not the least
of these repercussions were the call to war and the entire reframing of the
Bush administration, through which "one of the weakest, most personally
deficient presidents in U.S. history became one of the strongest" and most
bulletproof of public figures (Lewis 2006, 171).

The shift from destructive physical attacks to traumatizing cultural attack
thus redirected the social unrest and dissonance I discussed above from a
general dissatisfaction with the failure to achieve a widespread American
Dream to a nationalist fervor. By successfully channeling fear into faith in
a newly branded nation, and locating discontent in a shadowy and endless Other, the administration was able to push through a reactionary
domestic and foreign policy agenda that made the possibility of middle-
class citizens achieving the social and economic success necessary for the
American Dream increasingly remote (Heller 2005, 2). Because the "trauma"
was therefore rendered into an abstract and endless cultural landmark, it
dehistoricized 9/11 and distanced its political aftermath in both the foreign
and domestic spheres from the legacy of oppressive social policy and class
warfare. As R. Thomas Foster (2006) argues:

This dehistoricizing operation openly works to produce the attacks as a
traumatic experience that cannot be embedded in any historical narrative of the past, but only as the commencement of a supposedly "new"
struggle ("let's roll"). As such, the 9/11 attacks are explicitly represented
as unrepresentable and therefore as eliciting only "proper" nationalist
sentiment rather than historical knowledge. The incoherence of such
claims is the source of their power. (255)

Unfortunately, this means that when cultural scholars uncritically accept the
rhetoric of "trauma" when we speak of 9/11, we are complicit in both the use
of 9/11 as a tool of reactionary politics and its containment and displacement
into a veritable "trademark ... or national branding awareness" in which
government and industry "responded to this crisis by refashioning fantasies
of coherent, monolithic nationhood and consensual nationalism in accor-
dance with the new post-9/11 economic anxiety disorder" (Heller, 3).[2]

IN THE SHADOW OF NO TOWERS,
IRONY, AND POLITICAL ENGAGEMENT

Katalin Orbán argues that *In the Shadow of No Towers* in particular is interesting in this light, as its pages were written as serial comics for several
newspapers and magazines in the months following the event, and is thus
"a nearly contemporaneous monument" that "attests to both the power and
limitations of this instant memorialization and shows that these limitations
cannot be avoided by simply waiting a little longer to gain adequate historical distance ... if the event gets sufficiently buried under ... layers of national
public discourse" (85). Indeed, I argue that *In the Shadow of No Towers* is
an important discursive intervention because, far from being a representation of trauma, the volume only mobilizes the discourse of trauma as it
turns us away from the national and eternal to the local and every day, and
eventually dislocates us from complacency to engagement through ironic
multiplicity and fragmentation. It is of course necessary to see *No Towers*
in relation to Spiegelman's earlier masterpiece, *Maus Volume I* and *Volume
II*, published in 1986 and 1991, respectively. Most if not all reviews and critical examinations of *No Towers* do so, in fact. However, this should be done
with great care. *Maus* is subtitled *A Survivor's Tale*, but is Spiegelman's narrative of his father's experience as a Holocaust survivor and Spiegelman's
own sense of secondary guilt and generational trauma. *No Towers*, by contrast, is the story of Spiegelman's own experiences with the events of 9/11
and their political aftermath, and although it occasionally borrows imagery
from *Maus*, it does so in very particular circumstances that I will discuss
in depth below in order to destabilize binaries of "us" vs. "them" and victim
vs. perpetrator. These "over-articulated journal entries," as Spiegelman calls
them, were assembled into a coherent volume after their original publication and combined with historic cartoon strips that further fragment an
already fragmented narrative (Siegal 2005, 37).

The volume should also be understood within a particular industrial context, foregrounded in Spiegelman's introduction to the volume. Although the
cover of *No Towers* is a partial reproduction of the illustrated cover image
of *The New Yorker*'s response to the attacks, with two glossy black towers
that appear almost as shadows against a matte black background, the rest
of the images were published in minor leftist papers (mostly outside the
U.S.). Although Spiegelman has backed away from early assertions that his
comics were explicitly censored, he has also affirmed that there is an implicit
censorship in producing comics that he knew might pass censors or be what

a magazine might want (Siegal, 38–39). As one article from *The Independent* argued, although Spiegelman's history as an extremely successful and lucrative cultural icon should have made him a shoo-in for publication, "his habit of expressing uncomfortable truths was becoming awkward" and "he found himself being urged to tone down his work":

> You can see why the born-again US press steered clear—especially as the work moves on from the initial horror in New York to the subsidiary horrors of the "war on terror" and the changes it has wrought in US society. Yet there is also something shocking—and illustrative of those changes—in the thought that an artist of such towering reputation, apparently restored to the height of his creative powers, can scarcely get his work published in his own country. ("Art Spiegelman: Voice in the Wilderness")

Although this might seem hyperbolic, as the chapters in part 1 of this volume make clear the culture immediately after 9/11 was at the very least not conducive or receptive to critical voices, even those raised in jest. This persisted even into the 2004 publication of *No Towers*, in fact, as articles like *Time* magazine's scathing review make clear (e.g., Grossman 2004).

Why might this suppression occur? Comics aren't the most threatening medium, and Spiegelman's connection to the Holocaust (and thus the ability to cynically appropriate his work for pro-Israel or anti-Arab causes) makes him theoretically perfect for an abstract discussion of 9/11 as a traumatic national milestone and galvanizing event. Indeed, as Jamie Warner, David Holloway, and David Monje argue in this volume, other dissident voices (from *The Onion* to *Fahrenheit 9/11* [2004] to Jeff Danziger's cartoons) were quite marketable. What is it that made *No Towers* so problematic in the post-9/11 climate? Spiegelman himself argues in *No Towers* that his work only became marketable when the U.S. entered the 2003 political season, thus subsuming his critique within the accepted narratives of political wrangling (3). I argue, however, that it is precisely the connection to trauma that makes Spiegelman's work so potentially destabilizing; after all, "while most newspapers were publishing stories about the solidarity of all Americans, Spiegelman was exposing the irrationality of the national community" (Arizzi 2008, 7). Unlike texts such as those listed above, which were in most cases satirical engagements with dominant narratives, Spiegelman's narrative is heavily ironic. As Kevin Dettmar (2006) argues:

[I]f satire is the critique of that which we comfortably hold at arm's length, irony is the critique of those shortcomings with which we ourselves identify . . . irony, to the degree that it's able to shed satire's self-protective impulses, seeks always to reveal error or folly or malfeasance and, in so doing, begin the work of correcting it. Because the ironist recognizes that he [*sic*] shares at least some common ground with his "target," he is to that degree unwilling to demolish the ground beneath his feet. (134)

Although several critics (Chute 2007; Espiritu 2006; Kuhlman 2007; Orbán 2007; Versluys 2006) foreground traumatic identity and response to the attacks, reaction by the mainstream U.S. press to Spiegelman's work seems to suggest otherwise. Rather than seeing *No Towers* as an urge to "bear witness," "testify," or negotiate the "secondary" trauma of the Holocaust through the new "primary" trauma of 9/11, it might be more useful to understand the volume as questioning those very associations. Indeed, as scholars like Andreas Huyssen (2000) argue, this questioning is central to understanding *Maus* as well (69–70). In other words, it is the combination of trauma (as a foreclosure of discourse) and irony (as reopening it through fragmented and multiplied narratives) that makes *No Towers* such a challenge to dominant representations of the events.

The challenge occurs in three steps: first, Spiegelman's portrayal of the attacks themselves, and the trauma of his extremely personal experience of them; second, his engagement with the Bush administration's co-optation of the events into nationalist fervor and the "war on terror"; third, his connection between the trauma of the events and the trauma of the co-optation in terms of his feelings of guilt, failure, and powerlessness. In other words, Spiegelman inhabits the dominant discourse of traumatic response only to question its sufficiency for an understanding of post-9/11 politics. As he viscerally experienced 9/11 as a rupture of his everyday life, his increasing alienation from the portrayal of the events retains an authenticity that acts as a direct challenge to nationalist rhetoric.

This rupture begins at the beginning, so to speak. The book is massive, its size and cardboard pages reminiscent of both newspapers and children's books, both invested with a sense of disposability and nostalgia that are at once "monumental" and "ephemeral," to use Spiegelman's terms (as cited in Siegal, 37). Although the cover was drawn from *The New Yorker* cover, its drama is immediately displaced by an inserted full-color window of historically significant comic characters in free fall after being kicked by an angry goat with a beard and turban. As Wyatt Mason suggests, "the cover puts us on notice that our regularly scheduled tragedy is about to be pre-empted by a cartoon version," its sanctity displaced by disposability and caricature (32). The first two pages similarly displace 9/11's historical exclusivity or privilege, contrasting it with the attempted assassination of President McKinley in 1901, and the next spread is a narrative of Spiegelman's personal experience of the attacks and his subsequent foray into being a political cartoonist. From there the narrative and visual aesthetics become increasingly fragmented, and as other scholars have noted represent drastic challenges to easy interpretation through sequential narrative or visual continuity (Chute 2007; Frienkel 2006; Kulhman 2007). These challenges, as Frienkel suggests, are endemic to comics themselves, whose "narrativity depends on the 'gappiness' of the narration" (251). However, it is important to recognize with Wyatt Mason that this "gappiness" does *not* resolve itself into any easy continuity, but instead "produces an estrangement from the distress that it describes: it sets the reader adrift" (32). Although he does acknowledge that "this all seems by design," Mason's desire for psychological or historical closure (which he suggests is characteristic of *Maus*) is perhaps misplaced. As Frienkel argues, "this failure to satisfy its readers is precisely what constitutes the text's success" (255).

How does this failure happen, and is it a gesture towards Spiegelman's trauma (as most scholars assume) or a critique of trauma? At first, it would seem that it is the former; the continuous alienation forced by the materiality and visual structure of the book would seem to foreground primary trauma. Indeed, the first few spreads of the narrative seem to echo this personal perspective. The first page begins in medias res from a "last episode" (a reference to a previous comic that does not exist), as New Yorkers are "waiting for the other shoe to drop." In other words, we assume that they are waiting for another attack. The next few spreads continue this theme of stasis, as Spiegelman draws himself saying that "time stands still at the moment of trauma," in which he continually sees "that awesome tower, glowing as it collapses" (2)! He also begins his narration of himself and his family, as "our hero" freaks out and attempts to find their children, students at the high school at the foot of the towers. The connection between the smell of the smoke of the crematoria at Auschwitz and the smell of the crumbled towers again sustains a reading of *No Towers* as traumatic narrative (2), as does his reflection on the images he *didn't* see (e.g., the people jumping to their deaths rather than enduring the heat and smoke of the burning buildings) (3). The next four spreads, however, barely discuss the events at all, and the final seven spreads are a "review" of historic comics, both commentary and reproduced plates.

What are we to make of this seeming disjuncture between a supposed trauma narrative and a text that seemingly undermines that narrative? Assuming *No Towers* is about Spiegelman's trauma, shouldn't the whole book be about his personal experience of the events, or his traumatic state afterwards? Maybe, maybe not. But if we reread the plates from the beginning, we begin to see that the narrative of Spiegelman's experience is far from clear-cut. Indeed, the events are never seen as separated from their co-optation; in fact, the discussion of the politicization and containment of "9/11" the concept (as opposed to the events of 9/11) largely dominates even the personal experience Spiegelman relates in the narrative. The first comic we see in the main spreads, as a matter of fact, is not personal at all. It portrays a stereotypical U.S. family sitting on a couch in front of a TV, not unlike dozens of other such images from family sitcoms and other comics. A patriarch with a can of beer and a tank top snoozes on one end of the couch, next to a sleeping matriarch in a bathrobe with a cat on her lap and a little girl sucking her thumb to her other side. A calendar says "Sept. 10" in the background. In the next frame, the calendar reads "Sept. 11," and all four characters (cat included) are shocked awake with frizzy hair and bulging red eyes. In the third and final frame, however, they return to their original positions (albeit still with frizzy hair), and the calendar has been replaced by a U.S. flag. The "synopsis: in our last episode" frame sits at an angle next to that comic, with another U.S. flag behind it, and the middle comic is a triptych of the burning towers on the left, Dan Rather's face in the middle, and a television set with another U.S. flag on it to the right. This comic, however, has captions: Spiegelman says he saw the "crumbling towers ... live—unmediated," but immediately notes that on television they "aren't much larger than, say, Dan Rather's head," and that "logos, on the other hand, look *enormous*" (1). These two comics dominate the visual landscape, at the top and center; we see the glowing afterimage of one tower on the right and bottom left, along with Spiegelman's personal narrative, but the immediate, nationalistic co-optation of the events is key.

This counternarrative to the expected story of trauma continues throughout. On the second spread, Spiegelman relates his compulsive desire to bear witness on comic frames that rotate until their form suggests the twin towers; it is an echo of trauma, as I noted above, but again it is firmly connected to the administration's response. In this case it's literal; an "albatross" that looks much more like a bald eagle, with an Uncle Sam hat on its head, is tied to his neck and screeches "everything's changed!," "go out and shop!," and "be afraid!" as Spiegelman narrates. The frame below shows Spiegelman at his drawing table, sleeping with a mouse mask over his face, as caricatures of Osama bin Laden and George Bush stand above him and he feels "equally terrorized by Al-Qaeda and his own government" (2). To the right appears a floating vertical comic in black in white, titled "notes of a heartbroken narcissist," in which Spiegelman grows a beard as he looks into a mirror, shaves it after some "bad reviews," and finally turns into a mouse. Even the dominant cartoon, which continues the personal narrative of Spiegelman and his wife searching for their children, is co-opted by an image of the Arnold Schwarzenegger film *Collateral Damage* (postponed and reedited after the attacks, as its plot revolves around a firefighter's wife and children dying in a bomb blast), whose billboard blocks his view of the towers. A caption under the billboard reads "oddly, in the aftermath of September 11th, some pundits insisted that irony was dead." Again, this affirms the tone of the rest of the book, whose narrative increasingly revolves around post-9/11 politics and less around his personal trauma; indeed, the personal trauma is in many ways completely subsumed into the nationalistic narrative. Ironically, as we see with the *Collateral Damage* frame, image replaces reality on both a literal and a figurative sense even before the towers fall.

The one thing that might complicate this counternarrative is Spiegelman's "mouse" identity, first seen as he sleeps with a mouse mask, then as he turns into a mouse, and then on the third spread as he speaks to the audience directly as a mouse, albeit a mouse in black and white, dressed in a button-down shirt and vest and surrounded by the smoke from his cigarettes. This is significant, of course, because it is a direct reference to *Maus*, in which Jewish characters are drawn as mice and Nazis are cats. In both *Maus* and *No Towers*, however, this is complicated significantly. Spiegelman appears both as a mouse and as a human with a mouse mask on in *Maus*, as do other characters. Many scholars, notably Linda Hutcheon (1999) and Andreas Huyssen (2000), suggest that not only do the mice represent oppression rather than identity, but also that the masks suggest feelings of "insecurity and survivor-guilt" (Hutcheon, 9) and the fragmentation of Spiegelman's narrative, in which he reaches a "crisis of representation and the crisis of success" (Huyssen, 79). In *No Towers*, Spiegelman seems to continue this ambivalence. He only occasionally appears as a mouse, and other characters only appear as mice in the last spread, in which New Yorkers wait for the "other cowboy boot" to drop as the city prepares for the 2004 Republican National Convention. As he suggests when he first changes into a mouse on the second spread, in *No Towers* the metamorphosis is not only a measure of his feelings of oppression, but is also a measure of a sense of his own narcissism, in which his own reactions take precedence over the events happening around him. His mouse identity is explicitly disconnected from his Jewish identity, moreover; when Spiegelman speaks about understanding why some Jews didn't leave Berlin after Kirstallnacht (4) and when he confronts a homeless woman who shouts anti-Semitic accusations at him (6), he is human rather than a mouse. In his monologues about the towers' smell (3) and depicting himself in the aftermath of nightmares about John Ashcroft (6) and embedded journalists (7), conversely, he is a mouse, and his "mother" is at first human with a gas mask and then a monster. In other words, Spiegelman is only a mouse *in his own mind*; when he interacts with the world around him, when he lives the everyday reality of his life, he is human.

Although the disconnect between Spiegelman's personal trauma and social trauma seems like a subtle point, it is in fact a key aspect of *No Towers*. Far from foregrounding the events themselves, Spiegelman at first posits the overwhelming nature of the political and cultural aftermath of 9/11 in nationalist and hawkish rhetoric. More importantly, I argue, he actively dismisses his sense of personal trauma for most of the book, instead turning to the political realities of his everyday life. After he recovers his daughter, for instance, he attempts to "comfortably relive [his] September 11 trauma" but is interrupted by the war, the 2002 "anniversary," and the election (5). When "he's starting to get nostalgic about his near-death experience back in September '01," Spiegelman is again interrupted, this time by the color-coded "terror alerts," nationalist rhetoric, and the polarized political climate of "red" versus "blue" states (7), and a similar scene occurs on the next spread.

THE TURN TO EVERYDAY LIFE

These scenes deliberately defy interpretation through the lens of trauma theory as a personal expression of everyday reality. In fact, it is Spiegelman's everyday life that reconnects him to his city, his political beliefs, and above all his family. This is certainly no coincidence; it foregrounds fragmentation as a productive rather than alienating force. In other words, Spiegelman's everyday experiences of fragmentation displace any feelings of retreat, complacency, or fear that he suggests lead to an uncritical acceptance of nationalism and, eventually, unjust war. As Jenny Edkins argues in *Trauma and the Memory of Politics* (2003), 9/11 is a time in which "trauma time collided with the time of the state, the time of capitalism, the time of routine," in which "the state, or whatever form of power is replacing it, has taken charge of trauma time" (233). If that is the case, then Spiegelman's affirmation of everyday life, whether it is through a domestic scene (8), a party scene (9), or an argument with his wife before an interview about 9/11 (10), combats this assertion of symbolic control. Orbán calls this his newfound "rooted cosmopolitanism" in the "local community … and … material space, rather than in the symbolic national community represented by the flag" (73). Similarly, Erin Arizzi (2008) suggests that even Spiegelman's Holocaust references are more a connection to family than they are to the events themselves (11), and that the dominance of the domestic in *No Towers* is a nostalgic reaction away from fearmongering towards war and towards family and friends, albeit crazy ones (12). Although Wyatt Mason argues that the fragmentation in the narrative from personal to family to national space is a blinding abstraction that is unable to bear witness to a traumatic history (33), I argue that it is exactly that fragmentation that preserves the critical function of the narrative.

Why must this be the case? Why couldn't Spiegelman, or so many others that commented and discussed 9/11, make a coherent case against war while still preserving the sense of traumatic identity that prefaced it? Why were many of the humorous attempts to engage 9/11 so easily censored, and why did political movements find themselves unable or unwilling to fight the nationalist or self-pitying rhetoric on which the Bush administration relied? How did the politics of 9/11, in other words, transition to post-9/11 politics, and what did that transition mean?

I argue that Spiegelman is responding to the sincerity of trauma discourse with the ironies of the everyday, and that this shift from the national to the personal or immediate is actually what allowed many of the most effective critiques of post-9/11 domestic and foreign policy, as the chapters in parts 2 and 3 of this volume suggest. As Joseph Boskin argues, U.S. political humor is historically inundated with "black holes" that in large part have made it unable to critique broad systemic flaws or cultural inconsistencies (473–74), and that it focuses on political red herrings like the president (477–78) rather than anticorporate or culturally critical humor (478–79). The turn to ironic discourse is key to understanding how contemporary humor, from *The Daily Show* to *South Park* to *The Onion*, has managed to ground powerful political critique in the fragmented and multiple world of everyday life. As Arizzi argues, *No Towers* "is not about finding conclusive answers. Rather, it is meant to, on the one hand, encourage its reader to critique and engage with the American media and the American government; and on the other, to help its reader mourn" (4–5). This doubling of political affect and effect is essential to ironic discourse as political critique; Spiegelman's criticism of nationalism is not intended to reject his home, but instead to replace the mythic national home with the small, dissonant experiences of everyday life. As Frienkel notes, "in recent lectures Spiegelman has referred to this self-trumping irony as a *neo-sincerity*: a sincerity reembraced once cynicism is itself cynically renounced. At stake is not so much a *return* to faith or to innocence, as a lack of faith in *non*-innocence" (250). History, Frienkel suggests, is built not on coherent narratives or myths, but instead on "the gaps in memory, the displacements of mourning, the moments of misrecognition and failed reckoning" around which we construct our lives. This form of ironic narrative rejects the rhetoric of "heroes," "villains," "good," and "evil," as Espiritu argues, as that type of discourse is easily co-opted and closely tied to the forms of nationalism that form the basis of Spiegeleman's own, and his parents', traumas (184, 188–89).

In his essay on *Maus*, Andreas Huyssen asks a few questions that seem particularly relevant to *No Towers* and the turn towards irony in the post-9/11 public sphere: "How does one get past the official memorial culture? How does one avoid the trappings of the culture industry while operating within it? How does one represent that which one knows only through representations and from an ever growing historical distance? All this requires new narrative and figurative strategies including irony, shock, black humor, even cynicism" (81). Indeed, Kevin Dettmar (2006) suggests that what distinguishes post-9/11 politics from pre-9/11 politics is that the attacks and their aftermath "may have shaken irony out of the lazy cynicism into which it had settled and, rather than rendering it obsolete, has made ironic critique more urgent than ever" (139). In *No Towers*, the turn to everyday life as a displaced or fragmented site functions to push past the autistic understanding of community in nationalism, replacing it with a shared narrative that is never unified, never complete, and never ending.

This technique has a history, of course. As Lanita Jacobs in this volume and Bambi Haggins (2007) have argued, ironic identity and discourse have historically allowed oppressed communities to politically engage the dominant. By challenging common sense, which Richard Rorty (2007) considered to be its opposite, irony is able to energize social critique, especially in terms of humorous discourse which often relies on a sense of disjunction or incongruity. Rorty argues that "an ironist" does three things: doubts the discourse of her social system, realizes that phrasing arguments in that discourse cannot challenge the system, and recognizes that it makes more sense to understand the world through multiple points of view rather than her own preconceptions if she desires progressive social change (73). Although it is important to recognize, as does Linda Hutcheon in *Irony's Edge* (1994), that irony is fundamentally ambivalent as political discourse (that is, like satire it can be mobilized either for the left or the right) (10, 16, 29), because it "foregrounds human agency" (11–12) irony is often useful to oppositional movements and can "relate and relativize" rather than "exclude and finalize" (17). These features of irony make it an essential tool for progressive change in moments of extreme repression or nationalism like the immediate aftermath of 9/11, and allow it to invigorate works like *In the Shadow of No Towers* that seek to "complexify" rather than "disambiguate" (13). Although it carries with it an anger, or "an affective 'charge'" in Hutcheon's terms, irony's edge also allows silenced voices to slip past larger narratives of trauma, nation, and unity by retaining their connection to everyday life and by pointing out the inconsistencies between the experience of the political (a communal search for understanding, mourning, and contested space), on the one hand, and the mythology of politics (nationalism as a solution to a betrayed American Dream) on the other.

NOTES

1. I will refer to the volume as the abbreviated *No Towers* as well as the full title throughout this chapter.

2. See also Simpson (2006, 166) for a fascinating discussion of the repercussions of this sort of discourse.

WORKS CITED

Art Spiegelman: Voice in the Wilderness. 2003. *The Independent*, Sept. 11.

Arizzi, Erin. 2008. Toward a 'Rooted Cosmopolitanism': Reading *In the Shadow of No Towers* as a Call for Local Community. In *Conference Paper: National Communication Association*.

Birge, Sarah. 2007. Review of *In the Shadow of No Towers* by Art Spiegelman. *Journal of Medical Humanities* 28 (3): 181–183.

Boskin, Joseph. 1990. American Political Humor: Touchables and Taboos. *International Political Science Review* 11 (4): 473–482.

Chute, Hillary. 2007. Temporality and Seriality in Spiegelman's *In the Shadow of No Towers*. *American Periodicals* 17 (2): 228-244.

Dayan, Daniel, and Elihu Katz. 1992. *Media Events: The Live Broadcasting of History.* Cambridge: Harvard University Press.

Dettmar, Kevin. 2006. "Authentically Ironic": Neoconservatism and the Backlash. *Journal of the Midwest Modern Language Association* 39 (1): 134-144.

Edkins, Jenny. 2003. *Trauma and the Memory of Politics.* Cambridge: Cambridge University Press.

Espiritu, Karen. 2006. 'Putting Grief into Boxes': Trauma and the Crisis of Democracy in Art Spiegelman's *In the Shadow of No Towers. The Review of Education, Pedagogy, and Cultural Studies* 28 (2): 179-201.

Foster, R. Thomas. 2005. Cynical Nationalism. In *The Selling of 9/11: How a National Tragedy Became a Commodity,* edited by D. Heller. New York: Palgrave MacMillan.

Freinkel, Lisa Myobun. 2006. BOOK REVIEW: Art Spiegelman: *In the Shadow of No Towers. Visual Communication Quarterly* 13 (Fall): 1–9.

Fullerton, Carol S., James E. McCarroll, Robert J. Ursano, and Kathleen M. Wright. 1992. Psychological Responses of Rescue Workers: Fire Fighters and Trauma. *American Journal of Orthopsychiatry* 62 (3): 371-378.

Garrick, Jacqueline. 2006. The Humor of Trauma Survivors: Its Application in a Therapeutic Milieu. In *Trauma Treatment Techniques: Innovative Trends,* edited by J. Garrick and M. B. Williams. Binghamton, NY: The Halworth Maltreatment and Trauma Press.

Gournelos, Ted. 2009. Othering the Self: Dissonant Visual Culture and Quotidian Trauma in United States Suburbia. *Cultural Studies <=> Critical Methodologies* 9 (4): 509–532.

Grossman, Lev. 2004. The Way We Live Now. *Time,* Jan. 4, 87.

Haggins, Bambi. 2007. *Laughing Mad: The Black Comic Persona in Post-Soul America.* New Brunswick: Rutgers University Press.

Hajdu, David. 2004. 'In the Shadow of No Towers': Homeland Insecurity. *New York Times,* Sept. 12.

Heller, Dana, ed. 2005. *The Selling of 9/11: How a National Tragedy Became a Commodity.* New York: Palgrave MacMillan.

Hutcheon, Linda. 1994. *Irony's Edge: The Theory and Politics of Irony.* New York: Routledge.

———. 1999. Literature Meets History: Counter-Dicoursive "Comix." *Anglia-Zeitschrift für Englische Philologie* 117 (1).

Huyssen, Andreas. 2000. Of Mice and Mimesis: Reading Spiegelman with Adorno. *New German Critique* 81 (3): 65–82.

Jones, Malcolm. 2004. High Art. *Newsweek,* Aug. 3, 51–52.

Kuhlman, Martha. 2007. The Traumatic Temporality of Art Spiegelman's In the Shadow of No Towers. *The Journal of Popular Culture* 40 (5): 849–866.

Kunkle, Jeffrey. 2005. Standing in the Shadows of History. *Theory & Research in Social Education* 33 (4): 548–552.

Lewis, Paul. 2006. *Cracking Up: American Humor in a Time of Conflict.* Chicago: University of Chicago Press.

Mason, Wyatt. 2004. The Holes in His Head. *The New Republic,* Sept. 21, 30–33.

Moran, Carmen, and Margaret Massam. 1997. An Evaluation of Humor in Emergency Work. *The Australasian Journal of Disaster and Trauma Studies* 1997 (3).

Orbán, Katalin. 2007. Trauma and Visuality: Art Spiegelman's *Maus* and *In the Shadow of No Towers*. *Representations* 97 (4): 57–89.

Princenthal, Nancy. 2005. The Tall Towers of Art Spiegelman. *ArtUS*, Feb 10, 38–41.

Rorty, Richard. 2007. *Contingency, Irony, and Solidarity*. New York: Cambridge University Press. Original edition, 1989.

Siegal, Nina. 2005. Art Spiegelman. *Progressive*, Jan. 15, 35–39.

Simpson, David. 2006. *9/11: The Culture of Commemoration*. Chicago: University of Chicago Press.

Spiegelman, Art. 2004. *In The Shadow of No Towers*. New York: Pantheon Books.

Theokas, Christopher. 2004. Haunting Images of 'No Towers.' *USA Today*, Sept. 7, 1–2.

CHAPTER SIX

REPUBLICAN DECLINE AND CULTURE WARS IN 9/11 HUMOR

—David Holloway

Towards the end of Frédéric Beigbeder's *Windows on the World* (2004), a 9/11 novel that relates the deaths of a father and his children in the North Tower of the World Trade Center, there is a moment of characteristically Beigbederian black humor. With his tongue wedged firmly in his cheek, the narrator describes the "apocalyptic politeness" of post-9/11 New Yorkers, who have begun escorting blind people across city streets and surrendering their places in lines for cabs (Beigbeder 2004, 195). The rather bleak and intellectual joke depends on the reader recognizing the futility of these civic gestures, for, as Beigbeder tells us, the fragile late blooming of citizenship and republican virtue encoded in post-9/11 "apocalyptic politeness" occurs in an epoch when permissive liberalism and late capitalism have wrecked the republican moral compass.[1] As a restitution of civic virtue, helping the blind across New York City streets is too little, too late. So late, in fact, as to be comical, given what the narrator describes as the domination of twenty-first-century American social life by the rhythms of commodified and private desire, driven by the dynamics of the market, a permissive culture of instant gratification, and the lingering consequences, for Beigbeder's narrator, of the post-1960s sexual revolution.

The grim truth of Beigbeder's joke echoes throughout *Windows on the World*, where the permissive liberalism of Western societies since the 1960s is shown to have broken up the network of civic attachments that are forged, contractually, between and among citizens, and between citizens and the state. These attachments are integral to the cohesion of liberal capitalist societies, for they both help solidify the sense of rights, responsibilities, and citizenship, and help secure the illusions of egalitarian, democratic process, without which capitalism can only sustain and reproduce itself by force, or by intense forms of state control. Such civic attachments are particularly important in the segregated and highly privatized late capitalist U.S., where the sentimental ideal of citizenship in a classless republic still exerts a powerful ideological pull. In *Windows on the World*, these civic attachments have been swept away. Liberal capitalism has destroyed the things it needs to sustain and reproduce itself. "If the individual is king," as the narrator observes, "then only selfishness makes sense." He continues, "I blame the consumer society for making me what I am . . . incapable of loving anyone except myself" (Beigbeder, 143, 181–82). Where another famous Frenchman travelling in America, Alexis de Tocqueville, once saw a young republic unified organically around a set of egalitarian values whose "immense influence" extended across "the whole course of society" (de Tocqueville 1988, 9), after 9/11 Frédéric Beigbeder sensed only republican decline.

Beigbeder's joke about apocalyptic politeness articulates two related and overlapping themes that quickly became paradigmatic in early 9/11 humor. First, the joke articulates a traditional declinist narrative that is never far from the surface of American political culture, particularly in times of crisis and war, and which has roots all the way back to seventeenth-century New England, where Puritan anxiety about "backsliding" and the break up of the commonwealth produced the New England jeremiad, an enduring legacy of the colonial period. Traditionally, Euro-American narratives of republican decline chart the corrosive impact of a set of malign variables—big business, class, luxury, authoritarianism, excessive freedom, "alien" values or political traditions—on the institutions and mores of the republic. After 9/11 the theme of the republic as hijacked, stolen, or lost was again widely heard. The Bush administration was accused of acting illegally in federal and international law, and of eroding due process and accountability. Historians, political scientists and philosophers discussed republicanism's incompatibility with empire. The executive office of the United States government, it was said, had been infiltrated by a sinister cabal of neoconservative warhawks and corporate powerbrokers. These claims were sometimes reductive or simplistic, but their widespread dissemination contributed to the emergence of a discourse about a loss of popular sovereignty and a general attenuation of republican processes and institutions that was compounded by a series of high profile inquiries and reports describing state agencies and institutions as unfit for purpose on the day of the 9/11 attacks.[2]

Second, as in Beigbeder's joke, early 9/11 humor articulating traditional anxieties about republican decline was often framed by perspectives rooted in contemporary American "culture wars": the enduring conflicts over "identity" and "lifestyle" politics that first ignited, in their twenty-first-century forms, during the 1960s. At the end of the cold war, the term "culture wars" referred primarily to debates about or within "multiculturalism." These debates generally focused on race, ethnicity, gender, sexual orientation, and to a lesser extent class, as key markers of identity, with society construed as a body politic splintered into conflicting—and internally conflicted—interest groups and cultures. By 9/11, the scope of what many Americans understood by the term "culture wars," and the commitments they felt were intrinsic to identity, had broadened considerably to include a new diversity of divisions and disputes over religion, secularism, marriage, abortion, permissive sexuality, education, the environment, euthanasia, stem-cell research, the social impacts of popular culture, and, increasingly after 9/11, over America's role in the world.

Beigbeder's joke about apocalyptic politeness acts as a window on this spreading twenty-first-century definition of "culture wars," and also exemplifies the link between republican decline and contemporary "cultural" conflict that was often made in early 9/11 humor. The joke is funny because its context in the novel makes the civic behavior it describes incongruous and ironic, the main protagonist having sustained an unrelenting diatribe on the disintegrative social impacts of "raging liberalism" (Beigbeder, 291) and the breakup of the monogamous nuclear family—that molecular social unit of a lost cold war age for which the novel at times seemed overtly nostalgic. The narrator describes himself as "collateral damage" in the wreckage of the family, a product of the "disappearing father" and the end of sexual fidelity (Beigbeder, 181). Long before 9/11, in *Windows on the World*, New York was already Sodom on the slide, and the returning civic virtue of "apocalyptic politeness" is the flimsiest of gestures in a declining, decadent culture that has surrendered itself, almost entirely, to the corrosive logics of moral permissivism and private desire.

Making 9/11 meaningful in this way, through the intersecting prisms of humor, republican decline, and contemporary culture wars, was a notable trend in early representation of 9/11, with the attacks themselves widely described at the time (albeit problematically) as a Huntingtonian "clash of civilizations," a transnational culture war of epic proportions between "Islam" and "the West" (Huntington 1996, 1998). The examples discussed in this essay are politically diverse, and often politically ambiguous or contradictory. Underlying despair at the state of the union was a recurring theme, as 9/11 became the platform not just for discourse about foreign wars, but also for discourse about the tensions and conflicts shaping American society. Often, decline seemed irreversible. In David Rees's *Get Your War On*, a bleakly funny strip cartoon first published on the World Wide Web, the overriding theme seemed to be the disempowerment of citizens in the face of authoritarianism. Variations on this "postrepublican" theme were common in early 9/11 humor. In a Hollywood movie like *Team America: World Police*, or a TV series like *Rescue Me*, culture-war politics either appear to be antithetical to traditional republican mores, or to have supplanted them altogether as the normative political culture, fragmenting and stratifying "America" into multiple, sectional group-interests, corroding the sense of common belonging to a populist public sphere on which classical conceptions of republicanism traditionally depend.

One key figure in this shift was Michael Moore, whose controversial account of 9/11 and its aftermath, *Fahrenheit 9/11* (2004), won the 2004 *Palme D'or* at the Cannes film festival and sparked a major revival in the fortunes of political documentary in Western cinemas. While the ironic humor of *Rescue Me* or *Team America* often appeared mired in a brand of identity politics the texts found difficult to reconcile with traditional notions of republicanism, *Fahrenheit 9/11* welded liberal culture-war positions to a republican vision rooted in Jeffersonian assumptions about citizenship and participatory democracy.

At variance, politically, with postrepublican culture like *Team America* and *Rescue Me*, *Fahrenheit 9/11* nonetheless shared the same brand of bleak, *ironic* humor that was characteristic of the early post-9/11 period. Irony seems an entirely appropriate mode for writers and audiences attuned to the sensitivities of twenty-first-century American culture wars; irony's doubleness—its saying one thing but meaning another—making for relativist humor that is always alive to the "other" position or point of view. For Randolph Bourne, an intellectual founder of American multiculturalism, irony meant having "all the little parts of one's world . . . constantly set off against each other, and made intelligible only by being translated into and defined in each others' terms" (Bourne 1977, 134). To speak ironically, Bourne felt, was to abandon "fixed, immutable standards" (Bourne, 136). As the concluding part of this essay notes, however, in post-9/11 humor irony's propensity for saying one thing but also meaning another sometimes worked in less progressive ways, dressing pernicious, wholly reactionary, "postrepublican" culture-war positions as edgy, subversive, taboo-busting humor.

REPUBLICAN HUMOR

Fahrenheit 9/11 and Michael Moore's best-selling books-of-the-film, *Stupid White Men* (2002) and *Dude, Where's My Country?* (2003), were paradigm-defining texts. Their humorous representations of 9/11 and the Bush administration as triggers for accelerated republican decline, and their attempts to revive and reassert traditional notions of citizenship and participatory democracy, were overtly grounded in liberal culture-war positions (particularly on education, race, gender, class, the environment, and American foreign policy). *Fahrenheit 9/11*, in particular, reached mass audiences in the U.S. and around the world. Moore's depiction of the U.S. as a deeply divided society governed by incompetent, self-serving, authoritarian elites gave the film a populist, dissident chic that undercut prevailing representations of 9/11 as an assault on civilization, freedom, and democracy.

Moore's uses of humor to chart narratives of republican decline, and to energize countervailing narratives of republican redress, have deep transnational roots in the cultural histories of Western republics, where laughter has traditionally played an important role in the construction and reproduction of republican political cultures. In classical Rome, for example, wit had an explicitly civic function as a tool for the presentation of political rhetoric (Graf 1997), while one characteristic of the French Parliamentary Assembly of 1789–91, as Antoine de Baecque has shown, was the emergence of "a collective political humour established as a tool of persuasion and combat" (de Baecque 1997, 181). Debate about the appropriate uses of laughter, de Baecque demonstrates, "gripped" the revolutionary French Assembly during these years (de Baecque, 188).

It is a convention, if not a cliché of contemporary cultural studies, that hilarity in public space is associated with the disordering energies of *carnivale*, but the self-consciousness of debate about humor in the French Parliamentary Assembly suggests an ordering principle at work, a *discursive* function for laughter in the modelling and maintenance of a republican political order. In the French Assembly, humor flourished principally as a corrective to "out-of-place discourse, behaviour and actions" (de Baecque, 184), and thus also as a rhetorical purging of "unrepublican" mores from the political process. In Rome, too, senatorial wit was a discourse whose functions included the castigation of those who transgressed the rules of the senatorial class, preserving the integrity of the republic—or the integrity of the elites who presided in its name—by policing and reaffirming the norms of republican political culture (Graf, 32).

This discursive, or disciplinary, function of republican humor is reiterated in *Fahrenheit 9/11*, where one of Moore's objectives is to redress and purge what he depicts as the hijacking of republican high office by corporate-political elites.[3] *Fahrenheit 9/11* pursues this objective by positioning the Bush administration beyond the bounds of respectable republican conduct and legitimacy, employing ironic humor and polemical editing to expose contradictions, inconsistencies, and incompetence in executive-led homeland security initiatives and foreign policy. A sequence on the administration's post-9/11 ban on breast milk on airplanes runs into an interview with the part-time state trooper whose duties include single-handedly patrolling one hundred miles of unprotected coastline in Oregon. Footage of the president declaring victory in Iraq, on the flight deck of the USS *Abraham Lincoln* in May 2003, is cut against film of U.S. soldiers being blown to pieces by insurgents. Donald Rumsfeld discusses America's humanitarian prosecution of the Iraq war, accompanied by pictures of dead Iraqi children. The climactic sequence, a rousing denunciation of neoconservatism as permanent war in defence of a hierarchical, class society, runs into Neil Young's ironic grunge anthem, "Rockin' in the Free World."

Moore's ironic, agitprop humor is at its most effective when presented in the form of montage, typically as an agglomeration of episodic visual footage, music, and his own polemical voice-overs. From the combination and clashing of these different elements, Moore fashions powerful indictments of republican decline that emanate, he contends, from the combined influence of political elites and corporate capital. In one memorable sequence, slapstick news footage shows Bush playing golf and chopping logs on his ranch while final preparations for the 9/11 attacks unfold, to the tune of "Vacation" by the Go-Gos. The sequence ends on September 10, 2001, with footage of a young boy being tucked into bed by his mother, accompanied by Moore's caustic voice-over: "He [Bush] went to sleep that night in a bed made with fine French linens." Folded into the visual and musical accusation that Bush "fiddled" while the republic lay in mortal peril, the voice-over's reference to "fine French linens" reemphasizes his membership in a distant, privileged elite, while the president's depiction as a dependent child reiterates *Fahrenheit 9/11*'s central claim that Bush had failed in his primary role as protector of the American people, or figurative "father" to the nation.

Moore emphasized both the dangers of republican "backsliding" in the wake of 9/11 and the centrality of citizenship as a theme in his work in the special introduction he wrote for the edition of *Stupid White Men* published for English-speaking audiences outside North America, carefully contextualizing the book in republican political culture. In the new introduction, Moore recalled how his publisher, HarperCollins, which is owned by Rupert Murdoch's media conglomerate, News Corp., tried to prevent the book's publication; HarperCollins had decided that 9/11 made *Stupid White Men* commercially untenable, given its outspoken attacks on President Bush.

Moore told the story of how one American, Ann Sparanese, a librarian from New Jersey, led a citizens' revolt, campaigning for the book to be published and against restrictions imposed on First Amendment rights by big business and its representatives in government. In the populist terms of Moore's parable, the "junta" (the Bush administration) "and its cohorts in Corporate America (a separate, autonomous fiefdom within the United States that has been allowed to run on its own for some time)," were the antithesis of "the American people"—people like Anne Sparanese or Moore himself, and the "hundreds, and eventually thousands" of librarians Moore described rallying to Sparanese's cause, "leading the charge" against the erosion of constitutional rights by oligarchs (Moore 2002, 3, xix, xvi, xviii). Moore has been described as a Marxist, a revolutionary, and an anti-American, notably by HarperCollins authors David Hardy and Jason Clarke (Hardy and Clarke 2004, 61, 63), but none of these claims captures Moore's authentic political voice. In part, *Fahrenheit 9/11*, like the parable of Ann Sparanese, was a populist republican fable about the need for watchfulness when dealing with governments, and the dangers posed to the republic by corporate capitalism—traditional, populist, republican themes that resurfaced dramatically in the mainstream of U.S. thought and culture after 9/11.

Fahrenheit 9/11 was also a story about the defense of liberty through progressive acts of citizenship. "Giving a few hours . . . each week to be *citizens*," Moore wrote in 2001, is "the highest honor to hold in a democracy" (Moore 2002, 256, his italics). The film followed this precept to the letter, turning *Fahrenheit 9/11* into a grand statement of citizen-led participatory democracy. As in his previous films, *Roger and Me* and *Bowling for Columbine*, in *Fahrenheit 9/11* Moore starred in multiple roles as activist, director, celebrity, interviewer, and humorist, and was present, visually or audibly, as a distinct "authorial" presence throughout. *Fahrenheit 9/11* also featured Moore's characteristic "stunts," one slapstick sequence showing him riding around the Capitol in an ice-cream van reading the USA Patriot Act (2001) through a megaphone—a citizen exercising his citizenship in the only manner he can (his representatives in Congress having passed the Patriot Act without reading it, let alone debating it). The slapstick reinforces Moore's critique of republican decline by emphasizing the ridiculous lengths to which citizens must go to exercise their citizenship in Bush's America.

One mechanism that captured and carried this politics of republican redress was a slippage in Moore's narrative voice from first-person pronouns ("I," "my," "me") to collective ones ("our," "we," and "us"). Commonplace in his prose at the time, which often reads like a set of shooting notes for *Fahrenheit 9/11*, this slippage is also visible in the film, notably in the concluding act where the humor is largely displaced, the switch in tone alerting viewers to the lessons the film wants us to absorb ("read and laugh," as French republicans put it in the eighteenth century, "then re-read and ponder" [de Baecque 1997]). In the final sequence, Moore frames the military service of working-class Americans in Orwellian terms, quoting from Orwell's *1984* to depict militarism as an exercise in the maintenance of hierarchical social order in the United States. "I've always been amazed," the voice-over attests, "that the very people forced to live in the worst parts of town, go to the worst schools, and who have it the hardest, are always the first to step up to defend that very system. They serve so that we don't have to. They offer to give up their lives so that we can be free. It is remarkable, their gift to us. And all they ask for in return is that we never send them into harm's way unless it's absolutely necessary. Will they ever trust us again?" To function as a "citizen" is to realize and reinforce one's individuality by membership in a collective, public sphere, and the slippage between the "I" and the "we" in the climactic sequence of *Fahrenheit 9/11* (and the symbolic subordination of the former to the latter in linguistic acts of citizenship) brings the film to a close with a powerful reassertion of civic values and process.

Moore's "we" in his 9/11 work was usually an unfixed, decentered "we" that aimed to speak rhetorically to, and for, different groups at the same time. *Fahrenheit 9/11* spoke a common message to African Americans and white Americans alike, by turning black poverty and white poverty into the common, "color-blind" experience of class. Moore's writing at the time also highlights the common ground shared by groups who are often divided into hermetic blocks of competing "group interests" in the identity politics of contemporary American culture wars. The title alone of *Stupid White Men* drew attention to Moore's culture wars "multivoicing," indicating that gender and race would be equally important in his analysis of maladministration by an elite political/economic class. *Fahrenheit 9/11* harnessed its humor to a distinctive post-1960s identity politics with a view to building progressive coalitions between and among the diverse groups who shared a common interest, Moore argued, in defending the republic against big business and political authoritarianism. Even though Moore's 9/11 work usually addressed deeply divisive issues, by speaking simultaneously to different audiences in this "multivoicing" way, he attempted to unite Americans against Bush rather than divide them further among themselves.

These coalitions tended to be implied rather than explicit, but they were visible enough in the broad, inclusive chorus of ordinary American citizens the film summoned to speak against Bush. Black, white, multiethnic, male and female, old and young, working class, underclass, and middle-class Americans all appear in *Fahrenheit 9/11* as citizen-witnesses, to denounce a regime that is said to have betrayed them. Families, cops, peace groups, senior citizens, schoolkids, welfare workers, writers, FBI agents, politicians, businessmen, voters, servicemen and -women, and a host of other concerned citizens' groups, each with their own stake in the civic affairs of the post-9/11 republic, all speak directly to camera during *Fahrenheit 9/11*. Scripting the film in this way, so that it often seems to speak directly through the voices of the republican body politic, *Fahrenheit 9/11* effects a "merging of Moore's voice and the voice of the film with 'the people,'" with Moore's performances as director, activist, and humorist becoming also performances of a more civic nature—"performances, as it were, of the obligations that citizens owed to the world beyond themselves, in return for the protections afforded them by their membership in public space" (Holloway 2008, 102).

Moore's politics of republican redress in *Fahrenheit 9/11* are closely linked to a multicultural model of republican identity. "*Real* patriotism," he wrote, means "standing up so that all points of view are heard" (Moore 2002, xiii, his italics). This principle is traditionally associated in the U.S. with the rights and responsibilities of individuals, but Moore's 9/11 humor attached it seamlessly to liberal culture wars' emphasis on group-rights and identities. If Moore's republic in *Fahrenheit 9/11* was traditionally populist, one where the people stood opposed to the money trust, his was also a postmodern— which in this context means post-1960s—republican vision, which looked to multiculturalism as the fulcrum of traditional values in an age of republican decline. Artfully woven together by Moore's multivoicing, the film presented viewers with a republic that is strengthened and renewed by its multiculturalist identity-politics, and that can purge itself of Bush-era backsliding by recommitting itself to difference and to the principle of a union of differences.

These culture-war commitments are at their most overt toward the end of *Fahrenheit 9/11*, as Moore gathers the threads of his discussion about Iraq into a powerful sequence of interviews with Lila Lipscomb, a citizen from Flint, Michigan, whose son, Michael, was killed in Iraq. The sequence is emotionally and politically explosive. Lila is depicted by Moore as the model American citizen, her loss presented as compelling proof of republican decline and the betrayal of the people by elites. Lila, Moore's interviews tell us, is hardworking, self-reliant, honest, god-fearing, a friend to the underdog, the exploited, and the powerless, a loving and resourceful mother and a proud patriot who hangs the flag outside her home every morning. Edited into the footage of Lila hanging the flag—as resonant and profound an image of republican belonging as any in the American corpus—is a passage in which she displays the cross she wears around her neck. It is "a multicolored and multicultural cross," Lila says, which she wears because "all God's people come in many colors." The model American citizen, the one on whom our consent to the film's worldview substantially hangs in the movie's climactic final act, is a multiculturalist, a point powerfully underscored in subsequent scenes showing the interracial Lipscomb family gathered in their lounge, as Lila reads Michael's last letter from Iraq, in which her dead son denounces Bush's war.

In Moore's 9/11 culture-war humor, "standing up so that all points of view are heard" also means privileging positions that relativized America, turning the U.S. into just one local culture among others, with habits and totems that may appear strange or unfathomable to "others." The new introduction for the edition of *Stupid White Men* published for English-speaking audiences outside North America, in which Moore self-consciously contextualizes the book in native traditions of participatory democracy and citizenship, signifies a refusal to universalize Americanism that was provocative to say the least in the aftermath of 9/11, a period when the *National Security Strategy of the United States* announced that American values were "right and true for every person, in every society . . . across the globe and across the ages" (National Security Strategy 2002). By contrast, Moore's hyperbolic humility was conveyed in a series of humorous ironies. America under Bush, he said, was a "banana republic." Regime change was needed at home. The rest of the world, provocatively embodied by Moore as the United Nations, was described as the last best hope for America, rather than America as the last best hope for the world. What the American banana republic needed, Moore said, was "U.N. observers, U.N. troops, U.N. resolutions!" "Oh, say, can you see," he asked, "are the Belgian peacekeepers on their way? Hurry!" (Moore 2002, 3, 2).

POSTREPUBLICAN HUMOR

Moore's culture-war aesthetics of republican redress exemplified one important strand in early representation of 9/11. Generally, though, it was a bleaker, "postrepublican" irony that prevailed, in which notions like citizenship, participatory democracy, and civic virtue often appeared quaint or illogical, or did not appear at all, having been supplanted by culture-war politics that seemed to negate or transfigure such traditional republican commitments. "Postrepublican" humorists often seemed to agree with declinists like Moore that the republic was imperilled on and after 9/11 because "the people" had been betrayed by elites. Where they differed was in their tacit assumption that republican decline was intractable or irresistible, and already mature as a political trend in contemporary American culture. In *Fahrenheit 9/11* Moore did not simply chart decline, but also responded to it, using humor to forge acts of republican redress, simultaneously countering and compensating for decline by deploying humor as a progressive weapon in the broader network of culture-war conflicts the film engaged. In the bleaker milieu of postrepublicanism, this overtly civic function for humor often seemed muted, neutered, paralyzed, or lost.

One early example of postrepublican humor was David Rees's haiku-like comic strip, *Get Your War On*, which first appeared as an Internet Web page on October 9, 2001, two days after the U.S. began bombing Afghanistan.[4] *Get Your War On* depicted American workers debating the responses of their government to 9/11, using computer-generated "clip-art" figures for characters so that Rees's citizens were visually presented as anonymous, generic, commodified, and endlessly reproducible ciphers.

Get Your War On denounced the political and moral influence of the religious Right, and took sideswipes at the Bush administration's record on the environment. Its most intrusive dimension, though, was in the bland, bleached-out ethnicity of its clip-art characters, some of whom looked African American but were rendered generically colorless, evoking both a hypersensitivity to and a color-blind determination to repress ethnic or racial difference. Framed within this contradictory culture-war double bind, *Get Your War On*'s clip-art characters raged about the absurdities of war and the inequities of American society, using ironic humor to expose contradictions and inconsistencies in official accounts of 9/11 and war in Afghanistan. "We'll be sure to tell your grieving mother about the great college scholarships available to our soldiers who are alive," quipped one of Rees's characters, satirizing the attitude of officialdom toward U.S. soldiers leaving for Afghanistan. Another early subject was the dropping of food aid to Afghan refugees in areas riddled with mines. "It turns the relief effort into a fun game for the Afghan people," Rees's character observed, "a game called 'See if you have any fucking arms left to eat the food we dropped after you step on a landmine trying to retrieve it!'" (Rees 2002, np., October 9, 2001).

Most of all, however, Rees's generic post-citizens raged about their own inability to influence or impact the public world around them. "Maybe I should write a poem about my feelings since September 11th," one character wondered, "that might help!" Unable to find this poetic voice, the opening lines the character discards include "Dramatic self medication increase," "Visions of despair, illusions of hope," and "I'm starting to look like a damn ghost" (Rees 2002, np., October 30, 2001). "Do you have any alcohol left in your cubicle?" another character asked. "I've been studying current events again" (Rees 2002, np., October 14, 2001). In a familiar post-9/11 narrative of republican decline, Rees's characters denounced the Bush administration for eroding constitutional entitlements, subverting the Bill of Rights, and transforming the presidency into "a constitutional monarchy" (Rees 2002, np., November 29, 2001). The formal qualities of the clip art reinforced this discourse of attenuated popular sovereignty visually, reiterating the sense of citizen-impotence that was Rees's central theme. "How better to illustrate the horrific repetition of those days," as Colson Whitehead observed in his introduction to the book edition of *Get Your War On*, "than to have these representative citizens re-enact the same poses again and again, mouth the same platitudes and speculations over and over, without progress or relief." As Whitehead put it, Rees's clip-art citizens seemed "[f]rozen in ignorance. Paralyzed by helplessness" (Whitehead 2002, iv).

Where Moore's work mined native traditions of participatory democracy, using humor to take politics to mass audiences, *Get Your War On*, it was said at the time, helped build a sense of community among Americans who disagreed with their president's analysis of 9/11, but who found themselves marginalized at a time when domestic mass media and public opinion were overwhelmingly in favor of war. As the hyperlink to Rees's Web site was passed on, Whitehead suggests, "email by email his comics reinvigorated the community. We had been atomized by television, separated from each other," and *Get Your War On* told dissenters "at least we are not alone" (Whitehead, v). Rees also compensated, literally, for the republican dysfunction he charted in *Get Your War On* by donating all royalties from the first book edition to a land mine removal scheme in Afghanistan sponsored by the United Nations Association of the United States of America, a not-for-profit organization that promotes support for the U.N. in the U.S. With its charitable donations, and its function as a nodal point around which dissident communities could gather and grow, *Get Your War On* exhibited again the post-9/11 period's interest in defending and reinvigorating republican space and process; but even at its most satirical and savvy it had an air of damage limitation and an underlying despair that was clearly at odds with the republican optimism of Michael Moore.

Narratives of republican decline framed in the political vernacular of contemporary culture wars were also central to *Team America*, a comedic puppet movie modelled closely on the "supermarionation" style of *Thunderbirds* (the classic TV series created by Gerry and Sylvia Anderson in the 1960s), with the titular "Team" as a hypernationalist reworking of *Thunderbirds*' privateer security agency, "International Rescue," updated and retooled for the post-9/11 era. The story, in which the Team foil a joint plot by North Korea and al Qaeda to annihilate the West, quickly acquired the same kind of edgy reputation as *South Park*, the TV series for which the film's producers were previously best known. For some contemporary audiences the movie was an opportunity to laugh, if only in a loose allegorical fashion, at American national security strategy. The gonzoid forms of supermarionation puppet theatre seemed perfect for exploring, satirically, the banal polarities and simplistic certainties about America and the rest of the world that underpinned Bush administration foreign policy after 9/11. The Team wreak indiscriminate death and destruction wherever they tread, with the Eiffel Tower, the Louvre, the Pyramids, and the Sphinx among the more recognizable landmarks destroyed as collateral damage in the Team's war on terror. In this respect, at least, *Team America* appeared to merit its reputation as edgy, subversive humor geared to a progressive critique of American institutions.

For some audiences, the film also offered an opportunity to laugh at the reactionary cultural politics of Hollywood. When the hero, Gary Johnston, "the world's best actor," approaches a terrorist stronghold in Cairo, he walks like a western gunfighter. When he looks longingly at the glamorous Lisa, he does so with an exaggerated, puppet version of the Hollywood "male gaze." *Team America* featured blockbuster clichés in abundance: car chases, explosions, a love story complete with lurid puppet sex scenes, ludicrous backstories (one character had a morbid fear of gorillas, another a hatred of actors), and a ticking bomb whose clock was halted one one-hundredth of a second from disaster. In rare moments when he was given anything sentient to say, North Korean dictator Kim Jong-il added to the film's self-referential satirizing of Hollywood conventions by ridiculing the Team's penchant for happy endings. Viewed in this light, *Team America* inhabited the clichés it contained ironically, so as to subvert them from within, construing Hollywood as an ideological prop to empire and war. Assisted by the alienating effects of the puppetry, which made the Hollywood conventions of the film itself seem childish, *Team America* mocked Hollywood by wearing its hackneyed American-centrisms just a shade too ostentatiously to be "real," and with its eyebrows sufficiently raised to confirm its ironic intent.

It is dangerous, though, to presume that an unambiguous, unified, or uni-vocal cultural politics can be so easily found in Hollywood film. Hollywood narrative is rarely so committed as this, politically—its commercial logic often dictating that movies be pitched at a diverse consumer base, satis-fying as many different viewing sensibilities as can be accommodated in a given film. This leads to incoherent, ambiguous, and risk-averse politics (see Maltby 2003) more often than it leads to clear and committed state-ments on controversial issues like 9/11 and the war on terror. With irony as its governing narrative mode, *Team America* provides an almost textbook example of how this commodified politics translates into politically inco-herent filmmaking, enabling the film to tell two completely different stories at the same time (what it *appears* to say on one hand, and what it *also* says on the other), thereby proliferating the responses that are possible from dif-ferent audiences, while transferring responsibility for what the film means from its producers to its consumers.

This proliferation is assisted, in *Team America*, by the deadpan character of the film's humor, which can make the irony easy to miss. In the event that the irony fails, either because other aspects of the film get in the way or because audiences choose to ignore it, it is often difficult to differentiate between the film's supposed satirizing of reactionary conservatism and the sometimes ultraconservative culture-war positions the script itself appeared to endorse. It is perfectly possible, for example, for a conservative American audience to whoop and cheer entirely unironically when Hans Blix, Michael Moore, and Kim Jong-il are ripped apart, blown to pieces, and impaled on spikes, or when the Team saves the world from destruction at the end, because taken at face value there was very little in the film itself to discour-age such responses.

Indeed, despite its subversive sheen, *Team America* sometimes resembled a film-of-the-book treatment of Michael Medved's conservative culture-wars classic, *Hollywood vs. America* (1993), in which Hollywood liberals were excoriated for undermining core American commitments like mar-riage, religion, and patriotism. Taken at face value, without the leverage of irony, *Team America* certainly appeared contemptuous of liberals who publicly opposed the Bush administration over 9/11, depicting senior fig-ures in the Hollywood establishment as willing anti-American dupes of al Qaeda and Kim Jong-il's "Confucian-Islamic connection."[5] In the puppet bloodbath that brings the film to its knowing Hollywood climax, an entire catwalk of Hollywood liberals meets a variety of grisly ends. A Tim Rob-bins puppet is burned alive. Sean Penn and Danny Glover puppets are eaten by panthers (played by kittens). Susan Sarandon falls from a great height and is literally splattered all over the floor. Others, including Helen Hunt, George Clooney, Liv Tyler, Martin Sheen, Ethan Hawke, Janeane Garofalo, and Alec Baldwin are blown up, dismembered or decapitated, with the Baldwin puppet's beheading shown several times in rapid replay. Earlier, Michael Moore features as a suicide bomber who blows up the Team's headquarters in Mount Rushmore, and Hans Blix is ripped to pieces in Kim Jong-il's shark tank. Throw in a grisly death scene for Kim himself, and *Team America*'s spectacular supermarionation body count comprised a veritable catalogue of neoconservative hate figures. A communist dictator, a U.N. bureaucrat, the liberal Hollywood establishment, "terrorists," and a few French bystanders were all prominent casualties.

For audiences for whom the irony failed, or for whom the film's ironic humor provided a viewing pleasure that was secondary to its spectacular body count, *Team America*'s apparent contempt for liberals may have been matched by its hostility to ethnic and sexual difference. "Terrorists" jabber in a lazy, childlike approximation of Arab language sounds that are regularly identified in the DVD edition subtitles as "Arab gibberish." North Koreans speak "Korean gibberish." Terrorists from "Derka Derkastan" hang out at a bar on "Baka Laka Daka Street." Because he's North Korean, comedy James Bond–villain Kim Jong-il is given a speech impediment, which means that he can't pronounce the letter "l" ("I'm so ronery [lonely]," he sings, "poor rittle [little] me"). It is unlikely, in the heated culture-war contexts of the time, that the only laughter provoked by this kind of material came from liberals chuckling at the film's witty, self-referential irony.

The language of vicious homophobia is another part of *Team America*'s reactionary culture-wars vernacular. Terrorists are "cockfags." Hans Blix is a "fucking cocksucker" and a "buttfucking piece of shit." The hero, Gary, is a "buttfucking quitter." The Screen Actors Guild (or SAG) becomes "The Film Actors Guild" (or "FAG"). Against a domestic background that included vigorous political and public debate about, for example, gay marriage, it is perfectly possible for some viewers to sidestep the irony in the film's sexual politics, so normative is its homophobic language and so incongruously comic is such aggressive swearing in the mouths of puppets. For audiences such as these, the pleasurable experience of comic incongruity and the language of vicious homophobia are part of the same package, part of what makes the film funny, part of what gives it its subversive cachet (particularly, we might surmise, among audiences for whom "political correctness" is the culture of liberal elites). However ironic the film's representation of the Team itself, its lazy and irresponsible identity politics at times seemed too much part of the fabric of its humor, and too intrinsic to the pleasure of audiences, to be consistently described as functionally ironic.

The same is true of *Team America*'s antipathy to liberals, where the conventional pleasures of Hollywood "spectacle" during the climactic slaughter sequence, and the belly-laugh comedy of watching puppets do such incongruous things to one another, again seemed to override the superficial ironies of the surface narrative. Concluding films with sequences of redemptive, virtuous violence is a Hollywood staple, one way of initiating the patterns of resolution and closure that traditionally bring New Hollywood movies to a climax across a range of film genres. Westerns, gangster flicks, detective movies, war films, horror movies, thrillers, sci-fi, and—increasingly—children's films are just some of the genres which regularly use redemptive violence in this way. For experienced Hollywood audiences, these conventions surely operate at a more profound and moving level than the surface detail of *Team America*'s ironic Americanism. Many audiences will understand instinctively that the slaughter sequence in *Team America* signifies the onset of resolution—or a return to "equilibrium"—in the narrative. In conventional Hollywood terms, at the close of the film the graphic slaughter of the bad guys (liberals) makes sense: it feels normal, natural, and aesthetically right, in terms of the internal formal logic of Hollywood film. The main problem with *Team America*'s dependence on ironic humor, in other words, is that the irony consistently fails at key moments, leaving the film looking parochial, xenophobic, and aggressively heterosexual—positions the film still indulges and displays, albeit on the pretext of not really meaning them, even when the irony works.

What is most interesting about *Team America*, though, is the extent to which the culture-war politics it contains appear to supplant entirely, or to collapse from within, any viable sense of republican space or process in the broader political sensibilities of the film. Whereas Michael Moore uses liberal culture-war humor grounded in ridicule to construct narratives of republican redress, without the leverage of functional irony *Team America*'s depiction of anti-Bush Hollywood liberals amounts to a ridiculing of the idea of participatory democracy itself. "Why bother participating," seems to be the only question of substance the film actually poses to more conservative audiences, "when all participants are equally ridiculous?" *Team America*'s nihilistic culture-war comedy implies an evisceration of such traditional republican commitments, not just in its denigration of inclusivity and difference but also in the zero-sum appeal it makes to viewers to distrust all public actors equally. In *Team America* there is nothing to be done about 9/11 or the war on terror because, in a kind of Hobbesian culture war of all against all, the main players are all equally victimizers and dupes, with America's will to "police" the world depicted as merely one ridiculous political impulse among many others. Viewed in this way, there are no progressive levers and no authentic republican spaces to locate in the film, nothing that is truly "of the people" except ridicule. In consequence, *Team America*'s attacks on liberals and its denigration of ethnic and sexual difference becomes the omniscient postrepublican point of view in the film, fracturing anew the civic sphere that *Fahrenheit 9/11* tries to reassemble and reassert, that *Get Your War On* mourns in its passing, and which *Team America*, at least when its irony fails, appears to have abandoned altogether.

Something similar is true of the FX Network TV series *Rescue Me* (2004–), a black comedy-drama starring Denis Leary as Tommy Gavin, a New York firefighter haunted, literally, by ghosts of the 9/11 dead. *Rescue Me*'s humor is just as bleak, commodified, and "politically incorrect" as *Team America*'s, but is again complicated by its self-awareness and its use of irony to alienate viewers, occasionally, from the aggressively masculine, heterosexual gender politics that shape its humor. Scripted at times like a masculinist rejoinder to *Sex and the City*, *Rescue Me* links stories about the post-PC sexuality of its firefighters to stories about the fracturing of class identities, the breakdown of family relationships, and the unshakeable trauma of 9/11—a trauma that audiences follow through the gradual deterioration of Gavin's mental health. He is beset by ghosts, traumatized at work, alienated from his colleagues, and separated from his wife and family; everything in Tommy Gavin's life appears broken or in the process of breaking down. Contemporary accounts of the immediate post-9/11 period sometimes borrow from clinical and sociological models of trauma, defining trauma as the shattering of "a prior sense of what it means, in moral terms, to remain part of a collective" (Zelizer and Allan 2002, 2). If Tommy Gavin is waiting to be rescued, to have his trauma absorbed or healed by some therapeutic civic body or agency bigger and stronger than himself, all the script offers in the way of strong tokens of collective belonging are the viciously conflicted worlds of urban identity politics. In times of conflict and trauma, any wider sense of communal belonging, or of civic space and process, is generally crowded from view, despite the series's ostensible positioning in working-class New York and the occasional intrusion of class experience as themes. Like *Team America*, *Rescue Me* presents audiences with a fictive world in which identity politics, often in overtly reactionary forms, appeared to have subverted or superseded the potential for an authentic republican humor grown organically in a republican political culture.

More than anything, early 9/11 humor reveals the extent to which the attacks' meanings, for Americans, were shaped by debates about other social issues, with perspectives on 9/11 often stemming from entrenched domestic divisions and disputes as much as from discussion of foreign policy and international relations. After 9/11, Michael Moore's vision of a participative, multicultural citizenry unified against the hijacking of liberty by oligarchs was the exception, not the rule. In other significant humor of the Bush era, what 9/11 seemed to reveal was the stagnation of culture-war paradigms as models of republican theory and praxis. Viewed through this "late," or "decadent" culture-war prism, and read symptomatically, 9/11 humor grounded in narratives of republican decline implies that, as well as an international political and security crisis, 9/11 also spawned an incipient *ideological* crisis in the U.S. While core republican processes and institutions were said to be failing, or to have been eroded, or to have deviated from the functions allotted them by the Constitution, the attacks also brought to the surface of daily life far-reaching questions about citizenship, republicanism, and participatory democracy. These key totems of national belonging—on which powerful ideological abstractions like "freedom," "civilization," and "modernity" depend for their persuasiveness in times of crisis and war—presuppose the existence of adhesive common identities and "civic" bonds that have often been difficult to reconcile with the splintered identity politics of contemporary culture wars. In terms of American political history, the Bush era witnessed a new hegemony of the Right; a new coalition of forces between traditional "new Right" constituencies (the Republican Party, Christian conservatives, working-class conservatives, big business "energy" multinationals) and emerging forms of neoconservatism retooled for an era of U.S. hyperpower. The 9/11 humor of the Bush era reminds us that with this new hegemony there also came anxiety, and a counter-hegemonic narrative of entropy in American institutions and ideologies that sometimes deepened into a creeping sense of crisis in domestic Americanism itself.

NOTES

1. Please note that "republican" refers to the political ideology of republicanism (the ideologies of "the republic") rather than to the Republican political party.

2. See particularly *The 9/11 Commission Report* (National Commission 2004).

3. On humor as discipline or discourse in this loosely Foucauldian sense, see Billig (2005).

4. *Get Your War On* was also subsequently published in several book editions (Rees 2002, 2004, 2008).

5. "Confucian-Islamic connection" was Samuel Huntington's phrase. In one of the more heavily criticized passages of his essay "The Clash of Civilizations?" (1993), which enjoyed a new notoriety after 9/11 as debates about U.S. foreign policy blended fully with mainstream American culture wars, Huntington predicted an upsurge of dangerous new anti-Western alliances between non-Western "civilizations." In particular he warned of a sinister "Confucian-Islamic connection," designed "to promote acquisition by its members of the weapons and weapons technologies needed to counter the military powers of the West" (Huntington 1996, 23). As in *Team America*, one of the countries that Huntington said was at the hub of the emerging "connection" was North Korea.

WORKS CITED

Beigbeder, Frédéric. *Windows on the World*. London: Fourth Estate, 2004.

Billig, Michael. *Laughter and Ridicule: Towards a Social Critique of Humour*. London: Sage, 2005.

Bourne, Randolph. *The Radical Will: Selected Writings, 1911–1918*. Berkeley: University of California Press, 1977.

de Baecque, Antoine. "Parliamentary Hilarity inside the French Constitutional Assembly (1789–91)." In *A Cultural History of Humour*, edited by Jan Bremmer and Herman Roodenburg, 179–99. Cambridge: Polity, 1997.

de Tocqueville, Alexis. *Democracy in America*. New York: HarperPerennial, 1988.

Fahrenheit 9/11, DVD, directed by Michael Moore (2004; Lion Gate Films/Fellowship Adventure Group, 2004).

Graf, Fritz. "Cicero, Plautus and Roman Laughter." In *A Cultural History of Humour*, edited by Jan Bremmer and Herman Roodenburg, 29–39. Cambridge: Polity, 1997.

Hardy, David, and Jason Clarke. *Michael Moore Is a Big Fat Stupid White Man*. New York: HarperCollins/Regan Books, 2004.

Holloway, David. *9/11 and the War on Terror*. Edinburgh: Edinburgh University Press, 2008.

Huntington, Samuel P. "The Clash of Civilizations?" In *The Clash of Civilizations: The Debate*, by Samuel P. Huntington et al., 1–25. New York: Norton, 1996.

———. *The Clash of Civilizations and the Remaking of World Order*. London: Touchstone, 1998.

Maltby, Richard. *Hollywood Cinema*. Oxford: Blackwell, 2003.

Medved, Michael. *Hollywood vs. America*. London: HarperCollins, 1993.

Moore, Michael. *Stupid White Men . . . And Other Sorry Excuses for the State of the Nation*. London: Penguin, 2002.

———. *Dude, Where's My Country?* London: Allen Lane, 2003.

National Commission on Terrorist Attacks Upon the United States. *The 9/11 Commission Report*. New York: Norton, 2004.

Office of the President, *National Security Strategy of the United States of America, 2002*. The White House. http://www.whitehouse.gov/nsc/nss.pdf (accessed June 1, 2005).

Rees, David. *Get Your War On*. New York: Soft Skull Press, 2002.

———. *Get Your War On II*. New York: Riverhead Books, 2004.

———. *Get Your War On: The Definitive Account of George Bush's War on Terror, 2001–2008*. New York: Soft Skull Press, 2008.

Rescue Me. DVD (2004; FX/Sony Pictures Home Entertainment, 2005).

Team America: World Police. DVD, directed by Trey Parker (2004; Paramount/Paramount Home Entertainment, 2004).

Whitehead, Colson. "Introduction." In *Get Your War On*, by David Rees, iii–v. New York: Soft Skull Press, 2002.

Zelizer, Barbie, and Stuart Allan. "Introduction: When Trauma Shapes the News." In *Journalism After September 11*, edited by Barbie Zelizer and Stuart Allan, 1–24. New York: Routledge, 2002.

CHAPTER SEVEN

CRITIQUE, COUNTERNARRATIVES, AND IRONIC INTERVENTION IN *SOUTH PARK* AND STEPHEN COLBERT[1]

—Viveca Greene

On April 9, 2003—twenty days after the U.S. invasion of Iraq—Comedy Central aired the one hundredth episode of its top-rated show *South Park*. The episode "I'm a Little Bit Country," devoted to examining U.S. citizens' response to the invasion, concludes with Eric Cartman delivering a speech at a community rally:

> I learned something today. This country was founded by some of the smartest thinkers the world has ever seen. And they knew one thing: that a truly great country can go to war, and, at the same time, act like it doesn't want to . . . It's called "having your cake and eating it too."

Three years later, on April 29, 2006, another mainstay of Comedy Central, Stephen Colbert, headlined the White House Correspondents' Association dinner. Playing the Bill O'Reillyesque character from his show *The Colbert Report*, Colbert blithely declared:

> I stand by this man [President Bush]. I stand by this man because he stands for things. Not only does he stand for things, he stands on things. Things like aircraft carriers and rubble and recently flooded city squares. And that sends a strong message: that no matter what happens to America, she will always rebound—with the most powerfully staged photo ops in the world.

In the pages that follow, I argue that there are important differences between these two modes of social criticism that can be productively illuminated by the distinction between *stable* and *unstable* irony initially outlined by Wayne Booth (1975).[2] Both texts use irony as a tool of critique, but media producers, consumers, and scholars interested in emancipatory politics should be conscious of the divergent rhetorical strategies that the two forms of irony deploy. Ultimately I sketch the difference between ironic texts that are relatively unstable, undercutting politics and discourse altogether, and those that are relatively stable, subverting a given ideology without entirely repudiating a coherent political or ideological stance.

My goals are both theoretical and political. In taking seriously critiques of Booth's *A Rhetoric of Irony*, specifically those leveled by Stanley Fish (1998), I reconstruct Booth's distinction between stable and unstable ironies by attending to the ways in which ironic performances conjure (or neglect to conjure) what I refer to as *counternarratives*. So reconstructed, Booth's categories will provide an orientation for my readings of *South Park* and Colbert; I use these texts to differentiate between gradations of irony and their relationship to social criticism in a manner that moves us beyond the debate about whether irony is the property of a text or a context. As we shall see, this exercise will permit me to advocate for an irony of political engagement, not detachment, in a post-9/11 world—a kairotic one for counternarratives and politics of grounded commitment.

BOOTH'S DISTINCTION; FISH'S CHALLENGE

Irony as a rhetorical strategy can be used by the dominant and the subaltern, racists and antiracists, progressives and conservatives (Hutcheon 1995, 10). Although irony can, in principle, support any ideological position, not all forms of irony take aim at political issues or do the same ideological work. In *A Rhetoric of Irony*, Booth posits a distinction between what he labels "stable" and "unstable" irony. For Booth, the four defining marks of stable ironies are: (1) they are intended rather than accidental; (2) they are covert (not prefaced with an assertion of ironic content); (3) they are stable or fixed in the sense that the intention is not to undermine the validity of all meaning but simply the literal meaning; and (4) they are finite, which is to say not directed toward things in general (religion, language, truth) but toward specific manifestations of each (Catholicism, a presidential speech, a claim about the world). Unstable irony, conversely, occurs when the author "refuses to declare himself, however subtly, *for* any stable proposition, even the opposite of whatever proposition his irony vigorously denies" (240). In other words, what distinguishes the two is the presence or absence of an affirmative position on the issue at hand.

Booth outlines the four steps he believes readers take to "reconstruct" stable irony and ascertain its intended meaning. In step one, "The reader is required to reject the literal meaning," as he or she is "unable to escape recognizing either some incongruity among the words or between the words and something else he [or she] knows" (10). Step two involves the reader trying out "alternative interpretations or explanations" so as to make sense of the literal meaning of the statement (11). In step three, the reader makes a decision about the author's (or speaker's) "knowledge or beliefs," which is to say the reader makes a determination concerning authorial intention. Finally, in step four, readers "choose a new meaning or cluster of meanings with which they can rest secure" (12).

Booth's schema is not without its problems. In "Short People Got No Reason to Live: Reading Irony," Fish attacks Booth's analysis, insisting that it turns on an untenable distinction between the literal and intended meaning of a text. Fish argues that

> each of Booth's key distinctions—between meaning and significance, between a "central meaning" and that which is debatable, between the "work itself" and what different readers and different circumstances might add to it—is no more than a [false] distinction between a literal meaning, that which is indisputably and irreducibly "there," and interpretation, that which issues from some special perspective or set of circumstances. (179)

Fish goes on to argue that literal meaning is the result of an interpretive judgment (as "literal meanings" change based on interpretation), and he seeks to highlight the extent to which readings shift based on how various interpretive communities make sense of them.

The fact that any text is read consistently is, according to Fish, the result of preestablished "grounds of agreement" (189), and he sees irony not as a property of the text but as a reading strategy. Fish is, in fact, quite right to remind us that interpretive activity is central to meaning-making processes, ironic or literal, and that even literal meaning is "a product of perspective" (180). However, while Booth clearly overstates the significance of the text in securing meaning when he claims, for example, that a text's "central irony [can be] read identically by every qualified reader" (235), Fish errs in the other direction; his "act of totally vacating the text of inherent meaning is insupportable," as Jonathan Gray joins other scholars in noting (2006, 124). Nevertheless, Fish's critique of Booth reminds us to understand that irony is constructed through a complex interaction between texts, speakers, audiences, and contexts.

We cannot know if a given stretch of text should be read literally, at least not without recourse to the intentions of its author or speaker, and we can only gain access to the intentions of a speaker through a complex negotiation between speaker, text, and reader (i.e., what Fish calls the "interpretive community"), but this problem is, of course, endemic to all communication and not specific to irony. Fish himself acknowledges as much. In an endnote to his essay, Fish also observes that "[t]he distinction between stable and unstable ironies is a real one, but its reality is a function of the availability at a particular historical moment of certain modes of reading" (191). Rather than pick up where Fish leaves off in order to explore how "modes of reading" correlate with specific discourses, or question Fish's apparent denial that ironies are in any sense "the property of texts" (191), many scholars have employed Fish to entirely dismiss the distinction that Booth seeks to illuminate, and that, in fact, Fish himself accepts.

Although matters would be much simpler if ironic statements, performances, and texts fell neatly into the binary categories of stable and unstable irony (as they would if we *could* simply locate irony in a text), the line between the two is indeed a hazy one, a fact of which Booth himself is at least somewhat aware. Rather than think of stable and unstable irony as simple binary opposites, I regard them as relative terms and as two positions on a continuum that is highly contingent on context. Thus the two terms, elusive and contextually contingent as they are, can still be useful in characterizing ironic performances and the politics of critique that they sponsor, especially in times that call for careful consideration of the arena of cultural politics.

SOUTH PARK AND UNSTABLE IRONY

Named for the Donny and Marie Osmond hit song from the late 1970s, "I'm a Little Bit Country" explores how the program's main characters, (Eric) Cartman, Kenny, Stan, and Kyle, respond to a battle between pro- and anti-war groups (the former aligned, of course, with country music and the latter with rock 'n' roll). It ostensibly questions whether it is appropriate to respond to a controversial invasion with either of the two options provided by mainstream U.S. media: protest or unconditional support of the military. Following a student walkout to protest the war (but which seems to be mainly an excuse to get out of class), the boys and Mr. Garrison's other fourth-grade students are assigned to write a report on what the Founding Fathers would have said about the issue. To avoid doing actual research, Cartman drops a television Tivoed with hours of the History Channel into a pool of water so as to electrocute himself (and thus, by his media-influenced calculations, to "channel" history), which has the desired effect of transporting him back to 1776. He witnesses part of the Continental Congress in which they debate the prospect of going to war with England:

HANCOCK: Mr. Franklin, where do you stand on the war issue?

FRANKLIN: I believe that if we are to form a new country, we cannot be a country that appears war-hungry and violent to the rest of the world. However, we also cannot be a country that appears weak and unwilling to fight to the rest of the world. So, what if we form a country that appears to want both?

JEFFERSON: Yes. Yes, of course. We go to war, and protest going to war at the same time.

DICKINSON: Right. If the people of our new country are allowed to do whatever they wish, then some will support the war and some will protest it.

FRANKLIN: And that means that as a nation we could go to war with whomever we wished, but at the same time, act like we didn't want to. If we allow the people to protest what the government does, then the country will be forever blameless.

ADAMS: It's like having your cake, and eating it, too.

CONGRESSMAN 2: Think of it: an entire nation founded on saying one thing and doing another.

"Enlightened" by these dubious insights, Cartman returns from the past just in time to impart the wisdom of the Founding Fathers at a town rally that has degenerated into a pitched battle between protestors and supporters of the war:

I learned something today. This country was founded by some of the smartest thinkers the world has ever seen. And they knew one thing: that a truly great country can go to war, and, at the same time, act like it doesn't want to. You people who are for the war, you need the protesters—because they make the country look like it's made of sane, caring individuals. And you people who are antiwar, you need these flag wavers, because, if our whole country was made up of nothing but soft pussy protesters, we'd get taken down in a second. That's why the Founding Fathers decided we should have both. It's called "having your cake and eating it too."

Randy, Stan's father, quickly grasps this wisdom, summarizing it for the suddenly peaceable crowd: "[Cartman] is right. The strength of this country is the ability to say one thing and do another."

But how are we to hear or read this bit of parting wisdom that has pacified the warring citizens of South Park and addressed the episode's central conflict? The flashback cannot be understood to offer a reliable window onto history, as the debate concerning the Declaration of Independence misrepresents the history as we know it. And given the enormous differences in the ideological bases of the two wars, the conflation of the American Revolution with the war in Iraq is misleading (albeit one that President Bush himself pressed). Still, the claim that U.S. foreign policy has long been riddled by hypocrisy seems fair enough. In celebration of this hypocrisy, Cartman announces that "[t]he Founding Fathers want you to know that we can disagree all we want as long as we agree that America kicks ass." In response the town comes together in a patriotic duet heralding the marriage of hawkish foreign policy and strong antiwar sentiments. This rendition of the Osmond classic nears its crescendo with the town singing in unison, "Let the flag for hypocrisy fly high from every pole / We're a little bit country, and we're a little bit rock 'n' roll."

Clearly the celebration is laden with irony, but that is all that is clear. I will offer three possible readings of the episode so as to acknowledge the complexity of its politics, and then detail how "I'm a Little Bit Country" ultimately undermines each reading, leaving the reader with no stable ideological footing.[3] First, borrowing from Booth, perhaps we can hear or read this paean to hypocrisy as a stable ironic attack on the hyperpartisan nature of contemporary politics. In this regard, we might see *South Park* as offering a humorous criticism of how American politics, once defined in terms of its relentless centrism, now has turned into a pitched battle between opposing ideological camps that share little common ground.

But on closer analysis such a reading of the episode appears suspect. For what is the ideological position that it stakes out and defends? The only common ground that the warring factions find in "I'm a Little Bit Country" is the shared appeal of a politics of hypocrisy—hardly a position anyone would champion openly. Although it is true that *South Park* subjects both sides of the political divide to its characteristic style of ironic critique, this critique is not offered *pace* Booth from a relatively stable position (i.e., of the centrist caught in the fray). The episode doesn't espouse a negotiated position between these conflicting partisan perspectives; it assiduously refuses to espouse any politics at all, stopping at the level of observation. Its irony is launched from a destabilized position radically dislodged from any ideological camp and from which all of the political views and commitments the show represents find themselves the subject of ridicule.

Some viewers have interpreted this position of distance as ultimately hovering around conservative positions, a second possible reading we might consider. In an oft-quoted line, cocreator Matt Stone announces, "I hate conservatives, but I really fucking hate liberals" (qtd. in Anderson 2005, 75–76). Stone and Parker's distaste for so-called politically correct sentiments likely accounts, in part, for the show's popularity amongst some conservatives. As Brian Anderson (2005), author of *South Park Conservatives: The Revolt against Liberal Media Bias*, argues, "Lots of cable comedy, while far from traditionally conservative, is fiercely anti-liberal these days ... The number-one example of the new anti-liberalism is *South Park*" (75). We see this attack on display in "I'm a Little Bit Country" in its depiction of violent battles between supporters and defenders of the recently launched war. Both groups are made to look absurd, but this critical gesture reveals certain asymmetries. In the melee, a protester drives a "War Is Not My Voice" sign through the forehead of a pro-war demonstrator. Meanwhile, a pro-war demonstrator beats down a protestor with his "Support Our Troops" sign. That warmongers might be eager to bash in the heads of those that disagree with them can be seen as evidence of their savagery, but it reflects no betrayal of their basic position, which, after all, champions the use of violence as a means of settling political conflict. That war critics should resort to violence to defend their views, however, carries a different message altogether; here we encounter bona fide hypocrisy that takes the form of saying one thing and doing another—the very style of hypocrisy that the show locates at the heart of the American tradition and feigns celebrating.

But before we conclude that this episode of *South Park* is no more than the cartoon version of the Heritage Foundation's neoconservative propaganda, we should recall that antiliberal perspectives are altogether different from conservative perspectives. Although liberal positions and shibboleths are subject to relentless and withering ridicule, conservative causes fare little better on *South Park*. The defenders of war in "I'm a Little Bit Country" are invariably depicted as uneducated, beer-swilling simpletons who speak in the hollow clichés of knee-jerk patriotism, too ignorant to appreciate the contradictions that riddle their views. Thus, as Ethan Thompson argues, "nailing down the politics of South Park is a tricky—perhaps ultimately futile—exercise" (2009, 214). There are no sacred cows on *South Park*. As *Rolling Stone*'s Joe Levy put it in a CNN interview, "What the 'South Park' viewer wants to see is any symbol violated" (2008).

I have already argued that *South Park*'s politics cannot be described as centrist; nor, in its liberal bashing, can it be described as conservative. "I'm a Little Bit Country" radically refuses to commit to any politics of the present. It likewise refuses to find a positive counternarrative in the past, a third reading we must dismiss. One stable form of irony depicts the values of the present as a violation of those of the past. Particularly in the United States, this is a common form of critique, as the early republic of the founders provides the Edenic counterpoint to our postlapsarian politics. But "I'm a Little Bit Country" pointedly rejects this counternarrative. In his flashback to 1776, Cartman discovers that the founders themselves were profound hypocrites. If anything, then, our present politics have remained true and faithful to the nation's founding vision, in Cartman's telling, an uninterrupted history of unreconstructed bad faith—"of saying one thing and doing another." Certainly this is an ironic celebration, but one without stable counterpoint.

The obvious counterpoint to hypocrisy is "sincerity" or perhaps "authenticity," but not only are these hallmarks of the very piety that *South Park* attacks so strongly as the roots of U.S. hypocrisy in "I'm a Little Bit Country," they would also be odd virtues to embrace for a show predicated on the workings of irony. Indeed, Cartman's description of hypocrisy, of "saying one thing and doing another," all but supplies a pithy denotation of irony itself. In this regard, *South Park*'s unstable irony can be read as a peculiarly self-referential gesture that serves no higher purpose besides legitimating the show's own logic. In Cartman's flashback, the venerable Ben Franklin offers the solution to the contradictions the characters (in both time periods) have been wrestling with up until this point. Franklin's resolution is to "embrace" the contradiction rather than reconcile it: "We could go to war . . . but at the same time, act like we didn't want to. If we allow the people to protest . . . then the country will be forever blameless." In other words, we are free to act as violently and as corrosively as we want, as long as we also pretend to subject our actions to critique—the very bad-faith gesture that the nation was based upon.

Some scholars have defended *South Park*'s aesthetic of disruption and instability as allowing crucial interventions into dominant rhetorical constructions. Ted Gournelos argues, for example, that "through a chaotic approach to opposition, the series produces areas in which conversation can take place outside of the accepted or dominant discourse, and deploys those alternative spaces in a radical, and often internally dissonant, critical pedagogy" (2009, 32). Gournelos maintains that the show's political ambivalence "can both construct a community and direct that community toward a self-critical or self-aware set of practices" (97). By inviting viewers to think beyond simple binaries—conservative/liberal—and the limits of mainstream political discourse, the show asks its audience to arrive at independent critical conclusions. From this perspective, *South Park* might be seen as engaging in a form of Socratic irony, whereby basic assumptions and political commitments are subjected to a form of interrogation, not in the form of questions posed by Plato's straight-faced, syllogistic interlocutor, but in the form of ironic gestures that highlight contradiction and incoherence.

I argue that this reading doesn't fully account for how meaning is questioned and undermined in, at least, this particular episode that takes on the Iraq War. As we shall see, Colbert's ironic interventions presuppose and consolidate a clear counterpolitical narrative, one that we can describe as liberal-progressive. But what exactly is the counternarrative inscribed by "I'm a Little Bit Country"? If we follow the Platonic analogy, Socrates' goal was not simply to deconstruct the foundation of knowledge of his dialectical partners; it was to reconstruct from the terms of critique a positive basis of knowing. The episode, however, engages in no such reconstructive effort, as critique for critique's sake is less a counternarrative than the absence of one. Instead of leading viewers to think beyond political labels, the episode merely ossifies them.

"I'm a Little Bit Country" is a textbook example of unstable irony in that its only sure affirmation is, as Booth explains, "that negation that begins all ironic play" (240). The authors eschew "any stable proposition, even the opposite of whatever proposition [their] irony vigorously denies" (240). In other words, the only thing we can be reasonably sure of is that the tone of the episode is ironic, as sincerely venerating hypocrisy seems so implausible—and paradoxical. As we have seen, however, it offers no proposition in its stead. Thus, Parker and Stone leave us with nothing save the underlying message of all infinitely unstable ironic texts: "the universe (or at least the universe of discourse) is inherently absurd" (240–41). That Booth includes this parenthetical regarding "the universe of discourse" is particularly helpful in establishing the extent to which the show corresponds to his description of unstable irony; discourse itself is one of *South Park*'s most consistent targets.[4]

Through its failure to suggest a viable counternarrative, and in denying the audience a stable ideological foothold, "I'm a Little Bit Country" suggests some of the political limitations of unstable irony. Cynicism and distrust of power have a legitimate role in our contemporary political environment, but deriding all those who critique authority from a stable position bears the risk of suggesting little save ironic nonacquiescence (rather than resistance) to authority. Unstable ironic performances can degenerate into self-referential, self-legitimating gestures that reflect and can easily foster what Peter Sloterdijk (1987) calls a state of "enlightened false consciousness." As Terry Eagleton explains it:

> [I]deology is supposed to deceive; and in the cynical milieu of post-modernism we are all much too fly, astute and streetwise to be conned for a moment by our own official rhetoric. [Enlightened false consciousness is] the endless self-ironizing or wide-awake bad faith of a society which has seen through its own pretentious rationalizations ... The new kind of ideological subject is no hapless victim of false consciousness, but knows exactly what he is doing; it is just that he continues to do it even so. And to this extent he would seem conveniently insulated against "ideology critique" of the traditional kind, which presumes that agents are not fully in possession of their own motivations. (39)

Enlightened false consciousness aptly describes the critical space that "I'm a Little Bit Country" occupies, one in which we own and disown, which is to say embrace and ironize, hypocrisy as the ideological basis not simply for hegemonic militarism but also for ironic assault on these practices. Seen in this light, enlightened false consciousness finds convenient expression in the episode's unstable irony, as an ostensibly radical critique reveals itself to be—as I will now argue—no more than a gesture of (ironic) self-legitimation.

The final scene of "I'm a Little Bit Country" testifies to the episode's overall infinite ironic undercutting; the end turns from a celebration of the hypocrisy that makes a unified war effort possible to a celebration of the longevity of *South Park* itself. Breaking the fourth wall, Randy (dressed as Donny Osmond in a white pantsuit) says, "Well, goodnight everybody. It sure has been great bringing you a hundred episodes," and sings, "For the war, against, who cares? One hundred episodes!" Appearing dismayed by the absurdity of what they are witnessing, Stan, Kyle and Kenny stand by agape, while Kyle pinches his nose, covers his eyes, and gets the final word: "I hate this town. Ah, I really, really do." The show's celebration of its longevity sounds ironic and Kyle's lament sounds not just like a critique of the U.S., as represented by the town of South Park, but also metacritique, a gesture of disgust at the show's own reveling in nihilism. However, in the larger context of the show Kyle's disgust is just another example of *South Park* "having its cake and eating it, too"—by expressing disgust at itself, the show is able to legitimate its celebratory mood—one not all that dissimilar from the heady self-congratulatory mood of the nation embarking on war. "I'm a Little Bit Country" engages in a kind of social criticism, but in refusing to embrace any semblance of a counternarrative, it is all unstable values, embodying the very hypocrisy it seems to call out, legitimating nothing larger than at best, and only ironically, itself.

STABLE IRONY IN STEPHEN COLBERT

Three years after "I'm a Little Bit Country" first aired, and as public opinion turned against the war in Iraq, Stephen Colbert took the podium at the White House Correspondents' Association dinner. Present at the event were President Bush, First Lady Laura Bush, Chairman of the Joint Chiefs of Staff Peter Pace, and U.S. Attorney General Alberto Gonzales, as well as members of the news media. After a brief joke announcement about one set of bulletproof SUVs blocking another set of bulletproof SUVs outside the building, Colbert began his speech:

> Wow! Wow! What an honor! The White House Correspondents' dinner. To actually sit here at the same table with my hero, George W. Bush—to be this close to the man. I feel like I'm dreaming. Somebody pinch me. You know what? I'm a pretty sound sleeper; that may not be enough. Somebody shoot me in the face. Is he really not here tonight? Damn it! The one guy who could have helped.

With these words, Colbert sets an ironic tone for his address; clearly he does not consider Bush his hero, and he immediately juxtaposes the putative compliment with a jab at Vice President Dick Cheney for accidentally shooting a friend in the face while hunting. In so doing, Colbert accentuates the absurdity of the Bush administration and his own ironic stance. In the sixteen minutes that follow, Colbert figuratively does to Bush what Cheney actually (if accidentally) did to Harry Whittington in early February 2006 on the notorious hunting trip: he shoots him at close range. Colbert's ironic performance stunned members of the live audience, delighted legions of progressives, and left most members of the press unsure not how to interpret the speech, but how to respond to it. As David Carr (2007) wrote for the *New York Times*, "Because he failed to acknowledge both the propriety and the primacy of the establishment press, Mr. Colbert bombed inside the room, drawing disapproving looks from all quarters and little initial coverage."

In contrast to "I'm a Little Bit Country," Colbert provides a textbook display of Booth's concept of stable irony: his comments are intended, they are covert, they are fixed (in the sense that the intention is not to undermine the validity of all meaning but simply the literal meaning), and they are finite, directed toward specific political practices. Although we cannot know if a given stretch of text should be parsed literally or not without awareness of the context and recourse to the intention of its author, and in turn we can only gain access to the intentions of an author through a complex negotiation between author, text, and reader, it is precisely by playing with that relationship that Colbert effectuates a stable irony ideally suited to a politics of critical engagement.[5]

Many factors contribute to reading Colbert's address as ironic rather than literal. Some of these factors are contextual: Colbert's reputation, the nature of the event, the president's shrinking approval ratings. Others are textual and performative: his choice of words, jocular tone, and the rhetorical structure of his speech. All of these factors have an ideological dimension; much of what Colbert "literally" suggests is likely to strike even the most ardent Bush supporter as indefensible, and though the target of Colbert's jokes shift, there is an ideological congruence to them: they are pieces of an established critique of post-9/11 U.S. politics. Moreover, the text appeals, in a manner that "I'm a Little Bit Country" rejects, to core American principles—rational thought, democracy, and the notion that the news media ought to play a watchdog role—in such a way that it allows the reader to reconstruct its intended meaning. It is the "presence" of these principles, principles that are only present and affirmed by implication, and their ideological coherence, that distinguish Colbert's text from those that I have classified as unstable: works in which there is an "unlimited ironic undercutting" (Booth 259).

Colbert's remarks adhere to a signature rhetorical structure. As he moves from topic to topic, Colbert begins by stating a premise that at first blush can be heard either literally or ironically. He then follows this with hyperbolic commentary that reveals the original premise as ironic. When he says, for instance, "I believe the government that governs best is the government that governs least. And by these standards we have set up a fabulous government in Iraq," the defense of limited government sounds plausible at first hearing; by invoking Iraq, however, he subverts the party-line rhetoric. That the government in Iraq was, at the time, widely considered a disaster creates a dissonance with Colbert's adjectival choice of "fabulous." This dissonance between context and text suggests a larger rejection of the conservative rhetoric of limited government, supplying a perfect example of Fish's point that we need to know something about the relationship between text and context to detect irony. Even in this limited example, Colbert has communicated disdain for contemporary political practices, indicted conservative principles, embraced a Democratic ideology of robust government, and censured the war and U.S. ability to establish a functioning Iraq; this communicative act of critique is contingent on a shared set of meanings and a reference to larger contexts of shared background knowledge.

A similar strategy permeates other moments of the speech. For instance, when he says, "I believe in pulling yourself up by your own bootstraps. I believe it is possible. I saw this guy do it once in Cirque du Soleil. It was magical," again we might believe that Colbert accepts the conservative credo of bootstrapping. This surmise, however, cannot withstand Colbert's mention of Cirque du Soleil. Once the conservative ideal is shown to be no more than a circus illusion, a shadow is cast back on the original claim, which now sounds hollow and chimerical. Here again Colbert's irony functions to subvert not all politics, but a specific ideology; in so doing it delivers a stable ideological critique, reconstructing a coherent counternarrative.

In her discussion of the "political perils of irony," Hutcheon notes that "the many-voiced play of said and unsaid" in an ironic text results in people making different meanings (177).[6] Nevertheless, Colbert's performance gives us ample evidence to construct a sense of what he is against and what he is for: liberal democracy, effective government, and, as we shall see below, reasoned discourse.

Comparing himself, which is to say his public persona, to Bush, Colbert praises the president's refusal to bow to reason:

> It is my privilege to celebrate this president, 'cause we're not so different, he and I. We both get it ... We're not members of the factinista. We go straight from the gut. Right, sir? That's where the truth lies: right down here in the gut. Do you know that you have more nerve endings in your gut that you have in your head? You can look it up. Now, I know some of you are going to say, "I did look it up, and that's not true." That's 'cause

you looked it up in a book. Next time look it up in your gut. I did. My gut tells me that's how our nervous system works. Every night on my show, *The Colbert Report*, I speak straight from the gut, okay? I give people the truth, unfiltered by rational argument.

In this example, Colbert espouses kinship with Bush, praising the president for not being a technocrat and for making decisions in a visceral manner. But having derided the wonk paralyzed by statistics, Colbert then effectively defangs this condemnation, as he hyperbolically praises a decision-making process completely untethered to reality. This gesture frames a countervision: a defense of rational discourse based on a detailed comprehension of facts on the ground.

Colbert continues his performance by sketching how the country runs:

Listen, let's review the rules. Here's how it works. The president makes decisions. He's the decider. The press secretary announces those decisions, and you people of the press type those decisions down. Make, announce, type. Just put 'em through spell-check and go home. Get to know your family again. Make love to your wife. Write that novel you got kicking around in your head. You know, the one about the intrepid Washington reporter with the courage to stand up to the administration. You know, fiction!

As Colbert maintains, these are "the rules" for political reporting—or, at least, a slightly exaggerated version of them, in a post-9/11 America. His joke about the fictitious reporter who is fearless enough to confront the administration is a critique of the administration's control of the media and of the media itself, and suggests a counterposition demanding responsible political engagement: one that includes the idea that an independent press should provide a meaningful check on the president. As Jeffrey P. Jones argues, one of the most significant aspects of Colbert's performance is "the dual critique that his brand of satire is making—the ways in which news media and politicians are mutually constituting and enabling"—a critique Jones goes on to aptly describe as "double-fisted" (2010, 83).

Colbert's exaggerated tone, the incongruity between what his statements suggest, and the background knowledge they presuppose serve as markers or cues of irony for an audience familiar with Stephen Colbert's comedic persona and aware of various discourses that challenge the status quo. If in "I'm a Little Bit Country" we find a paragon of unstable irony that subjects the status quo to withering critique but offers the viewer "no firm place on which to stand" (Booth 249), in Colbert, by contrast, we find a strong example of stable irony—irony that conjures an effective counternarrative and oppositional politics.

CONCLUSION

Irony has enjoyed something of a renaissance since its short-lived death after 9/11. *The Daily Show, The Colbert Report, The Simpsons, South Park*: all these shows boast enormous popularity, not simply as vehicles of entertainment and humorous diversion, but as vital tools by which we make fun of, critique, and come to terms with the political challenges of the age. As Hutcheon notes, "'cultural politics' cannot be separated from 'real' politics or practical life. They share the same semiotic domain of signs, images and meanings" (1988, 202). As we have seen, however, the strategies of ironic critique that such shows deploy can differ significantly.

Although there are problems with condensing complex issues into conceptual binaries, the essence of Booth's categories provides a basis for a pragmatic (and politically productive) strategy to address and critique ironic texts. Fish shows the very distinction between stable and unstable irony to be vulnerable to deconstruction; yet if he helpfully reminds us that irony is more than simply something that a text does or signifies, that it works through a complex interaction between author, text, and received audience, his intervention ultimately serves less to render Booth's distinction untenable than it supplies it with greater nuance and sophistication.

My readings of Colbert's address and of a specific episode of *South Park* locate a fundamental difference in the ironic interventions of the two texts. Colbert's irony, I have argued, is relatively stable, in that it appeals to a clear counternarrative that makes explicit its political commitments. "I'm a Little Bit Country," by contrast, deploys an irony of instability, one that eschews an explicit counternarrative, and, in fact, subjects the very idea of political engagement to the critique of enlightened false consciousness.

For some, the global irony of *South Park* may seem the more radical gesture of critique. As Claire Colebrook (2004) observes: "Those who emphasize the stability of irony value, or assume the value of, a politics directed towards community and unity. Those who celebrate the destabilizing force of irony, by contrast, insist that politics is the rejection, contestation or disruption of shared norms" (45). As other authors in this collection discuss, irony took on a particularly important role with regard to political commentary and social criticism in the wake of 9/11; ironists often spoke the unspoken, challenged the political, social, and cultural status quo, and/or attempted to consolidate community (or countercommunities). My primary project here has been to reinsert the terms stable and unstable into discussions of irony and political engagement, because they help us recognize important differences at a time when ironic/satirical texts are widely popular and widely circulated. As Colebrook hints at above, "politics directed towards community and unity" and politics as the "rejection, contestation or disruption of shared norms" not only have different advocates but also differing attendant forms of irony.

As individuals and as citizens, we benefit from the existence of both notions about politics and forms of irony. In the world of Abu Ghraib, Guantanamo Bay, CIA black site prisons, and the emergence of the "Tea Party," however, and in light of a period of American popular culture in which the ironic treatment of 9/11 politics often tended toward what David Holloway elsewhere in this volume refers to as "postrepublicanism," the directed gestures of stable irony offered the stronger challenges to the power structures that arose in the wake of 9/11. There are times we are less served by a global irony that ridicules all causes and commitments, and political engagement itself, than by a targeted form of critique that both castigates and affirms, and that tells a story not of seeming infinite negativity but of possibility.

NOTES

1. Many thanks to Lawrence Douglas, Michael Morgan, Catherine Newman, and Ted Gournelos for their thoughtful feedback on this chapter.

2. Of course, there are many differences in the industrial and cultural frameworks in which the two pieces were produced and consumed, as well as inherent differences in comparing cultural productions in different media. However, my focus here is the properties that make the two texts illustrative of opposing sides of the unstable-stable irony continuum.

3. There are a number of monographs, edited volumes, and scholarly articles on *South Park* and its political commitments, and the significant level of disagreement among these works' authors testifies to the show's instability. For additional commentary on the "I'm a Little Bit Country" episode, see Gournelos (2009), Weinstock (2008), and Booker (2006).

4. In addition to describing the underlying features of stable and unstable irony, Booth attempts to distinguish between local and infinite instabilities, the former referring to irony that undermines something relatively focused and the latter an irony that undercuts or chips away at all meaning. The boundaries between various combinations of these categories are, as Booth acknowledges, "dim" and, for the purposes of my argument here, somewhat unnecessary though I see those pertaining to "I'm a Little Bit Country" as infinite with

regard to Booth's criteria. Regardless of how we categorize the episode with regard to these additional categories, however, there is no ground to stand on that isn't itself undercut.

5. A speaker's or reader's intentions are never transparent (questions of discerning intention is a problem that inheres in the very project of interpretation), but it is worth bearing in mind the fact that Fish is an intentionalist and his entire critique of literalism presupposes his intentionalism.

6. I do not mean to suggest that stable ironic texts are incapable of supporting rival readings; indeed, as LaMarre et al. (2009) found in their study of audience readings of a short clip from *The Colbert Report*, college students tended to interpret Colbert's statements and perceived his intended meaning in ways that supported their personal political beliefs and affiliations. Likewise, in their study of audience responses to *All in the Family*, Vidmar and Rokeach (1974) found selective perception influenced readings of the program and its primary characters, and I discovered a similar trend in responses to the satirical cartoon "The Politics of Fear" that graced the cover of *The New Yorker* magazine in July 2008. These studies examine relatively stable forms of irony, and though none of them specifically consider the distinction or contrast them with unstable texts, it seems likely that texts that eschew a counternarrative would sponsor an even greater range of disparate readings.

WORKS CITED

Anderson, Brian. 2005. *South Park Conservatives: The Revolt Against Liberal Media Bias.* Washington, DC: Regnery.

Booker, M. Keith. 2006. *Drawn to Television: Prime-time Animation from the Flintstones to Family Guy.* Westport, CT: Praeger Publishers.

Booth, Wayne. 1975. *A Rhetoric of Irony.* Chicago: Univ. of Chicago Press.

Carr, David. 2007. Carson-era humor, post-Colbert. *New York Times*, April 23. http://www .nytimes.com/2007/04/23/business/media/23carr.html ?_r=1&oref=slogin/.

Colebrook, Claire. 2004. *Irony.* New York: Routledge.

Eagleton, Terry. 1991. *Ideology: An Introduction.* London & New York: Verso.

Fish, Stanley. 1998. Short People Got No Reason to Live: Reading Irony. *Daedalus*, Winter 112: 175–91.

Gournelos, Ted. 2009. *Popular Culture and the Future of Politics.* Lanham, MD: Lexington Books.

Gray, Jonathan. 2006. *Watching with the Simpsons.* New York: Routledge.

Hutcheon, Linda. 1995. *Irony's Edge: The Theory and Politics of Irony.* New York: Routledge.

Jones, Jeffrey P. 2009. *Entertaining Politics.* Lanham: Rowman and Littlefield Publishers.

Kierkegaard, Søren. 1965. *The Concept of Irony: With Constant Reference to Socrates.* Trans. Lee M. Capel. Bloomington & London: Indiana University Press.

LaMarre, Heather L., Kristen D. Landerville, and Michael A. Beam. 2009. The Irony of Satire: Political Ideology and the Motivation to See What You Want to See in *The Colbert Report*. *International Journal of Press/Politics* 14, no. 2: 212–231.

Levy, Joe. 2007. Interview with Carol Costello. *CNN Newsroom.* CNN. March 31. Transcript. http:// transcripts.cnn.comTRANSCRIPTS/0703/31/cnr.01.html. Retrieved May 4, 2008.

Parker, Matt, and Trey Stone. 2003. "I'm a Little Bit Country." *South Park.* Comedy Central. April 9.

Sloterdijk, Peter. 1987. *Critique of Cynical Reason*. Minneapolis: University of Minnesota Press.

Thompson, Ethan. 2009. Good Demo, Bad Taste: *South Park* as Carnivalesque Satire in *Satire TV: Politics and Comedy in the Post-Network Era*. Jonathan Gray, Jeffrey P. Jones, and Ethan Thompson, eds. New York: New York University Press. 213–232.

Vidmar, Neil, and Milton Rokeach. 1974. Archie Bunker's Bigotry: A Study in Selective Perception and Exposure. *Journal of Communication* 24: 36–47.

Weinstock, Jeffrey Andrew. 2008. *Taking* South Park *Seriously*. Albany: State University of New York Press.

CHAPTER EIGHT

HUMORING 9/11 SKEPTICISM

—Michael Truscello

Two years after the publication of the *9/11 Commission Report* in July 2004, public opinion polls showed varying degrees of skepticism over the veracity of the report and the testimony of government and military officials. A Zogby poll in May 2006 showed 42 percent of Americans believed "that the US government and its 9/11 Commission concealed or refused to investigate critical evidence that contradicts their official explanation of the September 11th attacks" (911Truth.org, "Zogby poll," 2006). A Scripps Howard/Ohio University poll in August 2006 showed 36 percent of Americans believed their government was in some manner complicit with the 9/11 attacks (Hargrove 2006), and a *New York Times*/CBS News poll from October 2006 showed only 16 percent of Americans believed members of the Bush administration told the truth about pre-9/11 intelligence, while 81 percent believed the government was either "hiding something" or "mostly lying" (Angus Reid 2006). While many leading figures in mainstream American liberal and progressive media criticized the *9/11 Commission Report* when it was published in July 2004—*Harper's* magazine ran a cover story in October 2004 describing the report as a "whitewash" and a "cheat and a fraud" (DeMott, 2004)—two years later the same progressive media also authored vitriolic retorts to the self-styled "9/11 Truth Movement," members of which want a new investigation into the events of September 11. Skepticism of the *9/11 Commission Report* has, in fact, largely been relegated to Internet forums and alternative media; mainstream media cover 9/11 skepticism only in its most outlandish forms, such as the popular Internet film *Loose Change*, and conflate moderate skepticism with the often preposterous world of conspiracy theories.

✦ ✦ ✦

Humor has been employed by both skeptics and supporters of the official 9/11 narrative: for the skeptics, the humor often reflects a sense of outrage mixed with a sense of futility at what they perceive to be a state-sponsored act of terrorism and cover-up; for the supporters of the *9/11 Commission Report*, humor is often used to depict the skeptics as misguided conspiracy theorists. This essay examines three instances of humor that address 9/11 skepticism in order to illustrate a set of apparent paradoxes and ambiguities in the official 9/11 narrative. Although these examples of humor succeed comically with their designated in-groups, they fail politically to bridge the immense divide between the two positions. To bridge these disparate camps would require more of a cognitive transformation than these cartoons are capable of providing, given the social context of contemporary America in which 9/11 skepticism is routinely condemned by corporate media as heresy.[1] As Michael Mulkay argues, "humour depends on the active creation and display of interpretative multiplicity," the type of ambiguity and contradiction often presumed absent from serious or "unitary" discourse (1988, 3–4). The ambiguities and contradictions of the official 9/11 narrative produce particularly polarized responses, based on the centrality of 9/11 to radical reactionary U.S. policies and the relative lack of sustained academic study of the attacks of September 11, 2001, themselves. The use of humor in particular to draw attention to the omissions and distortions of the official 9/11 narrative exacerbates the production of cognitive dissonance for those who accepted the U.S. government narrative before contradictory evidence emerged. Although humor can, at times, reshape the contours of public discussion, the examples I address in this chapter point to the limits of humor in a mass mediated society; even when humorists are not inhibited in the subjects they broach, the overarching culture and media system of which they are a part restricts the ideological work they can accomplish. In the case of 9/11, the mere appearance of humor that addresses skepticism is a radical gesture.

Those who are already convinced the official 9/11 narrative is unproblematic tend to frame any expressions of skepticism as "conspiracy theory." Popular invocations of conspiracy theory often focus on ad hominem attacks, dismissing skeptics' beliefs on a priori psychological grounds rather than exploring the evidence for those beliefs, an approach that too often effectively forecloses additional discussion. At least two of the humorous pieces I have selected suggest moving beyond a priori assumptions about 9/11 on rhetorical levels, and also on the level of empirical evidence as a basis for skepticism. Of course, 9/11 skepticism is not homogeneous: some skeptics focus only on the compromises of the 9/11 Commission, while others believe certain events of that day are definitive proof of an alternative scenario. The pieces of humor I have selected, Kirk Anderson's comic "A Brief History of the 9/11 Commission," David Dees's photomontage "Jet fuel? That's a good one!," and the retort to 9/11 skeptics in the *South Park* episode "The Mystery of the Urinal Deuce," represent a sampling of possible skepticism.

The effectiveness of humor as a form of social protest is questionable. Many scholars claim that humor may act as nothing more than a cathartic release for oppressed groups (Hart 2007, 7). But humor can also be an effective rhetorical tool; as Marjolein 't Hart suggests, because criticism in the form of a joke can diffuse rational as well as repressive/oppressive argumentation styles, "Authority and power can melt, as the invitation to laugh *with* one another appeals to all-human feelings and breaks down official barriers. As such, humour certainly constitutes one of the 'weapons of the weak'" (8). Those who believe that important aspects of 9/11 are being concealed certainly face a number of "official barriers," most notably a lack of cooperation by the executive branch and the antagonism of the mainstream media. According to political economist and journalism critic Robert McChesney (who is not a skeptic of the official 9/11 account), 9/11 "highlighted the antidemocratic tendencies already in existence" in American journalism (2002, 91). McChesney calls the journalism of the post-9/11 period "propagandistic" (94), and derides the absence of debate over how to respond to the 9/11 attacks, while also denying any "explicit state censorship" (95). Even if McChesney is correct in his assertion that there was no official cover-up, however, the "distorted coverage" he emphasizes suggests that many questions about the events of 9/11 remain unanswered. Still, progressive pundits have largely focused their attention on the Bush administration's response to 9/11, generally assuming the important facts of the tragedies have already been revealed.[2]

9/11 skeptics often use humor to frame their arguments in a way that condenses or elides the true complexity of the evidence. While simplified frames often appeal to like-minded individuals, and do the essential work of translating "ideological beliefs into an existing, practical framework" of a social movement (Hart 2007, 9), they also present opponents with an expansive target for parody. The condensation of an extremely complex event into a cartoon or photomontage therefore requires a substantial effort to explain to the uninitiated what evidence lies behind forms of skepticism, and so much of this chapter is devoted to an overview of some of the evidence commonly referenced by skeptics. The popular opinion polls cited here point to the existence of a sizeable social movement, and despite its lack of a professional veneer the "boundary work" of many skeptics is compelling; "one condition must be met before humour can be utilized in social

8.1 A Brief History of the 9/11 Commission (July 24, 2004).

protest: the condition of a pre-existing collective identity, or a strict setting of the jokes. Humour never starts just out of the blue" (Hart 17). The collective identity signaled by the humor discussed below thus incorporates a broad spectrum of expertise and analyses of 9/11, from casual crackpot to dedicated research professional, from agnosticism to full-blown accusations of treason, and signals an important social instability derived from popular discourse surrounding the attacks whether or not the claims of the skeptics are themselves valid.

"A BRIEF HISTORY OF THE 9/11 COMMISSION" AND 9/11 AGNOSTICISM

Kirk Anderson's "A Brief History of the 9/11 Commission" (see figure 8.1), which appeared in the *Lexington Herald-Leader* on July 24, 2004, highlights the Bush administration's resistance to an independent investigation of the events of 9/11. If not for the efforts of the 9/11 families, in fact, there would not have been any investigation at all.[3] As Anderson foregrounds in his comic, the 9/11 Commission was reluctantly formed and systematically compromised. Anderson illustrates an escalating obfuscation from the White House, from its refusal to investigate 9/11 to its refusal to allow certain members of the executive branch to testify before the commission. Ultimately, as Anderson shows, the report blames no one and holds no one accountable. The humor of this cartoon is in both its depiction of the Bush administration as a collection of buffoons and its incremental revelation of injustice. The accretion of evidence that the 9/11 Commission is an example of justice denied, illustrated in the impish antics of Bush administration cronies, creates what Linda Hutcheon (1994) describes as "irony's edge," in which the obvious disjuncture of form and content in Anderson's cartoon plays on the cognitive dissonance of readers. While Anderson clearly does not agree with the tactics of the Bush administration, unlike some skeptics he avoids impugning individuals as coconspirators in the 9/11 plot. Anderson allows irony's edge to cleave unitary discourse on 9/11 into fragments of agnosticism. Of the many forms of 9/11 skepticism, the kind that accuses the 9/11 Commission of being neither independent nor comprehensive is the least controversial.

Two weeks after the 9/11 attacks, Secretary of State Colin Powell promised that the administration would release a paper outlining the evidence of Osama bin Laden's complicity in the attacks in which "[h]is guilt is going to be very obvious to the world" ("Evidence against bin Laden," 2001). Five years later, however, the FBI announced it had "no hard evidence" to connect bin Laden to the attacks ("FBI says," 2006). Bin Laden himself, in fact, denied any role in the attacks on three occasions, and specifically identified as possible suspects "intelligence agencies in the U.S., which require billions of dollars worth of funds from the Congress and the government every year."[4]

On December 14, 2001, the American government released a videotape it allegedly found in Jalalabad, Afghanistan, which purports to show bin Laden confessing to the crimes of 9/11 ("Tape proves Bin Laden's guilt," 2001). A week later, Dr. Abdel El M. Husseini told German television, "[The Pentagon's] translation is very problematic. At the most important places where it is held to prove the guilt of bin Laden, it is not identical with the Arabic" ("Mistranslated," 2001), and Dr. Gernot Rotter added: "The American translators who listened to the tapes and transcribed them apparently wrote a lot of things in that they wanted to hear but that cannot be heard on the tape no matter how many times you listen to it." Professor Bruce Lawrence, head of Duke University's Religious Studies program and editor of *Messages to the World: The Statements of Osama bin Laden*, called the tape "bogus" (quoted in Barrett 2007). According to the *Washington Post*, in 2010 a former CIA official revealed that the agency's Iraq Operation's Group had actually created "a video purporting to show Osama bin Laden and his cronies sitting around a campfire swigging bottles of liquor and savoring their conquests with boys," part of an effort to portray bin Laden as a pedophile. "The actors were drawn from 'some of us darker-skinned employees,'" a CIA employee said (Stein 2010). This revelation of a fake bin Laden tape, in addition to a long history of U.S. intelligence complex duplicity, reinforces the plausibility of suspicion that the bin Laden video in which he discusses 9/11 could be a fake.

Whether or not the "confession" tape is authentic is not of primary importance here. What *is* important is that the connections between bin Laden and the attacks are contested in empirical data but, aside from skeptic literature, not in public discourse.[5] Indeed, for many Americans the "confession" tape was all the evidence necessary to connect bin Laden to 9/11; however, for some of the victims' families, who fought for over a year for an independent investigation, it was not. On January 24, 2002, congressional and White House sources told CNN that "President Bush personally asked Senate Majority Leader Tom Daschle . . . to limit the congressional investigation into the events of September 11" (Bash, Karl, and King 2002). Vice President Cheney also warned Daschle not to investigate. On May 23, 2002, the president publicly announced his opposition to the formation of an independent commission (*CBS News*, 2002). The White House then stalled the creation of an independent commission, only relenting 441 days after 9/11. Senator Daschle had heard from Senator Trent Lott that the efforts to block the 9/11 Commission legislation were orchestrated by top Bush aide Karl Rove (Shenon 2008, 29). Commissioner John Lehman said Rove was "very much involved" with the commission, and was "the quarterback for dealing with the commission" (2008, 175–176).

On November 27, 2002, President Bush signed the 9/11 Commission Bill into law, and nominated Henry Kissinger as the commission's chairman. Considered by some to be a war criminal (Hitchens 2002), Kissinger's nomination was an exceedingly derisive gesture from the White House. He soon resigned, along with Vice Chairman George Mitchell, due to conflicts of interest. Their replacements had similar ethical difficulties: some commissioners worked for law firms that represented the airlines impacted on 9/11, several had strong ties to defense contractors and financial consulting firms, and others had legally represented the upper echelons of the Democratic and Republican parties (Arnold 2003). Chair Thomas Kean had a significant connection to a Saudi oil company, and as Bryan Sacks notes, Vice Chair Lee Hamilton "failed to show the virtues of independence and thoroughness both as chair of the Select Committee to Investigate Covert Arms Transactions with Iran in 1987, and again in 1992 as chair of the congressional task force charged with investigation of the 'October Surprise' allegations against the Reagan-Bush campaign in 1980" (Sacks 2006, 233).[6] Philip Zelikow, the commission's executive director, also "had good friends on Rumsfeld's staff, most importantly Steven Cambone, the undersecretary of defense for intelligence, [who] was Rumsfeld's most trusted aide" (Shenon 2008, 205). Even Henry Kissinger had representation on the commission in the form of John Lehman, who served under Kissinger at the National Security Council, and who was a member of the neoconservative think tank The Project for the New American Century along with Cheney, Rumsfeld, Cambone, Paul Wolfowitz, Richard Perle, and several others in the Bush administration. Anderson's depiction of the Bush administration's calculating approach to the investigation of 9/11 was more accurate than Anderson could have known when he drew the cartoon in 2004.

The scandal did not end with the belated start, the selection of commissioners, or the limited allotment of funds. By the admission of Kean and Hamilton themselves, the 9/11 Commission was "set up to fail" (Kean and Hamilton 2006, 14).[7] Critics point to the appointment of Executive Director Philip Zelikow as an insurmountable conflict of interest, especially since

Zelikow selected staff and had considerable control over the final edit of the report.[8] This is particularly questionable as Kean and Hamilton state they "seriously only considered one candidate," who was recommended by the White House, and "several commissioners had concerns about the kind of inquiry he would lead" (Kean and Hamilton 2006, 35). With Zelikow as the executive director of the 9/11 Commission, the White House and the national security complex were investigating themselves. As Richard Clarke said on the appointment of Zelikow, "The fix is in" (quoted in Shenon, 63).[9]

Most of the commission staff, recruited by Zelikow, were chosen because they had high-level security clearances, which would enable access to essential documents and thereby quicken the investigation.[10] All of the commission employees had to be cleared by the FBI and CIA to handle secret information (Kean and Hamilton, 34). This "preference" for staff from intelligence agencies, framed as a vital component of an expedient investigation, ensured that nothing incriminating of these agencies would appear in the report. The "bipartisan" composition of the commission—with equal numbers of Democrats and Republicans—similarly ensured that nothing terribly damaging to members of either party would appear. Information that required the highest security clearances was meted out by the White House only to select members of the commission, and ultimately, all of the information contained in the report had to be cleared by the White House, and then was additionally subject to censorship by Zelikow and May (May 2005, 134).[11] With so many layers of censorship, there was no need for a traditional "cover-up." The commission was structurally incapable of being seriously critical of the government or the national security complex. As 9/11 widow Lori van Auken remarked during the commission hearings, "We [the Family Steering Committee] feel that the Commission already has its report written. It's our sense today that they decided early on what they wanted the public to know, and then geared the hearings to fit this pre-conceived script" (quoted in Lance 2004, 3).

Although Anderson's cartoon suggests the Bush administration was adverse to full compliance with a serious investigation, it says little about the dubious information on which the final report relied. Essential information contained in the *9/11 Commission Report*, information that establishes a connection between Osama bin Laden and 9/11, is derived from reports of alleged interrogations of al Qaeda detainees by U.S. intelligence. The commissioners never met the detainees, and could not corroborate some of the evidence attributed to detainee confessions (*9/11CR*, 2004, 146). Kean and Hamilton admit where they could not corroborate information, "it was left to the reader to consider the credibility of the source—we had no opportunity to do so" (Kean and Hamilton 2006, 124). According to a document discovered by the ACLU in 2010, Cheney's counsel David Addington, Attorney General John Ashcroft, Defense Secretary Donald Rumsfeld, and CIA Director George Tenet had warned the commission in January 2004 that its request to question al Qaeda detainees was a "line" it "should not cross" (Kapur 2010).

Ernest May says the commission "never had full confidence in the interrogation reports as historical sources" (May 2005). In 2008 the CIA revealed that it had tortured three al Qaeda detainees including alleged 9/11 mastermind Khalid Sheikh Mohammed (KSM), which further obscures the veracity of comments attributed to these suspects ("CIA admits waterboarding inmates," 2008). The CIA also admitted it destroyed at least two videotapes of al Qaeda detainee interrogations, a clear case of obstruction of the 9/11 Commission (Mazzetti 2007). MSNBC found that more than 25 percent of the footnotes in the *9/11 Commission Report* were sourced to tortured testimony (Windrem and Limjoco 2008); significantly, most of these footnotes refer to chapters 5 and 7, which contain the allegations against bin Laden and details of the alleged al Qaeda plot. What if KSM turns out to have the same credibility as a source as once highly regarded detainee Abu Zubaydah? Zubaydah was touted by the Bush administration as a "high-value" detainee, a "number 2 or 3" person in al Qaeda and a confidant of Osama bin Laden, and even as one who planned 9/11. In 2010, the U.S. Justice Department backed away from all of these claims (Leopold 2010). Zubaydah, like KSM, was tortured repeatedly. The videos of his torture sessions were among those destroyed by the CIA.

The 9/11 Commission's entire mandate, in fact, was paradoxical: at once "to provide the fullest possible account of the events surrounding 9/11," and yet *not* "to assign individual blame" (*9/11CR*, 2004, xvi). Ultimately, the report blamed "deep institutional failings" (2004, 265) and the fact that "no one was firmly in charge" (2004, 400). Commissioner Bob Kerrey would later admit, "There are ample reasons to suspect that there may be some alternative to what we outlined in our version [of the history of 9/11]" (quoted in Manjoo 2006). Cofer Black, director of the CIA's Counterterrorist Center, felt "there were things the commissions [investigating 9/11] wanted to know about and things they didn't want to know about" (Froomkin 2006).[12]

Despite the deluge of evidence that problematizes the official 9/11 investigation, no serious interrogation of the report has taken place in mainstream media or academic circles. Critics of the commission and its report are framed as fringe-dwellers. Anderson's comic, in terse, incisive dialogue, exposes aspects of the Bush administration's dishonest gaming. Unfortunately, such

8.2 "Jet fuel? That's a good one!"

critiques were often dismissed as partisan haymaking (especially in 2004, an election year), and the early criticisms of the 9/11 Commission from the Left transformed into attacks on conspiracy theories. As with so many instances of Bush administration criminality, humor made from its handling of the 9/11 Commission could only produce grim but impotent snickers.

"JET FUEL? THAT'S A GOOD ONE!" AND THE CONTROLLED DEMOLITION THEORY

Some skeptics go beyond the agnosticism one might presume based on the compromises of the 9/11 Commission and declare 9/11 "an inside job"; this judgment often centers on the collapse of the World Trade Center towers. The obvious target of David Dees's photomontage "Jet fuel? That's a good one!" (see figure 8.2), which appears at his Web site (http://www.dees2.com/) along with many questionable images and was circulated online by skeptics, is the official explanation for the collapses of the World Trade Center towers. The South Tower collapsed at 9:59 a.m., 56 minutes after the impact of Flight 175; the North Tower at 10:28 a.m., 102 minutes after the impact of Flight 11; and Tower Seven at 5:20 p.m., despite no direct impact. Dees's photomontage of a picture of the South Tower collapsing with images of Donald Rumsfeld, Dick Cheney, and George W. Bush laughing implies that they were instrumental in destroying the towers and amused by the lack of skepticism present in media narratives. This particular image of the South Tower puts the image of the collapsing towers in the forefront of the viewers' minds, and, when combined with images of delighted government officials who are not supposed to be complicit with the attacks, creates what Arthur Koestler calls "bisociation," in which "humour occurs when there is a sudden movement between, or unexpected combination of, distinct interpretative frames" (Mulkay 1988, 26). In this case, the bisociative quality of Dees's montage may force some viewers to reconsider the nature of the collapses on 9/11, but its confluence of elements may repulse other viewers who consider them antithetical. Dees's montage, more than the other examples in this essay, preaches to the choir: the montage lacks subtlety because it is directed at an in-group of people that understands and agrees with its combination of interpretative frames.

That the cartoon could be so easily dismissed by nonskeptics is unfortunate because the argument it suggests, widely mocked in mainstream media, is not entirely without merit. According to engineering analyses of the WTC towers prior to 9/11, the towers were "sixteen times stiffer than a conventional structure" (Glanz and Lipton 2003, 134–136) and damage far worse than that experienced on 9/11 could be tolerated and that "the building would still be strong enough to withstand a 100-mile-per-hour wind" (2003, 133). Les Robertson, one of the original structural engineers, assured experts there is "little likelihood of a collapse no matter how the building [is] attacked" (2003, 227). After the 1993 bombing, John Skilling, the towers' chief engineer, said the towers could withstand an airplane impact "without collapsing" (2003, 131–132). Prior to 9/11, Skilling testified that the towers would withstand jet fuel fires in the event of a crash and "the building structure would still be there" (quoted in Nalder 1993). Frank A. Demartini, the on-site construction manager for the World Trade Center, claimed just months prior to 9/11 that the towers could withstand "multiple impacts of jetliners" (quoted in Dwyer and Flynn, 149).

As reported by *The New York Times*, "experts said no . . . modern, steel-reinforced high-rise had ever collapsed because of an uncontrolled fire" (Glanz 2001). The lack of a precedent for the collapses that happened three times on September 11 thus presented a compelling anomaly and cause for skepticism. In addition, demolition experts attested to the demolition-like appearance of the collapses, which were rapid, symmetrical, and total, and included high velocity horizontal bursts of debris well below the collapse wave. "The collapse of the WTC towers looked like a classic controlled demolition," according to Mike Taylor of the National Association of Demolition Contractors (Samuel and Carrington 2001). Structural engineer Ronald Hamburger told *The Wall Street Journal*, "It appeared to me that charges had been placed in the building." In the same article Charles H. Thornton, chairman of the structural engineering firm Thornton-Tomasetti Group, said, "I was absolutely flabbergasted when it [the collapses] happened–that it happened at all, and that it happened in less than three or four hours" (Hallinan, Burton, and Eig 2001). Van Romero, explosives expert and vice president for research at New Mexico Institute of Mining and Technology, told the *Albuquerque Journal* on 9/11, "My opinion is, based on the videotapes, that after the airplanes hit the World Trade Center there were some explosive devices inside the buildings that caused the towers to collapse" (quoted in Uyttebrouck 2001).[13]

The apparent paradox of expert testimony that says, yes, the collapses looked exactly like controlled demolitions, and official reports that say, no, there were no explosives in the towers, creates a space of ambiguity for nonexperts. The government investigations into the collapses did little to resolve matters. Two investigative reports were eventually published, one by the Federal Emergency Management Agency (FEMA) in 2002, and the other by the National Institute for Standards and Technology (NIST) in 2005. From the beginning, these investigations were plagued with compromises similar to the 9/11 Commission. A January 2002 editorial by Bill Manning in the respected journal *Fire Engineering* called the FEMA investigation "a half-baked farce" (Manning 2002). The FEMA report concludes, "With the information and time available, the sequence of events leading to the collapse of each tower could not be definitively determined" (FEMA 2002, "Executive Summary," 2). Regarding Tower Seven, FEMA states, "The specifics of the fires in WTC 7 and how they caused the building to collapse remain unknown at this time" (FEMA 2002, "Section 8," 7). Dr. S. Shyam Sunder, the head of the NIST investigation into

WTC7, admitted in *New York Magazine*, "We've had trouble getting a handle on building number seven" (quoted in Jacobson 2006). In August 2008, NIST released its WTC7 investigation in which it attributed the collapse to a "new phenomenon" called "thermal expansion." NIST declared WTC7 "the first known instance of fire causing the total collapse of a tall building." The study used no steel from WTC7, but instead spent three years constructing a computer simulation of the collapse.

The NIST study spent much more time and money than FEMA on its investigation of the Twin Towers and published a remarkable ten thousand pages in the final report; however, skeptics saw problems with the parameters of the investigation and the conclusions reached. For example, NIST does not attempt to explain phenomena after collapse initiation is achieved; its investigation "does not actually include the structural behavior of the tower after the conditions for collapse initiation were reached and collapse became inevitable" (NIST 2005, 82). NIST confirmed its inability to explain why the towers experienced total collapses in a letter it wrote September 27, 2007, in response to a Request for Correction written by a group of researchers and 9/11 family members: "In the case of the WTC towers, NIST has established that the failures initiated in the floors affected by the aircraft impact damage and the ensuing fires resulted in the collapses of the towers. . . . We are unable to provide a full explanation of the total collapse."[14] While NIST maintains it "found no corroborating evidence to suggest that explosives were used to bring down the buildings," it also admits it "did not conduct tests for explosive residue and as noted above, such tests would not necessarily have been conclusive."[15] Therefore, the parameters of NIST's study did not include the actual collapses, NIST did not test for explosive residue, and NIST cannot explain the total collapses; however, NIST asserts it is certain there is no evidence of the use of explosives in the WTC towers.

Supporters of the official narrative often cite the plane crashes as the obvious causes of the collapses; however, this is not the official U.S. government theory. NIST states: "The towers likely would not have collapsed under the combined effects of aircraft impact damage and the extensive, multi-floor fires if the thermal insulation had not been widely dislodged or had been only minimally dislodged by aircraft impact" (2005, xxxviii). The NIST theory also argues the fires were not very hot, never rising "above 600 degrees C for as long as 15 minutes" (2005, 180). In addition, when NIST tested their own physical models of the fires, they could not make the models collapse, even though NIST applied fires hotter and longer lasting than the fires of 9/11 (2005, 143). Given the failure of the physical models, NIST resorted to computer models of the WTC towers. For the computer models, NIST employed the most "severe" data for "each of the most influential variables," because with the moderate forms of data "it became clear that the towers would likely remain standing" (2005, 143–144).

The NIST investigation was criticized by Dr. James Quintiere, former chief of the Fire Science Division of NIST, who called NIST's conclusion "questionable" and called for an independent review of NIST's work. Quintiere is not alone in his criticism of the NIST investigation: over eleven hundred architects and engineers belong to the Architects and Engineers for 9/11 Truth, a group "dedicated to exposing the falsehoods and to revealing truths about the 'collapses' of the WTC high-rises on 9/11/01" (ae911truth.org).

Skeptics also find the oral histories of the first responders compelling. Many skeptics believe these eyewitness accounts support the controlled demolition theory. Professor Graeme MacQueen identified 118 witnesses to explosions, of the 503 witnesses in the oral histories (MacQueen 2006; all quotations are from MacQueen, unless otherwise noted); he found only 2 percent of the first responder eyewitnesses confirmed the official version of events. For example, Richard Banaciski witnessed an "explosion" in the South Tower: "It seemed like on television they blow up these buildings. It seemed like it was going all the way around like a belt, all these explosions." Gregg Brady heard "three loud explosions" under the North Tower, and Edward Cachia said that the South Tower "gave at a lower floor, not the floor where the plane hit, because we originally had thought there was like an internal detonation explosives because it went in succession, boom, boom, boom, boom, and then the tower came down." Assistant Commissioner Stephen Gregory saw "low-level flashes" before the South Tower came down: "You know like when they demolish a building, how when they blow up a building, when it falls down? That's what I thought I saw." *Wall Street Journal* reporter John Bussey also witnessed what appeared to be a synchronized event at the South Tower: "I . . . looked up out of the office window to see what seemed like perfectly synchronized explosions coming from each floor. . . . One after the other, from top to bottom, with a fraction of a second between, the floors blew to pieces" (quoted in Griffin 2006, 24). Firefighter Kenneth Rogers also witnessed synchronized explosions: "There was an explosion in the south tower. . . . I kept watching. Floor after floor after floor. One floor under another after another and when it hit about the fifth floor, I figured it was a bomb, because it looked like a synchronized deliberate kind of thing. I was there in '93" (2006, 30).

Government experts also put forward different explanations for the collapses; the official explanation endured a series of modifications: from the

8.3 Cartman points to Kyle during his slide show on 9/11 conspiracy, *South Park* (original airing: October 11, 2006).

"core meltdown" theory, to the "column failure" theory, to the "truss failure" theory, to the final theory of the NIST investigation, a hybrid version of the column failure theory in which fires made the trusses sag, which pulled the perimeter columns inward, which transferred column instability and led to global collapse.

If the causes of the collapses were not obvious to government experts, and the final theory rests on tenuous assumptions, unprecedented occurrences, and computer modeling, why should public skepticism be considered beyond the pale? Significantly, not only was the somewhat hyperbolic visual rhetoric of the Dees photomontage rejected by mainstream media and most of the American public, but so was any reasonable suspicion or skepticism. This may be due in part to the hyperbole on which responses like Dees's rely. Although such humor can theoretically broaden the base of skeptics by becoming a widely circulated example of what Henry Jenkins called "convergence culture," particularly through the use of image-editing programs for antiestablishment aims (Jenkins 2006, 206–239), its lack of connection to the commonly accepted narratives and its inability to strongly question those narratives through empirical evidence renders it easily dismissible. The bisociative bounce between interpretive frames required by

Dees's photomontage presents most people with an epistemological cavern too immense to cross, from believer to skeptic or vice versa. Mulkay acknowledges the challenge for particularly radical humor when he writes that "humor can be used to challenge existing social patterns, but only in so far as it is given serious meaning by means of criticism and confrontation that is already operative within the serious domain" (1988, 5). The frequent use of *guilt by association* arguments by opponents makes the move from believer to skeptic even more unlikely; for example, skeptics who support the controlled demolition theory, and the strident form of skepticism it implies, are often lumped in with Holocaust deniers and other hatemongers by so-called debunkers, even though such name-calling says nothing about the evidence. To laugh at this form of bisociative transition, then, can be portrayed by some debunkers as laughter in the face of the most heinous beliefs imaginable.

SOUTH PARK: "THE MYSTERY OF THE URINAL DEUCE" (OR THROWING THE SKEPTICISM BABY OUT WITH THE CONSPIRACY THEORY BATHWATER)

Perhaps the most popular and ambivalent piece of humor concerning 9/11 skepticism was the animated program *South Park*'s episode that aired on Comedy Central on October 11, 2006, "The Mystery of the Urinal Deuce." It featured the show's resident young bigot, Eric Cartman, presenting his 9/11 conspiracy theory to his grade school class in an elaborate slide show (see figure 8.3):

Cartman: *[His first image is that of the Twin Towers.]* We are told to believe that the fire from the jet fuel melted the steel framing of the towers *[the image gets animated as a cross-section of a wall is picked apart and the steel girders shown]*, which led to their collapse. But did you know jet fuel doesn't burn at a high enough temperature to melt steel? *[The other kids look at each other. Kyle's eyes are half-closed, showing his lack of interest.]* We were told the Pentagon was hit by a hijacked plane as well *[a picture of the Pentagon with the damage clearly visible; a helicopter hovers nearby]*, but now look at this photo of the Pentagon. The hole is not nearly big enough. And if a plane hit it, where is the rest of the plane?

So now, the inevitable question: if terrorists didn't cause 9/11, who did? *[Begins to use his fingers to show the numbers as he says them.]* Remember that there are in fact two towers. Two minus one is one; one, one-eleven; two minus one is one; one, one, and there are nine members on Silverstein's board of directors. That's nine-one-one. Nine-eleven. And take two minus one plus 9/11 and you get twelve, which leads us all to the mastermind of the 9/11 attacks. *[Click. Kyle now appears superimposed on the 9/11 picture already onscreen.]* Kyle!

Cartman's numerological theory is eventually put to the test as Stan and Kyle search for evidence that Kyle did not orchestrate 9/11, contrary to Cartman's accusation. In their investigation they discover a member of 911Truth.org (a real organization devoted to reopening the 9/11 investigation). He leads Stan and Kyle to the White House, where they confront President Bush and his cabinet. Here the *South Park* creators introduce a common a priori retort to 9/11 skepticism: the state (vaguely defined) would have to be all-powerful to orchestrate 9/11. When Kyle asks President Bush if he coordinated the 9/11 attacks, Bush responds, citing a litany of theories familiar to more radical 9/11 skeptics, concluding with, "It was only the world's most intricate and flawlessly executed plan ever, ever." The exchange also makes fun of the mental shortcomings of the real President Bush, here presented as a scheming mastermind. But the argument that "the government is too incompetent to pull off 9/11" is just another a priori argument, and as such carries no logical force. The *South Park* creators reveal the 911Truth.org activist to be a government operative, and the 9/11 conspiracies really products of the government itself.[16]

The *South Park* episode is in many ways typical of mainstream media discussions of 9/11 skepticism: it glosses the issue of evidence with a priori attacks; it labels all skepticism as anti-Semitic by having Cartman blame Kyle, who is Jewish, for 9/11; and it ignores the compromised 9/11 Commission. But there is a way of reading the episode as a less than damning comment on 9/11 skepticism. By putting the most outrageous theories in the mouth of Cartman, *South Park* seems to undermine those theories; that is, *South Park* may only be attacking extremism, and not 9/11 skepticism per se. The show prides itself on skewering extremists on both the left and right of the political spectrum, and Cartman "often plays a buffoonish exaggeration of a right-wing conservative" (Curtis and Erion 2007, 112–113). Are we really supposed to believe that all 9/11 skepticism is the equivalent of anti-

Semitism and numerological nonsense because *Cartman* says so? *South Park* normally champions rational skepticism, even though it gives voice to extremists, because, "while extremists are tolerated [on the show], they are not permitted to suppress the sort of free expression that is vital to the show itself" (2007, 113). Perhaps the real target of *South Park*'s satire in the "Urinal Deuce" episode is outrageous conspiracy theory, not 9/11 skepticism. As Ted Gournelos argues, *South Park* engages political rhetoric to "produce highly dissonant, multi-layered texts" (2009, 205). In the case of the "Urinal Deuce" episode, however, the dissonance was interpreted by 9/11 skeptics primarily as an endorsement for the official 9/11 narrative (911Truth.org, "South Park episode," 2006).

CONCLUSION

Humor may seem like the least likely medium for challenging the official narrative of 9/11, as it can appear abrasive and inappropriate when applied to tragic events, its success is generally contingent on its message's connection to established narratives, and, especially in the case of cartoons and photomontage, there is little space to provide empirical evidence for its author's/artist's claims. Mulkay believes humor often performs a reactionary role: "although humour appears to be a radical alternative to serious discourse in the sense that it is socially separated from the serious mode and is organized in terms of contrary discursive principles, it seems in practice overwhelmingly to support and reaffirm the established patterns of orderly, serious conduct" (1988, 212). However, many skeptics and a large percentage of the U.S. population feel their questions are appropriate, legitimate, and the result of information they have gleaned elsewhere, and the mainstream media have been reluctant to address those questions.

A significant impasse for a proper discussion of the ambiguities and unanswered questions of 9/11 is the assumption that one piece of skepticism represents all forms of skepticism, and in an unfettered forum such as the Internet this tactic of "guilt by association" can be applied generously. Most critics of 9/11 skepticism conflate its most egregious abuses with its legitimate concerns. This conflation eliminates agnosticism and the impetus for greater government transparency by reducing all skepticism to, in the words of *South Park*, "retarded" conspiracy theories. A spectrum of skepticism concerning the 9/11 attacks exists, as the discussion above illustrates, and has become a substantial social movement. If the only thing the work of humorists such as Anderson, Dees, Parker, and Stone achieves is to get people talking about the anomalies and ambiguities of the official 9/11 account, then that work will have achieved more than what the mainstream media or the progressive Left seem willing to do.

NOTES

1. The inability of skeptics to convince some people through rational argument may be in part due to the phenomenon known as "motivated reasoning." As sociologist Steven Hoffman told *Newsweek*, "Rather than search rationally for information that either confirms or disconfirms a particular belief, people actually seek out information that confirms what they already believe." Hoffman and other researchers studied why so many Americans believe Saddam Hussein was connected to 9/11. They concluded of people who continue to make this link despite the evidence, "[T]he fact of the [invasion of Iraq] led to a search for a justification for it, which led them to infer the existence of ties between Iraq and 9/11" (quoted in Begley, 2009). The events of September 11, 2001, have been accompanied by a more consistent government framing than the invasion of Iraq, and trying to convince some people of an alternative 9/11 scenario thus poses a significant challenge for skeptics.

2. Typical of this response is Noam Chomsky, who in his bestselling book *9-11* writes, "[D]espite what must be the most intensive international intelligence investigation in history, evidence about the perpetrators of 9-11 has been hard to find. . . . Nevertheless, despite the thin evidence, the initial conclusion about 9-11 is presumably correct" (2002, 120–121). Because of his celebrated status, Chomsky was strenuously pursued by 9/11 skeptics to endorse their cause. However, as Chomsky asserted at a public appearance, "Even if it [the idea of U.S. government complicity with the 9/11 attacks] were true, which is extremely unlikely, who cares? I mean, it doesn't have any significance. . . . It's just taking energy away from serious issues for ones that don't matter" (quoted in Peterson 2007).

3. The documentary *9/11: Press for Truth* examines the struggle of the "Jersey Girls," a group of 9/11 widows who pressured the government to sponsor an investigatory commission.

4. In one article he is quoted as saying, "I would like to assure the world that I did not plan the recent attacks, which seems to have been planned by people for personal reasons" ("Bin Laden says he wasn't behind attacks," 2001). In the Pakistani paper *Ummat* he similarly argued that "[t]he United States should try to trace the perpetrators of these attacks within itself; the people who are a part of the U.S. system, but are dissenting against it" (quoted in "Bin Laden denies involvement," 2001).

5. Of course the tape may be authentic, but questions remain: Why would a world-famous terrorist with a declared vendetta against the United States publicly declare his innocence in the most devastating terrorist attack on American soil, if he in fact orchestrated this terrorist masterstroke? Can the U.S. government provide proof of the provenance and chain of custody of this evidence? So far it has not, and to many the discovery of the tape seems too good to be true. *The Guardian* reported on December 16, 2001, that "several intelligence sources" suggested "that the tape, although absolutely genuine, is the result of a sophisticated

sting operation run by the CIA through a second intelligence service, possibly Saudi or Pakistani" (Vulliami and Burke 2001).

6. Hamilton's record in such investigations shows a willingness to deflect potentially damaging examinations of the Bush family. Hamilton, though a Democratic Party member, had lengthy friendships with top neoconservatives in the Bush administration, including Dick Cheney and Don Rumsfeld, who "let others in the White House know that Hamilton could be trusted" (Shenon 2008, 177).

7. They ultimately claimed that the commission was a success despite considerable obfuscation from the White House, which they called the "chief obstacle" (2006, 17).

8. According to Paul Sperry, "Though he has no vote, [Zelikow] arguably has more sway than any member, including the chairman. Zelikow picks the areas of investigation, the briefing materials, the topics for hearings, the witnesses, and the lines of questioning for witnesses. . . . In effect, he sets the agenda and runs the investigation" (quoted in Sacks 2005).

9. Zelikow's profile alarmed the Family Steering Committee so much they requested he resign. In addition to being a professor of history at Harvard and the University of Virginia, Zelikow coauthored a book with Condoleezza Rice, and was later appointed as a senior policy advisor to Rice at the U.S. Department of State in 2005; he served in the U.S. Department of State under the second Reagan administration, and joined the National Security Council under President George H. W. Bush; he authored the 2002 National Security Strategy for President George W. Bush, for whom he was also a member of the transition team following the 2000 election; he was a member of the Foreign Intelligence Advisory Board from 2001 to 2003; and Zelikow was a member of the Carter-Ford Commission on Federal Electoral Reform, members of which described him as "arrogant and secretive" (Shenon 2008, 59). Bryan Sacks also notes an often obscured item on Zelikow's resume: his directorship of the Aspen Strategy Group (ASG) in the 1990s. Emeritus members of the ASG include Rice, Cheney, Wolfowitz, Richard Armitage, I. Lewis "Scooter" Libby, and former *New York Times* reporter Judith Miller (Sacks 2005).

10. Professor Ernest May, a senior advisor to the 9/11 Commission, described the composition of the staff once a premium was placed on security clearance: "That meant preference for people who could be detailed from national security agencies or who had been on the staff of one of the congressional intelligence oversight committees. Of the fifty-odd men and women who counted as professional rather than administrative staff, at least half had such backgrounds" (May 2005).

11. Kean and Hamilton explain: "The White House wanted strict limitations on both of these fronts—limiting staff with access to White House documents to just two or three people, limiting the commissioners with access to certain materials to just the chair and vice-chair, and restricting the amount of notes the staff could bring back to the 9/11 Commission's office" (2006, 72).

12. Furthermore, the *9/11 Commission Report* described the origins of the financing for the 9/11 attacks as "of little practical significance" (2004, 172), and even after what was allegedly the worst intelligence failure in American history, no one within the intelligence community was fired or demoted as a result of demonstrable failures pertaining to 9/11; in fact, principal players were actually rewarded.

13. Romero later retracted his statement asserting the presence of explosive devices inside the towers, and is placed here alongside other experts who say they do not believe there were explosives in the towers.

14. http://www.911proof.com/NIST.pdf

15. In 2009 a group of scientists published results of a study of WTC dust in a peer-reviewed journal, which revealed unreacted thermitic material in the dust (Harrit et al. 2009). The finding suggested the chemical trace of a "highly engineered explosive" in the WTC dust. To date, no scientific studies have attempted to replicate these results.

16. The argument that 9/11 skepticism emerges from some kind of government propaganda promotes an argumentative endgame in the clash of 9/11 theories, by suggesting to those who find the official 9/11 narrative unproblematic that skeptics are actually the opposite of what they claim, not critics of the Bush administration but (un)intentional proponents.

WORKS CITED

9/11 Commission. *The 9/11 Commission Report*. Baton Rouge, LA: Claitor's Publishing Division, 2004.

911Truth.org. "South Park episode hits mark for toilet humor, but misses on 9/11 skepticism." October 26, 2006. http://www.911truth.org/article.php?story=20061013103151876 (accessed May 20, 2007).

———. "Zogby poll finds 70 million voting age Americans support new 9/11 investigation." May 22, 2006. http://www.911truth.org/article.php?story=20060522022041421 (accessed June 4, 2010).

Angus Reid Global Monitor. "Americans question Bush on 9/11 intelligence." October 14, 2006. http://www.angus-reid.com/polls/view/13469 (accessed June 4, 2010).

Arnold, Laurence. "9/11 commissioners connected to firms they'll be investigating." Associated Press, March 28, 2003. http://web.archive.org (accessed May 7, 2007).

Barrett, Kevin. "Top U.S. bin Laden expert: Confession video 'bogus.'" *Prison Planet*, February 19, 2007. http://prisonplanet.com/articles/february2007/190207Laden.htm (accessed May 20, 2007).

Bash, Dana, Jon Karl, and John King, "Bush asks Daschle to limit Sept. 11 probes." CNN, January 29, 2002. www.cnn.com (accessed May 7, 2007).

Begley, Sharon. "Why we believe lies, even when we learn the truth." *Newsweek*, August 25, 2009. http://www.newsweek.com/2009/08/24/lies-of-mass-destruction.html (accessed June 4, 2010).

"Bin Laden says he wasn't behind attacks." CNN, September 17, 2001. http://archives.cnn.com/2001/US/09/16/inv.binladen.denial/index.html (accessed May 20, 2007).

Boehlert, Eric. "The president ought to be ashamed." *Salon.com*, November 21, 2003. http://archive.salon.com/news/feature/2003/11/21/cleland/print.html (accessed May 7, 2007).

CBS News. "Bush opposes 9/11 query panel." May 23, 2002. http://www.cbsnews.com/stories/2002/05/15/attack/main509096.shtml (accessed May 7, 2007).

Chomsky, Noam. *9-11*. New York: Seven Stories Press, 2002.

"CIA admits waterboarding inmates." BBC News, February 5, 2008. http://news.bbc.co.uk/2/hi/americas/7229169.stm (accessed April 6, 2008).

Clarke, Richard. *Against All Enemies: Inside America's War on Terror*. New York: Free Press, 2004.

Curtis, David Valleau, and Gerald J. Erion. "*South Park* and the open society: Defending democracy through satire." In *South Park and Philosophy: You Know, I Learned Something Today*, edited by Robert Arp. Oxford: Blackwell Publishing, 2007.

DeMott, Benjamin. "Whitewash as public service." *Harper's*, October 2004. http://www .harpers.org/archive/2004/10/0080234 (accessed May 18, 2007).

Dwyer, Jim, and Kevin Flynn. *102 Minutes: The Untold Story of the Fight to Survive Inside the Twin Towers*. New York: Times Books, 2005.

"Evidence against bin Laden promised." *Seattle Post-Intelligencer*, September 24, 2001. http:// seattlepi.nwsource.com (accessed May 19, 2007).

"FBI says, 'No hard evidence connecting Bin Laden to 9/11.'" *Muckraker Report*, June 6, 2006. http://www.teamliberty.net/id267.html (accessed June 7, 2006).

FEMA, *World Trade Center Building Performance Study*. May 2002. Available online: http:// www.fema.gov/rebuild/mat/wtcstudy.shtm.

Froomkin, Dan. "The covered-up meeting." *The Washington Post*, October 2, 2006. http:// www.washingtonpost.com/wp-dyn/content/blog/2006/10/02/BL2006100200537 .html?nav=rss_opinion/columns (accessed April 6, 2008).

Glanz, James. "Engineers suspect diesel fuel in collapse of 7 World Trade Center." *The New York Times*, November 29, 2001. www.nytimes.com (accessed December 24, 2006).

Glanz, James, and Eric Lipton. *City in the Sky: The Rise and Fall of the World Trade Center*. New York: Times Books, 2003.

Gournelos, Ted. *Popular Culture and the Future of Politics: Cultural Studies and the Tao of South Park*. Lanham, MD: Lexington Books, 2009.

Griffin, David Ray. *Christian Faith and the Truth Behind 9/11*. Louisville: Westminster John Knox Press, 2006.

Hallinan, Joseph T., Thomas M. Burton, and Jonathan Eig. "Top structural engineers to do autopsy on Twin Towers to assess why they fell." *The Wall Street Journal*, September 19, 2001. http://www.absconsulting.com/news/wsjsept11.pdf (accessed April 10, 2008).

Hargrove, Thomas. "Third of Americans suspect 9-11 government conspiracy." *Scripps Howard News Service*, August 1, 2006. http://www.scrippsnews.com/911poll (accessed June 4, 2010).

Harrit, Niels, Jeffrey Farrer, Steven E. Jones, Kevin R. Ryan, Frank M. Legge, Daniel Farnsworth, Gregg Roberts, James R. Gourley, and Bradley R. Larsen. "Active Thermitic Material Discovered in Dust from the 9/11 World Trade Center Catastrophe." *The Open Chemical Physics Journal* 2 (2009): 7–31.

Hart, Marjolein 't. "Humour and social protest: An introduction." *International Review of Social History* 52 (2007): 1–20.

Hitchens, Christopher. *The Trial of Henry Kissinger*. New York: Verso, 2002.

Hutcheon, Linda. *Irony's Edge: The Theory and Politics of Irony*. New York: Routledge, 1994.

Jacobson, Mark. "The ground zero grassy knoll." *New York Magazine*, March 20, 2006. http:// nymag.com/news/features/16464/ (accessed May 7, 2007).

Jenkins, Henry. *Convergence Culture: Where Old and New Media Collide*. New York: NYU Press, 2006.

Kapur, Sahil. "Revealed: Ashcroft, Tenet, Rumsfeld warned 9/11 Commission about 'line' it 'should not cross.'" *Raw Story*, March 17, 2010. http://rawstory.com/2010/03/revealed-ashcroft-tenet-rumsfeld -warned-911-commission-line-should-cross/ (accessed March 21, 2010).

Kean, Thomas H., and Lee H. Hamilton. *Without Precedent: The Inside Story of the 9/11 Commission.* New York: Alfred A. Knopf, 2006.

Lance, Peter. *Cover Up: What the Government Is Still Hiding About the War On Terror.* New York: Harper Collins, 2004.

Leopold, Jason. "US recants claims on 'high-value' detainee Abu Zubaydah." *Truthout.org*, March 30, 2010. http://www.truthout.org/government-quietly-recants-bush-era-claims-about-%22high-value%22-detainee-zubdaydah58151 (accessed May 14, 2010).

MacQueen, Graeme. "118 witnesses: The firefighters' testimony to explosions in the towers." *Journal of 9/11 Studies* 2 (August 2006). http://www.journalof911studies.com/articles/Article_5_118Witnesses_WorldTradeCenter.pdf (accessed May 20, 2007).

Manjoo, Farhad. "The 9/11 deniers." *Salon.com*, June 27, 2006. http://www.salon.com/ent/feature/2006/06/27/911_conspiracies/index4.html (accessed April 6, 2008).

Manning, Bill. "Selling out the investigation." *Fire Engineering*, January 2002. www.fireengineering.com (accessed May 13, 2007).

May, Ernest. "When government writes history." *The New Republic*, May 16, 2005. http://www.tnr.com/doc.mhtml?i=20050523&s=may052305 (accessed May 7, 2007).

Mazzetti, Mark. "C.I.A. destroyed 2 tapes showing interrogations." *The New York Times*, December 7, 2007. http://www.nytimes.com/2007/12/07/washington/07intel.html (accessed April 6, 2008).

McChesney, Robert W. "September 11 and the structural limitations of US journalism." In *Journalism After September 11*, edited by Barbie Zelizer and Stuart Allan. New York: Routledge, 2002.

Miller, Alan. "Former chief of NIST's fire science division calls for independent review of World Trade Center investigation." *OpEd News*, August 21, 2007. http://www.opednews.com/articles/genera_alan_mil_070820_former_chief_of_nist.htm (accessed August 23, 2007).

"Mistranslated Osama bin Laden video—the German press investigates." *DC Indymedia*, December 23, 2001. http://dc.indymedia.org/newswire/display/16801 (accessed May 20, 2007).

Mulkay, Michael. *On Humour: Its Nature and Its Place in Modern Society.* Oxford: Polity Press, 1988.

Nalder, Eric. "Twin Towers engineered to withstand jet collision." *Seattle Times*, February 27, 1993. http://community.seattletimes.nwsource.com/archive/?date=19930227&slug=1687698 (accessed May 20, 2007).

National Institute of Standards and Technology. *Final Report on the Collapse of the World Trade Center Towers.* September 2005. http://wtc.nist.gov/.

Peterson, Kim. "9-11: The Truth Matters." *Dissident Voice*, March 13, 2007. http://www.dissidentvoice.org/Mar07/Petersen13.htm (accessed June 9, 2007).

Ridgeway, James. *The 5 Unanswered Questions About 9/11: What the 9/11 Commission Report Failed to Tell Us.* New York: Seven Stories Press, 2005.

Risen, James. "Rifts plentiful as 9/11 inquiry begins." *New York Times*, June 4, 2002. www.nytimes.com (accessed June 12, 2007).

Sacks, Bryan. "Making history: The compromised 9-11 commission." In *The Hidden History of 9-11-2001*, edited by Paul Zarembka. New York: Elsevier, 2006.

Sacks, Bryan. "Philip Zelikow: The Bush administration investigates the Bush administration." *9/11Truth.org*, November 28, 2005. www.911truth.org (accessed May 6, 2007).

Samuel, Eugene, and Damian Carrington. "Design choice for towers saved lives." *New Scientist*, September 12, 2001. www.newscientist.com (accessed September 19, 2006).

Shenon, Philip. *The Commission: The Uncensored History of the 9/11 Investigation*. New York: Hachette Book Group, 2008.

Stein, Jeff. "CIA unit's wacky idea: Depict Saddam as gay." *The Washington Post*, May 25, 2010. http://blog.washingtonpost.com/spy-talk/2010/05/cia_group_had_wacky_ideas_to_d .html (accessed May 25, 2010).

"Tape 'proves bin Laden's guilt.'" BBC News, December 14, 2001. http://news.bbc.co.uk/2/hi/ south_asia/1708091.stm (accessed October 2, 2005).

Uyttebrouck, Olivier. "Explosives planted in towers, N.M. Tech expert says." *Albuquerque Journal*, September 11, 2001. http://911research.wtc7.net/disinfo/retractions/romero.html (accessed April 10, 2008).

Vulliamy, Ed, and Jason Burke. "Bin Laden videotape was result of a sting." *The Guardian*, September 16, 2001. www.observer.guardian.co.uk (accessed May 25, 2007).

Windrem, Robert, and Victor Limjoco. "9/11 Commission controversy." MSNBC, January 30, 2008. http://deepbackground.msnbc.msn.com/archive/2008/01/30/624314.aspx (accessed April 6, 2008).

Woods, Toni-Johnson. *Blame Canada! South Park and Contemporary Culture*. New York: Continuum, 2007.

PART THREE Rethinking Post-9/11 Politics

CHAPTER NINE

LAUGHING DOVES

U.S. Antiwar Satire from Niagara to Fallujah

—Aaron Winter

A 2006 episode of Comedy Central's *The Daily Show* ridiculed an army-sponsored essay contest that solicited new ideas for "countering insurgency" in Iraq. Correspondent John Hodgman read a mock entry which detailed a scheme to "drop thousands of king cobras into Fallujah, each equipped with its own little parachute." The snakes would then "fight with their magical venom, and turn the Sunnis into Shi'ites and the Shi'ites into Sunnis" (Apr. 25, 2006). *The Onion* Web site suggested, likewise, that the Bush administration could "send 30,000 mall security guards to Iraq" (Nov. 10, 2004), "begin calling up Civil War re-enactors for active duty" (Mar. 27, 2007), or perhaps just "deploy 20,000 wishful thoughts" (Feb. 2, 2007). These satires captured one of the crowning ironies of Operation Iraqi Freedom: a military campaign prepared by a decade of think tank white papers had unraveled into a series of hastily improvised expedients.[1]

Readers of this volume know that the darkly humorous mode of antiwar critique we find in *The Daily Show* and *The Onion* has been a prevalent trope of oppositional politics in the past decade. What they may not know is that it was also prevalent two centuries ago. In 1811, for instance, when the Madison administration floated a dubious plan to invade British Canada by way of the Niagara peninsula, an editorial in *The Cynick* joked that the War of 1812 would be more easily won by "pick[ing] out from the mass of our male population, which heaven knows is ugly enough, the ugliest and most deformed men" and ordering them to "march immediately to the enemy's country, and fright the women out of their wits" (Nov. 30, 1811). *The Tickler* preferred subterfuge to shock and awe: "We would require but fifteen hundred men well disciplined to run on all fours; the first five hundred dressed in Sheep skins with the wool on, and taught to cry ba! Another 5 hundred in hogs skins with the bristles up, and taught to grunt; and another 5 hundred in bullocks hides with horns on ... well trained, and driven by officers as cattle merchants" (Mar. 4, 1812). The rowdy, decentralized, and openly partisan nineteenth-century media culture that birthed *The Cynick* and *The Tickler* bears many similarities to our twenty-first-century cacophony of blogs and cable news outlets. But the particular similarity that underpins this chapter is the crucial role played in both eras by American antiwar satirists, whom I refer to as "laughing doves" in a play on the hawk/dove terminology first coined in 1812.

Recent revivals of *Lysistrata* and *Hair* suggest that contemporary laughing doves do recognize some historical precedents for their work. But comparisons to the Age of Aristophanes can be too generic (is every war really the same?), and comparisons to the Age of Aquarius can be too specific (is every war really Vietnam?). So I want to supplement these with a different set of historical comparisons, principally to the War of 1812 (–1815), the U.S.-Mexican War (1846–1848), and the U.S.-Philippine War (1899–1913). In doing so, I will introduce a number of forgotten American antiwar satirists, and reintroduce a number of Americans who are remembered for everything *but* their antiwar satire (e.g., Abraham Lincoln, Mark Twain, William Dean Howells, Frederick Douglass, Herman Melville, and Nathaniel Hawthorne). I will jump back and forth from Niagara to Fallujah, and points in between, in the hopes of inducing the same stereoscopic vision of U.S. political rhetoric that I've experienced by spending my days poring over archival microfilm and my nights glued to the fake news. I will also jump back and forth between genres—poems, essays, cartoons, novels, television shows, movies, Web sites—in a manner that replicates the unique formal fluidity of satiric rhetorical modes both then and now.

Other chapters in this collection, and work I've published elsewhere,[2] explain how American satirists typically face the twin accusations of triviality and treason, and how they typically tease this contradiction into a crafty self-justification.[3] I will use my space here to delineate two other important continuities between nineteenth- and twenty-first-century laughing doves. In my first section, I will argue that satire shields U.S. antiwar rhetoric from pejorative "feminization" by compensating with a parallel form of macho violence. In my second section, I will argue that satire epitomizes the vacillation of U.S. antiwar rhetoric between a critique of racist jingoism and a reapplication of that same jingoism to alternate ends. In both cases, laughing doves flog a pro-war straw man not only for rhetorical effect, but also to stabilize their own equivocations. Along with *The Daily Show* and *The Onion*, I will discuss *The Colbert Report* (Comedy Central), Aaron McGruder's comic strip *The Boondocks* (Universal Press Syndicate 1999–2005), and two feature films: Joshua Seftel and John Cusack's *War, Inc.* (2008) and Jon

Hurwitz and Hayden Schlossberg's *Harold and Kumar Escape from Guantanamo Bay* (2008).

So let us now venture to an oddly familiar United States, where coastal elites and heartland populists hurl competing accusations of media bias and deficient patriotism, where an imminent threat to national security and a pledge to bring freedom to the victims of a diabolical dictator turn out to be convenient political fictions, and where a commander-in-chief celebrates a "mission accomplished" even as he demands unfettered funding for an open-ended counterinsurgency operation that will result in a troubling scandal over the morality of torture.

"OPERATION MACHO KICK-ASS"—GENDER AND *JOUISSANCE* IN WARTIME SATIRE

Laughing dove tactics were essential to nineteenth-century U.S. antiwar rhetoric because satire prevented hawks from monopolizing a claim to political masculinity, which was heavily associated during this period with personal and national displays of aggression.[4] Satire was the definitive idiom of masculine common sense and therefore the best means available of waging a war against war. Far from universal, this particular gender dynamic developed with the advent of liberal democracy in the United States during and after the War of 1812.

To an eighteenth-century Briton or British-American, isolationism was eminently manly. The body, the household, and the nation were organic units that proved their integrity through balance and self-control. Satire policed the borders of all three. Like the code of dueling that required a gentleman insulted by an equal to tender him a formal invitation to a pistol duel, but required a gentlemen insulted by a commoner to tenderize him with the handiest blunt object, the code of genre also assigned vulgar punishments to vulgar offenders. Jonathan Swift (1968) likened satire to a broomstick, "destined to make other things clean and be nasty itself" (239). American opponents of the anti-British foreign policy that eventually became the War of 1812 invoked this broomstick corollary by launching newspapers whose titles suggested violent discipline, including the *Corrector*, the *Lancet*, the *Porcupine*, the *Tickler*, the *Scorpion*, the *Scourge*, and the *Switch* (a tickler is actually a spiked whip). But relying on such imagery during a conflict many of their countrymen viewed as a second war for independence from Great Britain put Madison's critics on thin political ice. While most hawks were Republicans sympathetic to revolutionaries in Paris, most doves were Federalists sympathetic to bankers in London. Already suspiciously elitist and suspiciously anglophilic, they were now brandishing the most conspicuously snobby and British of all literary methods! Worse yet, the war itself was both a symptom of, and a catalyst for, an emerging social paradigm in which masculinity would need to be serially performed outside the self—in the marketplace, on the stump, and on the battlefield. This change made the antiwar position decidedly more vulnerable to metaphorical emasculation. One pro-war newspaper described Federalist dissent as "the impotent effort of petulant weakness" (*Democratic Republican* Aug. 17, 1812). Anxious refutations and reversals followed accordingly, as when dove satirists ridiculed the president as "Mrs. Madison's husband" (*Tickler* Nov. 10, 1812); his vice president, Elbridge Gerry, as "a political hermaphrodite" (*Federal Republican* Jun. 13, 1810); and his top general, Henry Dearborn, as "Old Granny Dearborn"(*Tickler* Sep. 1, 1812).

By the mid-1800s, both the generic character of U.S. satire and the social character of its participants had completed a parallel transformation. Aristocratic satire gave way to democratic "humor," a jostling rhetorical competition between members of a new ruling class that included every white male American. "Satire" was now a term reserved for antiques and imports, but it was still a process reserved for nasty punishment of inferiors; women and racial minorities are almost always the objects of nineteenth-century humor and almost never the subjects.[5] Consequently, when the war with Mexico began in 1846, dissenters were mocked as both effeminate and humorless, which were now two ways of saying the same thing. *New York Herald* publisher James Bennett classed antiwar activists with abolitionists and temperance crusaders, calling them "the old women of both sexes" (Hietala 1985, 213). Even outspoken critics of the war like Orestes Brownson distanced themselves from the "namby-pamby peace men," or radical pacifists (Johannsen 1985, 272). Reoriented from eighteenth-century elitist violence to nineteenth-century populist violence, the satiric genre again proved useful for reflecting hawkish imputations of effeminacy back toward the hawks themselves. The *John-Donkey* referred to President James Polk's cabinet advisers as "Georgina Dallas" and "Jemima Buchanan" (Jun. 10, 1848), while *Yankee Doodle* created imaginary dialogues between the First Couple (Apr. 2, 1847) in which Sarah Polk bemoaned her husband's inability to stay "awake" and pined for his mentor Andrew Jackson, the always erect "Old Hickory." But satire also performed a new function for antiwar rhetoric by yoking it to good-humored masculine common sense. Thus Lincoln made his national debut by dissecting the rationale for invading Mexico with the sarcastic "Spot Resolutions" (1847). The speech invited the president to specify precisely where the enemy had "shed American blood on the American soil," as Polk had claimed to bolster a thin justification he'd actually composed *before* receiving word of a skirmish in a disputed border area.[6]

During the war against Spain in 1898 and the subsequent war against Filipino nationalists who felt their American "liberators" had overstayed their welcome, American doves were once again mocked in gendered terms, as "misguided nannies" or "busy old women" (*Puck* Mar. 22, 1899). The most frequent insult was "Auntie," a term that alluded to both *anti*war and *anti*-imperialist dissent. As Richard Welch writes (1979), hawks cast opposition to the Philippine War "as a cross between treason and transvestitism" (52). Arguing that "the art of war" lacked "those little suavities that distinguish the function of five o'clock tea," hawkish satire magazine *Puck* ridiculed Congress (Apr. 17, 1901) for investigating the army's use of tortures like "the water cure" (i.e., waterboarding) in its interrogations of Filipino detainees, likening the legislature to a "Girl's High School Debating Club" and a "Home for Aged and Indigent Respectable Females." We may compare Rush Limbaugh's equation of the Abu Ghraib atrocities to college fraternity pranks that were "not as serious as everyone [was] making [them] out to be," and his call for those alarmed by them to have "a little levity" (Meyer 2004).

Given the advances of the women's suffrage movement, the mounting tensions between a rising tide of immigrants and an uneasy nativist majority, and the widespread fear that white-collar office labor was sapping the vigor and autonomy of the middle class, war struck many American men as a social panacea in the 1890s (Hoganson 1998). Peace was contemptible, claimed Teddy Roosevelt, who would serve in rapid succession as secretary of the navy, "Rough Rider" cavalryman, governor of New York, vice president, and president. It was "a condition of blubber-like and swollen ignobility, fit only for huckstering weaklings" (Tebbel 1996, 141). Only the most unimpeachably American and unimpeachably masculine war critic could weather this toxic climate of gender anxiety, and only satire could establish those credentials, which is why the surprising debut of "Auntie Twain" in 1901 as vice president of the New York Anti-Imperialist League makes him the most important laughing dove in U.S. history.

Twain never responded to the gender slur himself, but two of his literary allies and anti-imperialist fellow travelers used Twainesque satire to do so. In "Editha," Howells reframed thoughtful restraint as masculine and thoughtless aggression as feminine by skewering the story's title character,

an irrational and domineering shrew who bullies her boyfriend into joining the army. A parting shot asserted the femininity of military service per
se: "He looked well, in his uniform, and very soldierly, but somehow girlish,
too, with his clean-shaven face and slim figure" (1905, 223). In *Captain Jinks,
Hero*, Ernest Crosby extended Howells's scenario by depicting the hazing
rituals that his gullible hawkish protagonist undergoes at the "East Point"
military training academy as a vicious cycle of feminization; the ringleader
who initiates Jinks has a "squeaky voice" because he swallowed too much
tabasco sauce during his own initiation (1902, 23).

Because most Americans no longer suspect, as they did throughout the
nineteenth century, that the federal army is a corrupt European institution
lacking the democratic integrity of a self-organized state militia company,[7]
today's laughing doves are unlikely to ridicule U.S. soldiers in this fashion. They are equally unlikely to respond with countermisogynistic barbs
when they are dubbed "Aunties"—or "hopeless, hysterical hypochondriacs
of history"[8]—or perhaps "feminazis."[9] Instead, contemporary antiwar satire
tends to invert the gendering strategy of hawk rhetoric by creating cartoon-
ishly misogynistic or homophobic strawmen. Yet the cultural logic of this
latter technique nonetheless still depends on the continuing association of
satire/humor with a normative masculinity; here the hawk's masculinity is
hysterically funny because it is hysterically overwrought.

The Daily Show offers a case in point, with anchor Jon Stewart playing
the "straight" man in every sense of the word. Stewart's monologues file
a grievance against the feminization of dissent; he summarized the Bush
administration's rhetorical modus operandi as "chastising those who disagree and making them feel like pussies" (*DS* Aug. 13, 2007). But it is Stewart's bemused, paternal forbearance of his chickenhawk interlocutors that
performs his revenge, by modeling an alternate norm of male conduct.[10] The
first of these foils was "Senior Political Analyst" Stephen Colbert, who contended (*DS* Apr. 23, 2003) that "the media's role" in war coverage was merely
to give "accurate and objective description of the hellacious ass-whomping
we're handing the Iraqis." Challenged by Stewart that the term "ass-whomping" was overly "subjective," Colbert conceded it might be called an "ass-
kicking" or "ass-handing-to," and dismissed retired generals who criticized
Secretary of Defense Donald Rumsfeld as "queers" who were "light in the
combat boots."

When Colbert developed this hawk strawman into a more nuanced
satirical character for his spinoff show, he was replaced by Rob Corddry, who carped that doves might as well "pull out the couch and get a

banana daiquiri for the enemy," and rejected Stewart's praise of the military's increasing "sensitivity" to Iraq's cultural complexities: "Whoa, whoa, whoa, whoa! No, no, no, not sensitivity Jon, not in this administration's war on terror ... sensi-tough-ity perhaps" (*DS* Aug. 12, 2004; Jan. 11, 2006). Corddry plays a similarly hypermasculine character in *Harold and Kumar Escape from Guantanamo Bay*, an "undersecretary" of Homeland Security who wrongfully sentences the protagonists to the Cuban detention camp; they narrowly escape their ultimate punishment, which was to be coerced fellation of their wardens. When a subordinate questions the undersecretary's motives, Corddry snatches a framed photograph of a coworker's young daughter from a nearby desk and asks whether the man wants to see her "get raped," explaining that she symbolizes "America" and that political dissent is equivalent to "want[ing] to rape America." The latest incarnation of the *Daily Show*'s gender-baiting hawk strawman is Rob Riggle, whose imposing physical stature depletes some of the irony the character conveyed when played by the bookish Colbert or the diminutive Corddry. Yet Riggle's military background made him the ideal correspondent for the show's first taped segment in Baghdad, wherein he satirized the gendered connotations of the Petraeus "surge" by weighing the relative merits of naming it "Operation Fluffy Bunny" or "Operation Macho Kick-Ass" (*DS* Aug. 21–22, 2007).

Such satirical critiques of hawkish *jouissance*, to repurpose a term from Jacques Lacan,[11] rebut the Roosevelt/Limbaugh claim that war is a zesty frolic and that those who argue against it are wet blankets. By figuring hawks as sexually repressed martinets like Captain Jinks and Undersecretary Corddry, and associating doves with the Olympian levity of Twain and Stewart, antiwar satire can claim to be a more pleasurable tickler than war itself. All that remains is to select appropriate targets, and in this sense Bush's cabinet does just as well as Madison's. Thus Stewart nicknamed Rumsfeld "Bonkers McDeathwishman" (*DS* Nov. 12, 2002) and explained that Vice President Dick Cheney "want[ed] to bomb" Iraq "so bad" that he'd come to regard his more cautious NATO allies as "a handful of negative nellies who ... never want the U.S. to do anything fun" (Aug. 21, 2002). *The Onion*'s President Bush contended that "the Iraq war was the fun thing to do," regardless of its geopolitical consequences, and that it would therefore continue "for as long as his administration was enjoying itself" (Jun. 18, 2008). When the army's Middle East regional commander Tommy Franks resigned, the Web site reported that he would move on, in the manner of a disaffected rock musician "to pursue solo bombing projects" (Jun. 12, 2003).

More impressive than these ad hominem thrusts is the way that contemporary laughing doves have mobilized the trope of hawkish *jouissance* to eviscerate a complacent or opportunistic news media for rehashing administration propaganda. In the midst of the stunned interval after the World Trade Center attack when U.S. citizens, reporters, and satirists alike were observing a voluntary self-censorship, McGruder admitted, through *The Boondocks*'s youthful protagonist Huey Freeman, that it was "hard to laugh, or smile, or be funny" (Sep. 24, 2001). But he cast a wary eye on the admiration of Huey's bellicose brother Riley for the "cool titles and logos" that the cable news channels used in their coverage of the war against the Afghan Taliban (Sep. 27, 2001). *The Daily Show* echoed this sentiment (Apr. 10, 2003), reairing a sequence of war footage that Fox News had set to a bombastic Wagneresque score, then dubbing over it with music suggesting pornography. The virtuoso of this particular tactic of antiwar satire is surely Colbert, who portrays a jingoistic cable news pundit who lusts to "use multimillion dollar weaponry to act out [his] own personal juvenile fantasies" (*DS* Mar. 4, 2003), dismisses *New Yorker* columnist George Packer as a "Gloomy Gus" for criticizing the Iraq war (*CR* Feb. 9, 2006), and explains to foreign policy analyst Fareed Zakaria that "a centrist" is "just someone who doesn't have the balls to be a fanatic" (*CR* Oct. 19, 2005).[12] Indeed "balls" are a central obsession of *The Colbert Report*, which promises viewers that they will experience vicarious *jouissance* when the host "feels the news at" them (Oct. 17, 2005). When the show filmed a week of episodes as part of a USO tour in Baghdad (Jun. 8–11, 2009), its logo became a military seal for "Operation Iraqi Stephen," with one quadrant displaying a large pair of brass testicles.

Such portrayals of the pro-war attitude as a fetish, a way to seek perverse pleasure outside of heterosexual domesticity in the guise of an overeager defense of its values, would seemingly trace to Stanley Kubrick and Terry Southern's *Dr. Strangelove* (1964). *War, Inc.* makes this inheritance explicit, having one character refer to the condition of a war-torn "Turaqistan" setting as "Strangelove in the desert." Ben Kingsley's archvillain is a cross between Dick Cheney and the Wizard of Oz who remains hidden throughout the movie behind a bank of video screens; like Peter Sellers's Nazi nuclear expert, this "viceroy" is wheelchair-bound and implicitly impotent. Stewart paid similar homage when he quipped (*DS* Apr. 28, 2003) that the "ideology" of Rumsfeld's deputy Paul Wolfowitz was "a wheelchair away from Dr. Strangelove's." But, as I have suggested, the hawkish *jouissance* critique actually originated in Twain's generation, when the first international peace organizations were emerging in close tandem with the first wave of Euro-American feminism.

One reason that the Strangelove template is more legible to us is that it is more recent, but another is that it registers an important demographic reversal that occurred in the twentieth century. Circa 1901, Roosevelt was one of the older proimperialists at the age of forty-three, while Twain was one of the younger anti-imperialists at sixty-six. Hence the sting of "Auntie," and the anxious rebuttal of "Old Granny." But today we regard doves as connotatively "young" and hawks as connotatively "old." This is also the strand of cultural logic that connects *Hair* with *Harold and Kumar*, though as *Escape from Guantanamo Bay* suggests via a scene at a hedonistic "bottomless party" that develops an elaborate visual pun on the movie's "anti-Bush" politics, antiwar hairstyles per se have changed since the 1960s.

If my analysis seems gratuitously prurient, consider that the most hirsute pubic area in the aforementioned scene is likened to "Osama Bin Laden's beard." As in *Dr. Strangelove*,[13] an impotent gerontocracy's zealous warmongering results from a jealous mistrust of youthful sexual vitality. Nonetheless, the conspicuous absence of feminist critique in mainstream antiwar satires like *Harold and Kumar* suggests that the most fitting comparison for the contemporary laughing dove rhetoric is the recapitulation of zero-sum chauvinism we find in their nineteenth-century predecessors. One could object, perhaps, that Stewart portrays a nebbish, that Colbert's hypermasculine performance effects a queering of gender roles,[14] or that McGruder's protagonists are all prepubescent. But this would ignore the gymnastic efforts[15] of *The Daily Show* and *The Colbert Report* to distance their own dovish tendencies from those of the overtly feminist satirical projects favored by activist collectives like Code Pink, the Raging Grannies, or the Missile Dick Chicks,[16] or the fact that *The Boondocks* devoted six weeks of strips to exploring the paternalistic premise that "if there was a man in the world who [National Security Advisor Condoleezza Rice] truly loved, she wouldn't be so hell-bent to destroy it" (Oct. 14, 2003). On the balance, satire is still a male prerogative in the United States, and the reason that these laughing doves are able to deliver an ass-kicking to the purveyors of hawkish masculinity is that they are culturally authorized to perform this macho operation.

"PLEASE LEAVE A MESSAGE AT THE ULULATION"— WARTIME SATIRE AND ITS IMPERIAL OTHERS

If the attempts of U.S. laughing doves to deflect misogynistic barbs have, for most of the last two hundred years, taken place in an echo chamber that reorients and reiterates this misogyny, their attempts to contest the racist slant of many hawk arguments reveal commitments that are even more nominal, and even more conflicted. This terrain will be easier to manage if we reverse our historical circuit and begin in the 1890s.

In an era of lynch law in the South, reservation removal and yellow terror in the West, and nativist antilabor violence in the Midwest and Northeast, hawkish satire magazines like *Puck* helped rationalize a new transpacific U.S. empire in the Philippines (and Alaska, Hawaii, Guam, Samoa, etc.) by adapting the racist imagery of the existing U.S. empire that spanned the North American continent "from sea to shining sea." This procedure rendered Filipinos an amorphous combination of African American, Hispanic, and Amerindian stereotypes; one U.S. senator called the islands a "witch's caldron" that contained a devilish "brew" of "all hues and colors" including even "spotted" and "striped" (Halili 2006, 26). Filipinos frequently appeared as ignorant, surly children, signifying arrested development and limited capacity for political sovereignty. Animal imagery was also common, as cartoonists likened them to snakes, donkeys, and swarming bees. Revolutionary nationalist leader Emilio Aguinaldo, whom Twain scandalously dubbed the "George Washington" of the Philippines (Twain 1992a), figured as a diminutive parody of a Spanish cacique, a puppy, a monkey, a frog, or a mosquito.

American soldiers in the Philippines experienced a "race war" (Kramer 2006, 89), as such stereotypes colored their view of its inhabitants. Their letters home, which jeered the "gugus" as unsympathetic subhumans, in turn reinforced the accuracy of those depictions. Thus one soldier reported that "the fun was fast and furious" as dead Filipinos piled up "thicker than buffalo chips," while another opined that "picking off niggers in the water" was "more fun than a turkey shoot" (Miller 1982, 67). Meanwhile the domestic press labeled doves "Filipiniacs" (*Judge* Feb. 25, 1899) or "domestic Filipinos" (Feb. 18, 1899), with some cartoons picturing them in grass skirts or blackface. *Judge*'s ingenious cover cartoon "Who is Behind Aguinaldo!!!" (Oct. 26, 1900) was die-cut so that Aguinaldo's face could be opened to reveal that of William Jennings Bryant, who challenged William McKinley on an antiwar presidential platform. One cartoonist even depicted Twain as a grass-skirted "Old Savage" with a bone through his nose, wielding a club (*Minneapolis Journal* Mar. 23, 1901).

Yet much of the opposition to U.S. empire in the Philippines, like much of today's opposition to U.S. empire in Iraq and Afghanistan, derived from a xenophobic populism that judged supporting the welfare of undeserving foreigners to be a waste of domestic resources. Thus Chicago's *Verdict* opined that "public interest . . . never can be roused over the doings and misdoings of an alien population, who walk like flies on the ceiling with the whole round earth between them and us" (Jan. 2, 1899), concluding that the United States had "all the colored folk on [its] muster rolls of citizenship that [it] need[ed]." Hawks derided the uneasy union of this populist/racist dove sentiment and the elitist/antiracist dove sentiment of Twain and his peers as an alliance of "Harvard and the slums" (Schirmer 1972, 15). The political strength of any U.S. antiwar movement can arguably be gauged by the coherence of this pairing.[17]

During the Civil War, Lincoln was satirized by the Union's antiwar intelligentsia as a slave to the interests of slaves, a claim that galvanized populist dissent during the New York draft riots. Publications skeptical of the war with Mexico nonetheless conceded Mexican inferiority. Thus *Yankee Doodle* ran Melville's urbane swipes at General Zachary Taylor and Secretary of War William Marcy (Jul. 24–Sep. 11, 1847), but also declared that Mexicans were "ungrateful, kinky-headed, copper-colored rapscallions" who "ought to be 'civilized' off the face of the earth" if they failed to appreciate "the efforts which YANKEE DOODLE and Gen. TAYLOR were making on their behalf" (Dec. 12, 1846). This satirical vocabulary was scarcely distinguishable from that of hawkish editorials which argued that the "greasers" south of the border were "reptiles in the path of progressive democracy who must either crawl or be crushed," or that of the American militiamen stationed in Puebla who mocked an Ash Wednesday ritual by rubbing burnt cork over their faces in the style of minstrel performers (McAffrey 1992, 69, 72–73). Yet the antiwar camp also included abolitionist James Russell Lowell, whose *Biglow Papers* is the most devastating laughing dove satire of the century before *Strangelove*. Lowell's master stroke was a poetic dialogue between two yokels, one who refuses to enlist because his "Testyment" tells him "plain an' flat" that war is "murder" (the eponymous Hosea Biglow—*Boston Courier* Jun. 17, 1846), and another who believes Mexico is a racially inferior "ourang outang nation" exempt from such moral considerations (the Colbertesque Birdofredum Sawin—*Boston Courier* Aug. 18, 1847). Here racism appears as a derangement of common sense rather than a consequence of it.

The War of 1812 furnishes no hawk racism against the British enemy, naturally, but abounds in dove vitriol against British-allied Amerindians and against ethnic minority groups suspected of supporting the war to gratify their own anti-British grudge. The *Tickler* lampooned Pennsylvania governor Simon Snyder's German accent, publishing letters from "Soimon Schnoider zu de Presedent von all de Unoided Schdades" that expressed admiration for "Ole Crenny Deerburn" (Jul. 21, 1813). Madison's treasury secretary Albert Gallatin was likewise mocked for his Swiss origins. Many satires featured villains who wrote in French dialect, in keeping with the Federalist conspiracy theory that Madison was urged to war by Napoleon. Thus "Nicholas Pedrosa, Hair Dresser" wrote weekly letters to the "Prentair" of the *Alexandria Gazette,* analyzing the political condition of "de Nitestate" (United States), complaining bitterly of the "Federalees," and bragging that "de Fransh nation is universellement acknowledge to be de most enlightened under de whole creation of de worle" (Mar. 23, 1812; Jun. 1, 1812; Dec. 4, 1811). Irish immigration was blamed for diluting the collective intellect of the American public: "If the truth were fairly known," sneered one poet about a political caucus of Madisonian Republicans, "In ten men there you'd scarce find one, / But what five years ago, quite frisky, / Was trotting hogs and tippling whiskey" (*Tickler* Mar. 29, 1809).

Because the apartheid regime of the nineteenth-century United States gave white men the exclusive right to ridicule, and made racial minorities and women the major targets of that ridicule, satire was an oppositional tactic more or less unavailable to nonwhite and nonmale antiwar activists. The grand exception to this rule is Douglass, an African American laughing dove who amused abolitionist audiences in 1848 with a speech juxtaposing "the delectable business of kidnapping and slave-driving" with "the achievements of our gallant army in Mexico, shooting, stabbing, hanging, destroying property, and massacring the innocent" (*North Star* Jun. 2, 1848). But the most intriguing case is that of Finley Peter Dunne, a *Chicago Journal* muckraker who also wrote under the pseudonym of a wisecracking Irish-American bartender named Mr. Dooley. Dooley's thick brogue marks him as a minority speaker.[18] At the turn of the twentieth century, the Irish were dubiously "white," and frequently stereotyped as alcoholic, belligerent, and foolishly sentimental. Dunne's columns on the Spanish-American War in 1898 catapulted him from regional to national fame; upon Twain's death in 1910 he became the unofficial dean of U.S. satire. Roosevelt, a frequent butt of Dooley's ridicule, praised Dunne as a "laughing philosopher" and "a force that count[ed]" in U.S. politics, but scolded him for overemphasizing "certain ugly and unpleasant tendencies in American life" (Eckley 1981, 70).

One of those ugly tendencies was the brutal occupation of the Philippines, and Dunne surely ruffled Teddy's fur by offering an exceedingly heterodox defense of guerrilla warfare as a legitimate expression of Filipino nationalism (1906, 53): "'Tis on'y ar-rmies fights in th' open. Nations fights behind threes an' rocks." Yet Dooley just as often voices the imperialist's

position. During the torture scandal, he endorsed "the ol'fashioned American wather cure" for the "pore benighted haythens" in the Philippines, calculating that any rebel who swallowed "four gallons" would gratefully "ask to
be wrapped in th' flag" (Dunne 1902, 118–19). This is sarcastic, to be sure, but
it nonetheless establishes a strangely shifting viewpoint that befits Dooley's
ambiguous racial status. Dunne repeats this trick by making Dooley and his
steadiest customer Hennessy enthusiastic supporters of the pseudoscien-
tific program of "Anglo-Saxon" supremacism that became the central plank
in Roosevelt's pro-war argument. It seems they believe Irish-Americans
like themselves to be Anglo-Saxons—and so too Scottish-Americans like
McKinley, Dutch-Americans like "Teddy Rosenfelt," as well as Americans of
African, Swedish, and Jewish descent (1899, 56). Because Roosevelt's terminology is fatally incoherent, Dunne stretches it to fit his own, more inclusive
version of national identity.

Dunne affords us an interesting comparison to McGruder, whose *Boondocks* strips often attacked racial profiling in domestic antiterror policy as
a scapegoating ritual that bolsters state power. While we find similar gestures in *The Onion*,[19] McGruder has drawn a more provocative connection
to a broader legacy of American racism. Hence a news report about a bomb
scare on a commercial flight informs Huey that the suspect was a "swar-
thy looking man" who was apprehended when he "sneezed loudly" (Oct. 13,
2001). Likewise, McGruder's President Bush announces that he is abolish-
ing racial profiling, but for a few "narrow exceptions" that include "people
of color who wear bandannas, do-rags, and clothes five sizes too big, who
are out in public and not accompanied by a white friend, any black person
with the last name Rice whose first name isn't Condoleezza, Jerry, or Uncle
Ben ... Mexicans with tattoos, Mexicans without tattoos, Puerto Ricans who
look Arab, [and] Arabs who look Puerto Rican" (Jul. 7, 2003). Both Dunne/
Dooley and McGruder/Huey generate satiric friction out of their dual status
as American citizens and racial subalterns.

Of course, the majority of contemporary laughing doves are more akin
to Lowell, not only in their racial status (white) and their political content
(which often critiques hawkish anti-Arabism or anti-Islamism), but also
in their preferred technique (the self-refuting straw man). Indeed Lowell's
"Birdofredum Sawin" closely anticipates Colbert's naïve jingo, who calls his
studio "the Eagle's Nest." Sawin's patriotic conviction that "every man" in the
United States must fight for the right to do "jest wut he damn pleases"—
unless he is "a nigger or a Mexican" (*Boston Courier* Jun. 17, 1846)—leads
him to enlist in the army. Colbert's patriotic conviction that "there's got to

be a way to just bomb some sense into th[o]se people" leads him to support the invasion of Iraq (*DS* Dec. 29, 2002). He later complains about being forced to "learn the difference between Sunnis and Shi'as merely because [the American] army is in that country" (*CR* Apr. 11, 2007). A kindred *Onion* article warns that Syria is "harboring more than 15 million known Arabs" (Apr. 30, 2003); *The Daily Show*'s Jason Jones concludes of the region's religious diversity, "It's crazy! Sects, subsects, everyone hates each other. I don't know what Jesus was thinking when he put all our oil over there" (Dec. 14, 2006). Such willful ignorance about Middle Eastern culture satirizes not only the half-baked stratagems of Rumsfeld and Wolfowitz, but the American public's apathetic reluctance to question them. As with the contemporary misogynistic/homophobic straw man, the audience is encouraged to read these characters ironically and close the loop by connecting their ostensible objections to racism with a more skeptical view of racialized prowar rhetoric.

But as Lowell's *Biglow Papers* and Twain's "To the Person Sitting in Darkness" (1992b) attest, this "Harvard" irony may prove such a Gordian knot that "slum" nativism offers a viable axis for cutting across it. Because it is almost always articulated from a perspective that preserves the racial Other as exotic (and mute), it is often unclear whether vitriol for the straw man truly becomes sympathy for the scapegoat. How do we interpret *Onion* articles like "Dead Iraqi Would Have Loved Democracy" (Mar. 26, 2003), "Coalition: Vast Majority of Iraqis Still Alive" (Jun. 23, 2004), or "Iraq's Little Victories," which reports that "U.S. medics saved an Iraqi man's life when they successfully removed the shards of his wife's skull from his face" (Dec. 15, 2008)? Pace Paul Lewis (2006), if these are "killing jokes," then who exactly is being killed? Obviously it is difficult for satire to express genuine sympathy; that is not its function. Yet these laughing dove satires reveal a boundary of empathy or identification that characterizes contemporary antiwar rhetoric more generally, even in its sentimental mode.[20]

It is especially productive to analyze Stewart's persona when probing this boundary of laughing dove rhetoric. Stewart isn't presenting a pure farce like *Harold and Kumar* or *Lysistrata,* a pure journalistic genre parody like *The Onion* or *The Tickler,* a gadfly sting like *The Boondocks* or the Spot Resolutions, or a matroyshka of interfoliated ironies like *The Colbert Report* or *Mr. Dooley.* He is attempting something more—to construct a stable satiric ethics, a voice of reason. I therefore judge *The Daily Show*'s occasional traces of anti-Arab nativism to be not so much a pander to majority views, or an accidental slip, but a deliberate expression of how difficult he finds this undertaking. Take, for instance, Stewart's common practice of dubbing video clips of diplomatic meetings between Middle Eastern heads of state with an ironic British schoolmarm voice, or its converse—his fascination with ritual ululation. Both denote the Other's illegibility. The two tactics combined in a fascinating segment that ridiculed Bush's plea for Arab rulers to join the fight against "Islamofascism" (*DS* Oct. 6, 2005). Stewart imagined the president placing phone calls to various countries asking for their support, which went unanswered until he finally reaches an answering machine that chirps, "Hello this is Yemen. And this is Oman. Please leave a message at the ululation." At which point there was, of course, a ululation.

Stewart's ambivalent use of Middle Eastern stereotypes has been evident since the start of *The Daily Show*'s terrorism coverage. Recall the utter incomprehension he expressed toward the Afghan pastime of *buzkashi* (Dec. 19, 2001). After explaining that it was a "sport in which riders on horseback compete for the corpse of a decapitated goat," he remarked, "Is there nothing in that country that isn't royally fucked up? Am I wrong about that? Playing ball with a goat?" Obviously this could be read as a parody of Bush or Rumsfeld, but Stewart's periodic reversion to this position is precisely the point. The most fascinating case of *The Daily Show*'s ambivalent antiracism came more recently, when the show's staff created a bushy-bearded puppet character named "Gitmo" to represent a detained al Qaeda (Jun. 19, 2008). Gitmo is a simple device for conveying a complex satiric argument—that the imperial gaze itself is partly responsible for the creation of its terrorist Other. "Wouldn't you want a chance to prove your innocence, maybe go free?" Stewart asks Gitmo. "Yes, yes, Gitmo go free," the puppet answers, "Gitmo go home. Gitmo go home to Damascus, get back in taxi cab, fill it with C-4, and drive into east entrance of British embassy!" The puppet then loudly ululates. "Wait, Gitmo!" exclaims Stewart. "You just said you weren't a terrorist!" The puppet responds, "When they caught Gitmo, Gitmo wasn't, but Gitmo is now," before emitting another round of ululation. Gitmo is utterly sympathetic, with disproportionately large eyes and an obvious association with Elmo, the most childlike character on *Sesame Street;* Gitmo's title graphic labels him "Cuddliest Ex-Detainee." Yet it is also specifically inhuman, and specifically a fictional construct. The coup de grace is that Stewart always makes sure to "accidentally" move Gitmo out of his camera frame so that we can see in the other camera that he is the puppeteer.

In a kindred piece, Stewart discusses President Obama's difficulty in relocating inmates from the detention facility (*DS* May 19, 2009). A video montage shows U.S. politicians making exaggerated, nativistic refusals to incarcerate the inmates in their own states. "You know I'm actually starting to feel sorry for these detainees," Stewart quips, over a picture of suspected 9/11 organizer Khalid Sheikh Mohammed. "Maybe if they had bigger eyes." The picture is then distorted to show Mohammed with large, Elmo-like eyes. In the search for stability these segments instead produce satiric vertigo, making it increasingly difficult to determine how sympathy should be distributed. Perhaps there is a category slippage here, similar to the one we find in Dunne and McGruder; Stewart's comic persona is ethnically Jewish and he may be gesturing to a dual identity in which he is both an American and a Semite. What is obvious from the "Gitmo" segments is that Stewart is sketching a limit beyond which he cannot pass. This limit is precisely that engendered by the U.S. imperial project itself. It is what Edward Said calls Orientalism, a condition in which Westerners project their own hopes and fears upon the Middle East so completely that the region itself is no longer legible in its particulars.

For Stewart to make this gesture constitutes a cogent criticism of U.S. policy, but it also expresses a form of mimetic despair that reinscribes the policy's original limitation; it is ultimately impossible for him to confront the object that he is supposed to be analyzing. We may compare the superb ending sequence of *War, Inc.*, in which the villainous viceroy orders a missile strike that will ultimately destroy the movie's pedantic bad conscience—symbolized by Kingsley's own headquarters, hidden inside a Popeyes Chicken franchise in the bombed-out Emerald City—but also its flimsy good conscience—symbolized by an airplane carrying Cusack's small band of heroically enlightened antiwar/anticapitalist American dissidents.[21] As the missile arcs over the Turaqi desert the last thing we see is a Bedouin sheepherder wearing a replica jersey of the American basketball star Kevin Garnett. If the Gitmo puppet fails as a satisfying object of sympathy, this Other fails as a satisfying object of obliteration. Like all mirror images, it is at once too exotic and too familiar.

CONCLUSION

I would no more praise contemporary laughing dove rhetoric as a subtle engagement with imperialist semiotics than I would condemn it as a vapid act of bad faith. At its best, like all satire, it is never successful as a moderating force, but rather as a nasty broomstick that sweeps the discourse clear so that more positive gestures can follow. Its greatest value has been a dogged insistence on historical fact over political fantasy, which is to say truth over "truthiness." I note, for instance, a scene in *War, Inc.* that takes place in a Hellenic amphitheater outside the Turaqi capital. Like the veridical Turkey, Iraq, and Syria, the fictional Turaqistan belongs to a classical Mediterranean world with no fixed "East" and "West," which clarifies the Middle East as a finite ideological construct instead of an infinite epistemological regress. *The Boondocks* undertakes a similar repeal of the clash of civilizations narrative that has so thoroughly disfigured recent U.S. political rhetoric. Thus Huey picks up his phone, which has been wiretapped by the FBI, and offers to surrender intelligence about "several Americans who have helped train and finance Osama Bin Laden." When asked how he has obtained this information, he responds, "A little investigating. It wasn't that hard, actually." He then proceeds to grant the investigator's request to "give [him] some names" by slowly spelling "Ronald Reagan" (McGruder Oct. 6, 2001).

A little investigating into the historical archive opens a broader view of our contemporary moment. Given the frustrating duplicity of so many hawk arguments proffered since 9/11, juxtaposing today's antiwar satire with its occasionally distasteful nineteenth-century antecedents may curb our understandable but nevertheless misguided desire to sanctify Stewart, Colbert, McGruder, et al. But this chapter is not meant as a leftist purity test. I even suspect that a more honest construction of the pro-war position is possible, and I have bracketed the legitimate moral and geopolitical questions it would urge. What I do mean is that we must not confuse our appreciation of today's laughing doves with a committed political act per se. It's good venom indeed, but it's not quite magical.

NOTES

1. E.g., "Rebuilding America's Defenses" (Kagan, Schmitt, and Donnelly 2000).

2. See Winter 2009.

3. Cf. Jones 2005.

4. See Freeman 2002; Altschuler and Blumin 2001.

5. This terminological shift was durable; show me the satire section in an American bookstore and I'll show you a publisher who titles this book differently. I suspect that Americans still prefer "humor" because the appealing fiction of laughter without objects still affirms the appealing fiction of politics without power.

6. Polk's Democratic supporters responded by nicknaming the future president "Spotty Lincoln."

7. According to Hawthorne (1862), it "clogged . . . the free circulation of the nation's life-blood."

8. Comments Spiro Agnew directed to an "effete" press corps for asking questions about Vietnam (Safire 2008, 454).

9. Rush Limbaugh's favorite misogynistic epithet.

10. Cf. Morreale 2009.

11. Lacan first used *jouissance* to refer to an intense feeling beyond the psyche's threshold for pleasure that was therefore potentially painful; it took other connotations in his later philosophy and that of respondents like Gilles Deleuze, Julia Kristeva, and Slavoj Žižek.

12. Among other Agnewesque sound bites decrying "pacifistas," "whine-inistas," and "hindsight huggers."

13. Or *Lysistrata.*

14. Cf. Gournelos 2009.

15. See *Daily Show* Oct. 28, 2002; Dec. 11, 2002; Feb. 4, 2003; Feb. 18, 2003; Mar. 6, 2003; Apr. 25, 2003; Sep. 27, 2005, and *Colbert Report* Feb. 1, 2006; Aug. 16, 2006.

16. See Kutz-Flamenbaum 2007.

17. Consider the role of the draft in galvanizing cross-class alliances during Vietnam.

18. Dooley, a favorite of William Safire, John F. Kennedy, and Lyndon Johnson, remained popular through the 1960s. His present obscurity may owe to his reliance on dialect (Morath 2004), though the Dooleyism "politics ain't beanbag" did cameo in a recent Paul Krugman column (2008).

19. A grimly ironic *Onion* editorial (Jan. 20, 2008) entreats a return to the racial "panic" of autumn 2001: "What happened to that country I used to know and love, where a Korean grocer could be killed out of irrational xenophobia merely because someone thought he was an Arab? . . . You may say, 'I am only one person. What can I do?' But all of our efforts are needed if we are to maintain a state of constant anxiety . . . Twice a week, for at least 15 minutes, take the time to worry about any Muslims who may live in your area . . . Each and every one of us, no matter how big or small, possesses the ability to jump to conclusions.'"

20. Cf. Greene 2009.

21. Cf. Klein 2004.

WORKS CITED

Altschuler, Glenn, and Stuart Blumin. *Rude Republic: Americans and Their Politics in the Nineteenth Century*. Princeton: Princeton UP, 2001.

Crosby, Ernest. *Captain Jinks, Hero*. New York: Funk & Wagnalls, 1902.

Dunne, Finley Peter. *Dissertations by Mr. Dooley*. New York: Harpers, 1906.

———. *Mr. Dooley in Peace and War*. Boston: Small and Maynard, 1899.

———. *Observations by Mr. Dooley*. New York: Harpers, 1902.

Eckley, Grace. *Finley Peter Dunne*. Boston: Hall, 1981.

Freeman, Joanne. *Affairs of Honor: National Politics in the New Republic*. New Haven: Yale UP, 2002.

Gournelos, Ted. *Popular Culture and the Future of Politics: Cultural Studies and the Tao of South Park*. Lanham, MD: Lexington Books, 2009.

Greene, Jody. "Melancholia's Meerkat: A Poetic Leap." *PMLA* 124.5 (2009): 1719–28.

Halili, Servando. *Iconography of the New Empire: Race and Gender Images and the American Colonization of the Philippines*. Quezon City: Philippines UP, 2006.

Hawthorne, Nathaniel. "Chiefly about War Matters. By a Peaceable Man." *Atlantic Monthly* 10.57 (1862): 43–61.

Hietala, Thomas. *Manifest Design: Anxious Aggrandizement in Late Jacksonian America.* Ithaca: Cornell UP, 1985.

Hoganson, Kristin. *Fighting for American Manhood: How Gender Politics Provoked the Spanish-American and Philippine-American Wars.* New Haven: Yale UP, 1998.

Howells, William Dean. "Editha." *Harper's* (January 1905): 214–24.

Johannsen, Robert. *To the Halls of the Montezumas: The Mexican War in the American Imagination.* New York: Oxford UP, 1985.

Jones, Jeffrey. *Entertaining Politics: New Political Television and Civic Culture.* New York: Rowman and Littlefield, 2004.

Kagan, Donald, Gary Schmitt, and Thomas Donnelly. *Rebuilding America's Defenses: Strategy, Forces, and Resources for a New Century.* Washington D.C.: The Project for a New American Century, 2000.

Kramer, Paul. *The Blood of Government: Race, Empire, the United States, and the Philippines.* Chapel Hill: UNC Press, 2006.

Krugman, Paul. "Blizzard of Lies." *New York Times,* September 11, 2008.

Kutz-Flamenbaum, Rachel. "Code Pink, Raging Grannies, and Missile Dick Chicks: Feminist Performance Activism in the Contemporary Antiwar Movement." *NWSA Journal* 19.1 (2007): 89–105.

Lewis, Paul. *Cracking Up: American Humor in a Time of Conflict.* Chicago: Chicago UP, 2006.

McAffrey, James. *Army of Manifest Destiny: The American Soldier in the Mexican War, 1846–1848.* New York: NYU Press, 1992.

Meyer, Dick. "Rush: MPs 'Just Blowing Off Steam.'" *CBS News Online.* http://www.cbsnews .com/stories/2004/05/06/opinion/meyer/main616021.shtml.

Miller, Stuart. *"Benevolent Assimilation": The American Conquest of the Philippines, 1899–1903.* New Haven: Yale UP, 1982.

Morath, Max. "Translating Mr. Dooley: A New Examination of the Journalism of Finley Peter Dunne." *Journal of American Culture* 27.2 (2004): 147–56.

Morreale, Joanne. "Jon Stewart and *The Daily Show*: I Thought You Were Going To Be Funny!" In *Satire TV: Politics and Comedy in the Post-Network Era*, edited by Jonathan Gray, Jeffrey Jones, and Ethan Thompson, 104–23. New York: NYU Press, 2009.

Safire, William. *Safire's Political Dictionary.* Oxford: Oxford UP, 2008.

Schirmer, Daniel. *Republic or Empire: American Resistance to the Philippine War.* Morristown: Schenkman, 1972.

Swift, Jonathan. "Meditation on a Broomstick." In *The Prose Works of Jonathan Swift* Vol. 1, edited by Herbert John Davis and Irvin Ehrenpreis. Oxford: Blackwell, 1968.

Tebbel, John. *America's Great Patriotic War with Spain: Mixed Motives, Lies and Racism in Cuba and the Philippines, 1898–1915.* Manchester, VT: Marshall Jones, 1996.

Twain, Mark. "Review of Edwin Wildman's Biography of Aguinaldo." In *Mark Twain's Weapons of Satire: Anti-Imperialist Writings on the Philippine-American War*, edited by Jim Zwick, 86–108. Syracuse: Syracuse UP, 1992.

———. "To the Person Sitting in Darkness." In *Mark Twain's Weapons of Satire: Anti-Imperialist Writings on the Philippine-American War*, edited by Jim Zwick, 22–39. Syracuse: Syracuse UP, 1992.

Welch, Richard. *Response to Imperialism: The United States and* the Philippine-American War,

Winter, Aaron. "The Laughing Doves of 1812 and the Satiric Endowment of Antiwar Rhetoric in the United States." *PMLA* 124.5 (2009): 1562–81.

CHAPTER TEN

"HUMMER RHYMES WITH DUMBER"

Neoliberalism, Irony, and the Cartoons of Jeff Danziger

—David Monje

Editorial cartoons, in addition to injecting humor into otherwise serious discourses, are a longstanding means of revealing disingenuous political rhetoric. They have, in cartoonist Patrick Olivant's words, the capacity to "galvanize public opinion and kick-start discussion" (Olivant 2004, 24). At their best, as Chris Lamb (2004), Jeffrey Jones (2004), and many others have argued, cartoons often expose lies and contradictions by visually, metaphorically, and semantically confronting the inconsistencies in political discourse. Jeff Danziger's syndicated editorial cartoons following September 11, 2001, zeroed in on the Bush administration's responses to the attacks by (literally) drawing connections between cold war policy, the events of 9/11, and present-day Afghanistan, between big oil, the rise in popularity of gas-guzzling Hummer SUVs and the invasion of Iraq, and between the West's culture of consumption and the war on terror.[1] Using selections from his work in the years following 9/11, this chapter illustrates how Danziger deployed irony as a discursive strategy to explicitly critique the neoliberal underpinnings of the cultural, political, and military response to the attacks on 9/11.

This chapter also argues, along with others in this volume, that not only did 9/11 not signal "the end of the age of irony," as predicted by Roger Rosenblatt in *Time*, but that the attacks (or rather the popular and governmental response to them) in fact fueled the age-old use of irony as a critical, rhetorical tool. Rosenblatt, writing on September 16, 2001, put his plea for a revival of seriousness and nonironic realism this way:

> With a giggle and a smirk, our chattering classes—our columnists and pop culture makers—declared that detachment and personal whimsy were the necessary tools for an oh-so-cool life . . . The ironists, seeing through everything, made it difficult for anyone to see anything. The consequence of thinking that nothing is real—apart from pranc-

ing around in an air of vain stupidity—is that one will not know the difference between a joke and a menace.
No more. The planes that plowed into the World Trade Center and
the Pentagon were real. The flames, smoke, sirens—real. The chalky
landscape, the silence of the streets—all real. (2001)

The phenomenon Rosenblatt describes doesn't fit traditional, dictionary
definitions of irony. Rather, Rosenblatt describes the cynical, ironic detachment of a certain segment of disillusioned and disappointed American liberals. It's a kind of irony that R. J. Magill Jr. calls "chic ironic bitterness" in
his volume of the same title (2007). Magill, contrary to Rosenblatt, argues
that this ironic stance is "a liberating cultural and personal force; one that,
when used wisely, can be a psychological strategy for maintaining personal
integrity in a complex and often contradictory world" (2007, 12).
    It is the deployment of irony as a critical tactic that provides a backdrop
for my argument in this chapter. As Hutcheon argues, the transideologi-
cal nature of irony suggests "the need for an approach to irony that would
treat it not as a limited rhetorical trope or as an extended approach to life,
but as a discursive strategy operating at the level of language (verbal) or
form (music, visual, textual)" (1995, 10). Editorial cartoons deploy irony in
this way by strategically—through visual and textual means—ironizing the
object of critique, be it a politician, a policy, a political party, a war, etc. For
Jeff Danziger, the cultural and political responses to the events of 9/11 were
ripe for this sort of critique.
    There is a kind of situational irony in the cultural milieu that Rosenb-
latt describes, but it is less the detachment and cynicism of the "chattering
classes" than that the source of the detachment and cynicism is the very same
neoliberal political and economic rationality that places human liberation in
the invisible hand of the market and downplays the role of ethical, political,
and moral commitments in human relations (cf. Magill 2007, Harvey 2005,
Brown 2001). Under this version of economism, citizens—articulated primarily as consumers—are free mostly to choose how to spend their money.
As neoliberal subjects, we are expected to express our individuality first and
foremost through our relation to the market as consumers and producers,
and only secondarily (or not at all) through our care or empathy for others.
David Harvey, for instance, argues that neoliberalism, as an ethic, seeks to
maximize the social good by "maximizing the reach and frequency of market transactions, and it seeks to bring all human action into the domain of

10.1   Jeff Danziger, "Mayor Giuliani Urges Everyone to Come to New York and Buy Something" (September 28, 2001). Reprinted by permission of Jeff Danziger.

the market" (2005, 3). In the discourse regime of neoliberalism, the rational self-interest of the individual is articulated as a kind of Darwinian basis for all human relations.

In the neoliberal culture of economic determinism the consuming individual is sovereign. "Detachment and personal whimsy" as modi vivendi are proselytized to us through billboards, subway ads, and television and radio commercials, and are exemplified by ever more finely targeted marketing and narrowcasting on the Internet and cable television. By constituting the citizen as consumer, and consumption as participation, the discourse regime of neoliberalism encourages individuals to imagine that any problem or desire can be successfully managed through a market interaction. It should come as no surprise that for critics such as Rosenblatt this overarching ethos of individualism gives rise to a cynical, postmodern ironic detachment.

Rosenblatt's declaration of "the end of the age of irony" was not only wrong; it was based on a mistaken understanding of the discursive and political role of irony. The self-absorbed and pervasive nihilism that Rosenblatt takes for irony does in fact represent a kind of domestic social malaise manifest in popular discourses and media artifacts of the late 1990s and

early 2000s. These range from a culture of over-the-top consumption, wan-
ton risk-taking in business and finance, unquestioning faith in the "invisible
hand of the market" and the social Darwinism of Wall Street, to the inane
distractions of "reality TV" and the sanctification of consumerism as a new
kind of individual social agency by advertisers and the media outlets eager for
consumers' dollars. From Nike's ubiquitous and long-lived "Just Do It" campaign to the fall of the Soviet Union and the unprecedented global expansion
of free market capitalism, the decade of the 1990s seemed to many Americans to be the final vindication of the doctrine of American exceptionalism.
Francis Fukuyama established the baseline for this with his declaration, in
1992, that the fall of the Soviet Union signaled the end of human ideological
struggle (between liberalism, fascism, and communism) with the ascendency
of liberal democracy and the free market (Fukuyama 1992).[2]

DRAWING CONNECTIONS

Danziger epitomizes the culturally hegemonic discourse of this perspective
in his cartoon published on September 28, 2001 (see figure 10.1). Reproducing the widely recognized bumper sticker slogan of the nineties "When the
Going Gets Tough, the Tough Go Shopping," the cartoon emphasizes the
primary function of the neoliberal subject as consumer. It is no coincidence
that Giuliani and Bush both appealed to the American public to get back to
work and shopping shortly after 9/11—the economy as conceived by neoliberalism depends on the uninterrupted flow of capital from the consumer.
    The subtle irony Danziger conveys with this cartoon depends on the rela-
tionship between neoliberal globalization, its proponents, and its discontents.
Rosenblatt's "age of irony" is the culture-wide acceptance of the so-called
logic of the market. Individuals in this neoliberal social configuration are
expected to maximize their own well-being by way of rational choices that
will allow the market to function smoothly and properly.[3] In other words,
the "detachment and personal whimsy" that "were the necessary tools for an
oh-so-cool life" in Rosenblatt's jeremiad are, by other accounts, the ultimate
resolution of human nature—the culmination of Western democracy and
the path for all humanity to follow (Fukuyama 1992). It is an ironic situation.
It is even more ironic that the style of liberal individualism and free market
capitalism promulgated by Fukuyama and his followers prior to September
11, 2001 (and symbolically embodied in the World Trade Center buildings),
depended largely on a ready source of cheap energy (with Middle Eastern

Bush Republicans Heed the President's Call to Conserve Fuel...

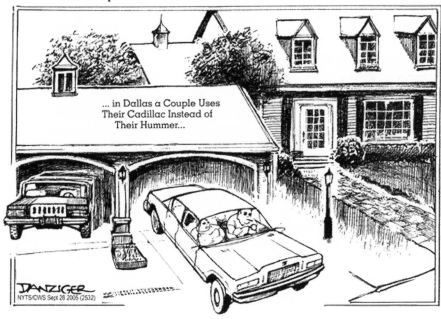

10.2 Jeff Danziger, "Few notice that Hummer rhymes with dumber" (September 28, 2001). Reprinted by permission of Jeff Danziger.

oil as a major source) and the continued uneven global distribution of capital (Harvey 2005). In "Mayor Giuliani Urges Everyone to Come to New York and Buy Something," Danziger deploys these ironies as a subtext in the cartoon to criticize what to many seemed like a poor way to respond to 9/11, as well as to highlight the antiglobalization ethos of al Qaeda and its supporters.

The American military adventures in Afghanistan and particularly in Iraq have been accompanied by discourse regimes of patriotic nationalism and their cultural representations. Most obviously, of course, is the proliferation of American flags on cars and front porches and in windows and offices across the nation. However, although it is quite literal and ubiquitous, the flag is less emblematic of American dependence on oil and militarism than the Hummer. Euphemistically categorized as a "sport utility" vehicle, the domesticated version of the military's High Mobility Multipurpose Vehicle, or Humvee, as it is known, has become an icon of American conspicuous consumption. The original Hummer H1, sold by General Motors, is renowned for its very poor fuel economy, large size, and its deployment as a hypermasculine status symbol. In less polite company, the Hummer, in any of its civilian models, is an overpriced, gas-guzzling symbol of unrestrained machismo and wastefulness.

Danziger exploits this in the titular cartoon of this chapter (see figure 10.2). The caption for this cartoon in Danziger's 2006 collection *Blood, Debt, & Fears* reads "Few notice that Hummer rhymes with dumber" (153). The cartoon, which depicts an overweight suburban couple from Dallas, labeled Bush Republicans, is a biting critique of the attitudes and lifestyle of Bush's self-identified base constituency. Danziger selects roughly equivalent status symbols—the Hummer and the Cadillac—both gas-guzzlers, both extravagantly large and expensive, to represent the connection between Bush's imagined America and its dependence on foreign oil. The irony, of course, is that these symbols of the proper neoliberal subject as conspicuous consumer are also symbols of the precarious global situation that is the context for international disequilibrium. The agents of the 9/11 attacks targeted what they understood to be material representations of secular, democratic, neoliberal globalization: the World Trade Center towers, the Pentagon, and presumably the White House. From al Qaeda's perspective, these institutions represent America's political and economic ambitions and the military that is deployed in their attainment.

Danziger's comic and satirical cartoon highlights the ironies of this situation by depicting Bush's base as composed of people so ignorant or careless that they believe driving a Cadillac over a Hummer is a meaningful decision. A few gallons plus or minus will make little difference in a world driven by heedless consumption and increasingly scarce resources. In Danziger's view, these are relevant objects of criticism, and irony and humor are his instruments of critique.

Irony as a discursive strategy always has at its foundation the most serious matters (Hutcheon 1995). Contrary to asserting that nothing is real, and that nothing matters, irony in this sense is an effort to highlight the seriousness and exigencies of the real by exposing fallacious rhetoric, false assumptions, and other misrepresentations of a given state of affairs. An example of Danziger's use of irony as a critical vehicle follows George W. Bush's September 20, 2001, "Address to a Joint Session of Congress and the American People," in which Bush asserts his now-infamous good v. evil paradigm:

> We will starve terrorists of funding, turn them one against another, drive them from place to place, until there is no refuge or no rest. And

we will pursue nations that provide aid or safe haven to terrorism. Every nation, in every region, now has a decision to make. Either you are with us, or you are with the terrorists. [Applause.] From this day forward, any nation that continues to harbor or support terrorism will be regarded by the United States as a hostile regime. (Bush September 20, 2001)

This statement, which is more reminiscent of the mythically simple world of good and evil forces in George Lucas's *Star Wars* franchise than of the complex geopolitical situation emerging after 9/11, was seen by many critics—both within the United States and abroad—as reproducing the very enmity intended by the agents of the violence. Danziger points out the irony in figure 10.3. The depiction of Osama bin Laden gloating over the news that the attacks had deepened the perceived battle between good and evil points to another ironic situation for the Bush administration and its deployment of divisive discourse: one of the potentially intended political effects of terrorism is to disrupt the dominant political order by provoking an overreaction and thus escalating the situation rather than allowing for recourse to diplomacy and law. Although, according to Charles Tilly, the uses and agents of "asymmetrical deployment and threats of violence against enemies outside the forms of political struggle operating within the current regime" vary widely across political, ethnic, religious, and regional situations, terror is nearly always meant to be coercive (Tilly 2004, 5–13). By declaring a unilateral global war on "terrorists" and "terrorism," George W. Bush effectively articulated bin Laden, the Taliban, and al Qaeda as enemies in a war, rather than as criminal militants subject to international law. Rather than downgrading and marginalizing the coercive efficacy of the terrorist attacks, Bush elevated them to acts of war. This rhetorical move rationalizes the counterstrike by the United States military, but it also, ironically, provides a retroactive rationale for the initial criminal attacks and articulates the terrorists as somehow durable, ideologically pure, and organizationally coherent in their nature.

This is especially problematic, as Danziger's cartoon implies, since it legitimizes al Qaeda and its strategic deployment of terror. It does so on a number of levels. I draw on Tilly, again, who argues that "terror works best when it alters or inhibits the target's disapproved behavior, fortifies the perpetrators' standing with potential allies, and moves third parties toward greater cooperation with the perpetrators' organization and announced program" (2004, 9). Most important to the discussion of irony is that Bush's declaration of war on terror serves each of these strategic purposes with regard to

News for Osama

LISTEN, O GREAT ONE...
THE AMERICANS HAVE
DIVIDED THE WORLD INTO
THOSE WHO ARE FOR THEM
AND THOSE WHO ARE
AGAINST THEM...

WELL, WELL...
THINGS ARE GOING
ACCORDING
TO PLAN...

10.3 Jeff Danziger, "News for Osama" (September 21, 2001). Reprinted by permission of Jeff Danziger.

the announced program of al Qaeda. First, by declaring a war between the United States and "all terrorists of global reach," Bush alters the behavior of the United States by going against the longstanding international practice of multilateral approaches to dealing with rogue political actors (such as economic sanctions, trade embargoes, and diplomatic solutions). Second, by dividing the world into two factions, as Danziger's cartoon highlights, Bush legitimizes al Qaeda, thereby buttressing its standing within its sphere of political and ideological influence and among its members, its allies, and potential members and allies. Finally, the "us against them" discourse leaves little opening for al Qaeda's neighbors and other third parties—the Taliban and other regional political parties, other Mujahedeen, and Iran and Pakistan, for example—to negotiate with the United States. This final effect of the Bush doctrine is perhaps an unintended one, but in the end may be the most acutely ironic in that it inhibits international diplomacy and dissent while encouraging further bifurcation. By refusing hearings with the "harboring" governments or with the militants themselves, the response of the Bush administration effectively left no alternative open other than acquiescence

Taliban Forces Await the Alliance Attack

10.4 Jeff Danziger, "Taliban Forces Await the Alliance Attack" (September 25, 2001). Reprinted by permission of Jeff Danziger.

or war. Danziger's representation of bin Laden's satisfaction upon hearing Bush's declaration of war concisely and effectively highlights the deep, and consequential, ironic situation that results.

Another situational irony that was highlighted by the attacks of 9/11 is that the Taliban in Afghanistan came to power in part through a decade of material, logistical, and training support for the Mujahedeen from the United States against the Soviet occupation during the Carter and Reagan administrations.[4] At first a guerilla army, the Taliban fought with weapons left over from the Soviet occupation and the international response to it. Much of this context is alluded to in the single pane of the cartoon "Taliban Forces Await the Alliance Attack" (see figure 10.4). Danziger seems to be pointing out the irony that the Taliban exists as an enemy force thanks to the multifarious political, economic, military, and colonial conditions of its genesis as the ruling government of Afghanistan, in which the Soviet Union, the United States and some of its allies, and others played significant roles.

Danziger metonymically highlights this complex and multifarious history in this illustration, which maps the national origin of each of the weapons that arm the Taliban forces and calls to the viewer's attention the ironic situation that the Taliban exist in part as a result of prolonged military intervention by some of the same governments that comprised the anti-Taliban Northern Alliance. This cartoon not only reminds us of the irony of the situation, but also tells a cautionary tale that politicians need to be mindful of whom they arm and for what purposes. In a subtle but telling way, "Taliban Forces Await the Alliance Attack" names the nations that to some degree benefited from, or are responsible for, the rise of the Taliban through their own reckless, instrumental, and neglectful support of what they saw as a stop-gap against the spread of Soviet communism in South Asia. In the case of Russian weapons, the Taliban have long had access to arms left over from the Soviet occupation. This cartoon also draws attention to the fact that the Taliban fighters are not necessarily a state-sponsored militia, thus emphasizing the atypicality of the conflict while drawing attention to the complex historical context that led to the rise of the Taliban regime in the first place.

The war in Afghanistan that began in October 2001, dubbed "Operation Enduring Freedom" by the Pentagon, was, according to the *9/11 Commission Report: Final Report of the National Commission on Terrorist Attacks upon the United States*, intended to unseat the ruling Taliban government and to facilitate a disruption of the activities of al Qaeda in Afghanistan (2004, 206). In the same section, the *9/11 Report* also asserts that plans for the elimination of al Qaeda in Afghanistan and Pakistan were being made by the deputies of the National Security Council even before the attacks on 9/11 (ibid.). Osama bin Laden and al Qaeda's connections to the Taliban were also known before 9/11, according to the *9/11 Report* (ibid.). George W. Bush (Sept. 20, 2001), in his speech to a joint session of Congress on September 20, 2001, publicly, and more colorfully, articulated the position of the United States towards Afghanistan, the Taliban, and al Qaeda: "And tonight, the United States of America makes the following demands on the Taliban: Deliver to United States authorities all the leaders of al Qaeda who hide in your land." This demand, he continues, is nonnegotiable, and failure to comply will result in war. There are several ironies at work in this situation, not least of which is the fact that Bush's demand of the Taliban that "they hand over the terrorists, or they will share in their fate" was not so much a demand as a rationalization for plans that were already in the works prior to 9/11 (ibid.). Not only were the Taliban unlikely to willingly hand over the al Qaeda leaders, they were probably entirely incapable of doing so in a way that would, or could, have satisfied Bush's demand. In fact, according to CNN (October 7, 2001), the Taliban offered to try bin Laden in Afghanistan,

Problems in Revenge

10.5   Jeff Danziger, "Problems in Revenge" (September 14, 2001). Reprinted by permission of Jeff Danziger.

in Islamic court, on October 7, 2001, but the offer was rejected as inadequate by the United States. And again, after the United States and its allies began their bombing campaign, Bush rejected a Taliban offer to hand bin Laden over to a neutral third country if the bombing ceased, saying, "They must have not heard: There's no negotiations" (Harris, October 15, 2001). Bush's refusal to consider diplomacy reinforces the appearance that the decision to strike the Taliban predated the seemingly precipitating events of 9/11.

In the days following the attack on 9/11, there was a lot of buzz about who was responsible, and the media widely reported calls for revenge against the perpetrators. George W. Bush (September 13, 2001) articulated a similar will to revenge against the perpetrators, declaring, "Justice demands that those who helped or harbored the terrorists be punished—and punished severely. The enormity of their evil demands it. We will use all the resources of the United States and our cooperating friends and allies to pursue those responsible for this evil, until justice is done." Danziger suggests, in the cartoon "Problems in Revenge," that such talk of retaliation is problematic, and its effectuation necessarily asymmetrical (see figure 10.5). Again, the salient irony here, combined with its inherent criticism of the Bush administration's response to the attacks, is that by declaring them "acts of war" (akin to the Japanese bombing of Pearl Harbor) the attacks are articulated not as crimes with diplomatically available juridical solutions, but are rather essentialized as an ongoing military threat to national security that demands foremost a militarized response. Of course, as Danziger illustrates, there is, in the Taliban's Afghanistan, no specific target upon which retaliation can be taken. There is no "there" there, so to speak. As the child peering around the broken wall also reminds us, the demands of justice, when sought with military force, may unfortunately involve the innocent. This is not to suggest that Danziger is arguing that justice should not be pursued, or even that a military response would necessarily be out of order, but that "revenge" may not be the best discursive strategy or military action in the search for a solution.

The cartoon "Problems in Revenge" also reminds us that Afghanistan under the Taliban was already, long before September 11, 2001, a war-torn nation, with few resources, little viable infrastructure, a broken political economy, and a fragmented social order. Bush's ultimatum, by representing Afghanistan, and the ruling Taliban, as a monolithic state capable not only of harboring al Qaeda, but also of somehow rounding up all its leaders—on a moment's notice—seems to demonstrate a consequential misunderstanding of the context from which the situation in that country emerged.

Retrospectively, the ironic force of "Problems in Revenge," as well as "Taliban Forces Await the Alliance Attack," is compounded by the fact that while the Taliban were removed from power, Afghanistan has hardly become a stable, thriving democracy in the years since Operation Enduring Freedom was begun, and although al Qaeda has taken heavy damages, they still exist, and Osama bin Laden has yet to be captured. The Obama administration has inherited the ongoing military situation in Afghanistan, and in February 2009, signed orders to send additional troops into what Obama called a "deteriorating situation" in the country. According to CNN (February 18, 2009), Obama said in a written statement, "The Taliban is resurgent in Afghanistan, and al Qaeda supports the insurgency and threatens America from its safe haven along the Pakistani border."

CONCLUSION

Rosenblatt's loathing for irony, and his indignant assertion that the events of 9/11 were "real," are more moral and political claims than they are ontological ones. His fear that we have collectively lost our capacity to tell the difference between "a joke and a menace" seems either curiously naïve or disingenuous. One hopes that he and his readers know that the danger of such a lapse in our judgment is a rhetorical hyperbole calculated to simultaneously express exasperation and function as a plea to reform the culture. Nevertheless, his understandable loathing for the hollowness of much American popular culture seems to have clouded his judgment regarding the uses and meanings of ironic discourse.

Danziger's discursive deployment of ironic critique in the examples above not only contradict the assertion that the age of irony had come to an end with the events of 9/11, but also affirms that the deployment of this type of irony can, in fact, yield insights into the state of human affairs. Specifically, Danziger criticizes the Bush administration's mischaracterization of the situation that gave rise to the conflict between itself and the agents of violence on 9/11, and foregrounds the complexity and multifarious influences of the conditions that led to the enmity between al Qaeda, its supporters, and the forces of neoliberal globalization. Danziger questions the facile way that "our way of life" is characterized as unproblematic and disconnected from global events. The iconic moments and symbolic references he chooses to depict in his editorial cartoons are packed with ideological content, and it is this content that he engages with in his cartoons. It is a type of critical judgment and political punditry that relies on both a capacity for ironic interpretation and a fairly wide awareness of contemporary global affairs. In the examples discussed in this chapter, Danziger exposes underlying connections (between the constitution of the neoliberal subject as detached consumer and the need for cheap energy) and situational ironies (the U.S. training and support of the Taliban—including Osama bin Laden—during the cold war) that suggest the possibility of alternative discourses to those promulgated by political leaders.

NOTES

1. Danziger's cartoons are syndicated by both the New York Times Syndicate and the Cartoonists and Writers Syndicate and enjoy wide audiences in newspapers in North America and internationally.

2. Fukuyama previewed this perspective in an essay in *The National Interest*, Summer 1989, entitled "The End of History?" but it reached a wider audience and was popularized by the book.

3. Rational Action Theory, also know as Rational Choice Theory, is the academicized version of this perspective that has been popularized by the business press and self-help

business books. It is now a staple of business and economy blogs on the Internet, even as it loses some of its currency in the social sciences.

4. Ronald Reagan, for example, said, "We must stand by all our democratic allies. And we must not break faith with those who are risking their lives on every continent—from Afghanistan to Nicaragua—to defy Soviet-supported aggression and secure rights which have been ours from birth." United States Department of State (undated).

WORKS CITED

9-11 Commission (2004). *9/11 Commission Report: Final Report of the National Commission on Terrorist Attacks Upon the United States.* Washington, D.C., National Commission on Terrorist Attacks Upon the United States (9-11 Commission).

BBC (2006). Leader of Afghan Mujahideen Dies. http://news.bbc.co.uk/2/hi/south_asia/5211604.stm, accessed on June 23, 2009

BBC (2009). Who Are the Taliban? http://news.bbc.co.uk/2/hi/south_asia/1549285.stm, accessed on August 17, 2009.

Booth, Wayne C. (1975). *A Rhetoric of Irony.* Chicago: University of Chicago Press.

Borch, Frederic L. "Comparing Pearl Harbor and '9/11': Intelligence Failure? American Unpreparedness? Military Responsibility?" *The Journal of Military History,* Volume 67, Number 3, July 2003, pp. 845–860.

Botti, David (2008). Newsweek.com, Soldier's Home. http://www.blog.newsweek.com/blogs/soldiershome/archive/2008/02/26/obama-s-comment-on-taliban-weapons.aspx, accessed on February 14, 2009.

Brown, Wendy (2001). *Politics Out of History.* Princeton, NJ: Princeton University Press.

Bush, George W. (September 20, 2001). "Address to a Joint Session of Congress and the American People." http://georgewbush-whitehouse.archives.gov/news/releases/2001/09/20010920-8.html

———. (September 13, 2001). National Day of Prayer and Remembrance for the Victims of the Terrorist Attacks on September 11, 2001, White House. Accessed from http://georgewbush whitehouse.archives.gov/news/releases/2001/09/20010913-7.html on February 14, 2009.

CNN.com (October 7, 2001). Accesses on February 12, 2009, from http://archives.cnn.com/2001/US/10/07/ret.us.taliban/.

———.(February 18, 2009). "Obama approves Afghanistan troop increase." Retrieved on February 20, 2009, from http://edition.cnn.com/2009/POLITICS/02/17/obama.troops/?iref=mpstoryview.

Danziger, Jeff (2006). *Blood, Debt, & Fears.* Hanover, NH: Steerforth Press.

Fukuyama, Francis (1992). *The End of History and the Last Man.* New York: Free Press.

Giroux, H. (2003). *The Abandoned Generation: Democracy Beyond the Culture of Fear,* 153–197. New York: Palgrave Macmillan.

Harris, John F. (October 15, 2001). "Bush Rejects Taliban Offer On Bin Laden; No Evidence Links Anthrax Mail To Al Qaeda, U.S. Officials Say." *Washington Post,* Final Edition, Section A, p. 1.

Heller, Dana (2005). *The Selling of 9/11: How a National Tragedy Became a Commodity.* New York: Palgrave Macmillan.

Hess, Stephen, and Sandy Northrop (1996). *Drawn & Quartered: The History of American Political Cartoons*. Montgomery, Ala.: Elliott & Clark Publishers.

Hutcheon, Linda (1994). *Irony's Edge: The Theory and Politics of Irony*. New York: Routledge.

Lamb, Chris (2004). *Drawn to Extremes: The Use and Abuse of Editorial Cartoons in the United States*. New York: Columbia University Press.

Magill, R. Jay, Jr. (2007). *Chic Ironic Bitterness*. Ann Arbor: University of Michigan Press.

Mayhall, Stacey L. (2009). "Uncle Sam Wants You to Trade, Invest, and Shop! Relocating the Battlefield in the Gendered Discourses of the Pre- and Early Post-9/11 Period." *NWSA Journal,* Volume 21, Number 1, Spring 2009, pp. 29–50.

Noon, David Hoogland (2004). "Operation Enduring Analogy: World War II, the War on Terror, and the Uses of Historical Memory." *Rhetoric & Public Affairs*, Volume 7, Number 3, Fall 2004, pp. 339–364.

O'Keefe, Mark (2006). Five Years After 9/11, The Clash of Civilizations Revisited. Interview on the Pew Forum on Religion and Public Life Web site. Accessed 7/14.09 from http://pewforum.org/events/index.php?EventID=125.

Olivant, Patrick (2004). Why Political Cartoons Are Losing Their Influence. *Nieman Reports,* Winter, Volume 58, Number 4, 2004, p. 25. Cambridge, Harvard.

Pooley, Eric (2002). Mayor of the World. *Time.* Retrieved from http://www.time.com/time/subscriber/poy2001/poyprofile.html, accessed on February 9, 2009.

Rosenblatt, Roger (September 16, 2001). "The Age of Irony Comes to an End." *Time.* Retrieved from http://www.time.com/time/magazine/article/0,9171,1101010924-175112,00.html on July 18, 2007.

Simpson, David (2006). *9/11: The Culture of Commemoration*. Chicago: University of Chicago Press.

Tilly, Charles (2004). "Terror, Terrorism, Terrorists." *Sociological Theory*, Volume 22, Number 1, March 2004, pp. 5–13. American Sociological Association, Washington, DC.

United States Department of State (undated). Reagan Doctrine, 1985. http://www.state.gov/r/pa/ho/time/rd/17741.htm, accessed on February 9, 2009.

White, Hayden (1973). *Metahistory: The Historical Imagination in Nineteenth-Century Europe*. Baltimore and London: Johns Hopkins University Press.

CHAPTER ELEVEN

LAUGHING ALL THE WAY TO THE BANK
Enron, Humor, and Political Economy

—Gavin Benke

It hardly needs pointing out that for many U.S. citizens, the terrorist attacks of late 2001 were a shock to the political, economic, and cultural system. Though it may now seem trite to say that "everything changed" after 9/11, in the immediate aftermath there was no question that the tone of public discourse was different. Week after week, aggressively frightening images appeared on the fronts of magazines: the October 1, 2001, cover of *Time* featured a close-up of Osama bin Laden with the phrase "Target: Bin Laden" in bold letters, and the October 8 *Newsweek* cover depicted a U.S. Marine wearing a gas mask with the phrase "Biological and Chemical Terror: How Scared Should You Be?" plastered on the center of the page. The attitude of mainstream media articles was often jingoistic. Lance Morrow's editorial in the *Time* Special Issue that followed the attacks, titled "The Case for Rage and Retribution," juxtaposed the issue's many disturbing photographs with an argument for "a policy of focused brutality," in which the nation needed "to relearn why human nature has equipped us all with a weapon (abhorred in peacetime societies) called hatred" (Morrow 2001). Even as the months wore on, this attitude proved to have sticking power, as Jonathan Alter's piece in that November's *Newsweek*, "Time to Think about Torture," demonstrates.

In tandem with this new mood, usually even-handed news outlets took it upon themselves to revamp Bush's image following the attacks. If Bush had been floundering in the earliest months of his presidency, 9/11 became a catalyst for his rehabilitation. For example, Eric Pooley and Karen Tumulty's piece in the September 24 issue of *Time*, "Bush in the Crucible," referred to Bush's famous bullhorn declaration at Ground Zero as possessing a "grace that was both convincing and, somehow, unmistakably American" (Pooley and Tumulty 2001, 49). The change in the national mood also had an impact on U.S. entertainment. As Lynn Spigel and other contributors to this collection have noted, immediately following the attacks, "Dave Letterman, Jay

Leno, Craig Kilborn, Conan O'Brien, and Jon Stewart met the late-night audience with dead seriousness" (Spigel 2005, 120).

If 9/11 was the dominant news story of 2001, Enron's bankruptcy was not far behind. Just over a month following the terrorist attacks, the energy company stunned Wall Street analysts by announcing losses of over a billion dollars. Though it seemed inconceivable in mid-October, this revelation would be the catalyst for a shockingly swift collapse of what was, at the time, the seventh-largest corporation in the United States. Though the company's stock price had been declining for most of the year, and CEO Jeff Skilling's sudden resignation in August had raised red flags for some who followed the company, it was the October 16 announcement that led to the media focusing on Enron's extensive use of "Special Purpose Entities"— corporations that, in effect, only existed on paper and did "business" with Enron, allowing it to seem more profitable than it actually had been. Financial news outlets like the *Wall Street Journal* began aggressively reporting what increasingly seemed like the company's dishonest business practices. The initial announcement certainly damaged its reputation, and Enron followed it by restating its profits going back several years. Although the company appeared to be an economic powerhouse throughout the late 1990s, it now seemed more like an elaborate con.

Within the span of a month, from mid-October to November 2001, the company's credit rating and stock price collapsed. By the end of the year, shares of Enron were, for all intents and purposes, worthless. Enron employees, many of whom held significant amounts of the company's stock, suddenly faced uncertain futures. Finally, the company filed for bankruptcy on December 2, 2001. At the time, it was the largest bankruptcy in U.S. history.

◆ ◆ ◆

Yet before December, Enron scrambled to stay afloat. Amid a sea of bad press and a declining stock price, 9/11 provided CEO Kenneth Lay with a handy comparison that could, in theory, reconstruct the image of his company that would align with the suddenly militant and defiant atmosphere. "Just like America is under attack by terrorism, I think we're under attack," Enron's CEO pronounced to a group of employees in late 2001 (Smith and Emshwiller 2003, 152). Ken Lay's statement was not just wild hyperbole, but was also woefully out of step with the national mood. Contrary to Lay's statement, most Americans did not view Enron as a victim, but, like 9/11, as a harbinger of an unstable world. Even a year later, in naming Enron

"Whistleblower" Sherron Watkins one of *Time* magazine's "Persons of the Year," the authors referred to Enron and WorldCom (another recently disgraced corporation) as the "Twin Towers of false promises" (Lacayo and Ripley 2002).[1]

Enron quickly became a problem for the Bush administration. Much like the newly minted president, Enron was a product of Texas. Both Lay and the company, which had begun its life as a natural gas pipeline operation, were headquartered in Houston and had long ties to the Bush family. While Bush was governor of Texas, he and Lay shared both a friendly relationship and a free market ideology that saw government regulation as an impediment to business.[2]

This association was not lost on the media. Reporters for *Time*, *Newsweek*, and other news sources pointed to the long friendship between the two, and Enron swiftly became the punchline for a raft of politically oriented jokes in a variety of settings, from written satire to cartoons, and even entire Web sites. Despite the complex, esoteric nature of the company's misdeeds (and the seemingly inherently unfunny nature of accounting), the scandal provided comics and political wits with a great deal of material. Naturally, some of the initial satire focused on the convoluted logic of Enron's accounting methods. However, Enron humor was not solely focused on accounting jokes; much of this satirical treatment turned on the close ties between Enron and the Bush White House. Arrogant, greedy, dishonest executives with direct links to the Bush administration created a perfect source of fodder for comedy and satire.

Although the obvious links between Bush and Lay seemed to demand political humor, as well as legal investigation, it was the historical moment that transformed what would have been quotidian pieces of humor into sharp jabs at one of the Bush administration's deeply held political philosophies. In short, they were articulate moments of protest in the face of a specific (and powerful) political economic regime at a time when *any* criticism of Bush was rare.

Such politically minded Enron humor was a liability for the new administration, as well as an avenue for dissenting voices in a potentially hostile political climate. Satire about Enron throughout the 2000s provided a forum for thinking about the relationship between the government and corporate power and influence. For both a company and a presidency devoted to the idea of limited government and the "free market," humor that linked Enron to Bush was potentially devastating. As *Time* reporters Richard Lacayo and Amanda Ripley would opine a year later in 2002, Enron called into question the nature of capitalism itself. They wrote that "with communism vanquished, capitalism was left with no real enemies but its own worst impulses. It can be undone by its own overreaching players" (Lacayo and Ripley 2002). Though the passage did not spell it out in explicit terms, the type of capitalism here appeared to be the extreme laissez-faire variety that both Ken Lay and George Bush espoused.[3]

As geographers Neil Brenner and Nik Theodore point out, however, the free market and its attendant neoliberal philosophy is a specific type of government intervention on behalf of business in which "states and markets [are presented] as if they [are] diametrically opposed principles of social organization, rather than recognizing the politically constructed character of all economic relations" (Brenner and Theodore 2003, 6). Various satirists thus labored to use the Enron scandal as a means of censuring not only the Bush administration but neoliberal ideology itself by pointing out the disingenuous nature of the rhetoric of so-called "deregulation."[4]

BAD PRESS FOR ENRON

Given the magnitude of the bankruptcy, as well as many of the seedier details—from document shredding to employees unable to sell declining Enron stock in their retirement plans even as senior executives were selling theirs—it was inevitable that Enron would be a major news story in 2001 and 2002. However, it was the connection between Ken Lay and George Bush that made what could have been a mere business scandal into a problem for the new administration. Liberal intellectuals, such as Thomas Frank, wasted no time in pointing out the various connections between the company and Bush's coterie. As he wrote in Salon.com in mid-December of 2001, "The company, of course, was largely responsible for the grooming of George W. Bush as a national figure. As governor of Texas Bush used to fly around the country in Enron corporate jets. In later years Enron distinguished itself as the single largest donor to his campaign for the presidency" (Frank 2001).[5]

Though the earliest national Enron coverage focused squarely on the complexity of its business deals, by early 2002 many media outlets had picked up a political angle as well. *Time*'s February 4, 2002, cover story by Michael Duffy and John F. Dickerson, for example, featured a photograph of the White House with the words "How Sticky Will It Get?" and explicitly painted Enron as a political scandal. At one point, the authors went so far as to assert that "[o]ver the last year, the Bush team had quietly performed a host of political sacraments for the Texas company before it began to go bust, and vice versa" (Duffy and Dickerson 2002, 19). Published on the eve of the State of the Union address, Duffy and Dickerson's article argued that Enron threatened to derail Bush's message. The two reporters interpreted the revelation that Karl Rove "recommended that Enron hire a key G.O.P. consultant during the early days of Bush's presidential campaign" as "one more unwelcome story at a time when the President is hoping that his big speech will change the subject back to heroism and unity and patriotism, the themes that have helped make him so popular of late" (19). The story itself was accompanied by a poll suggesting a majority of the public thought the Bush administration was covering *something* up. Perhaps more revealing, the poll also suggested that 51 percent of the survey's participants felt the Bush administration cared more about big business than it did ordinary Americans (19). This last point indicated that even in the immediate post-9/11 environment, in which Bush was repeatedly foregrounded as a "regular guy" (e.g., brush-clearing, flannel-wearing, dog-playing), he could be cast as an elite.

This distrust of the Bush administration's loyalties could also be found in various tropes and forms that revealed a suspicion towards corporate and political power. In the news media, such sentiments were most often expressed through Watergate references. A January 2002 issue of *Time* splashed the question "What did they know and when did they know it?" in large type across the first pages of its Enron story. Though this story primarily dealt with the company's shenanigans (and not Washington's), the two were connected through the phrasing of the question, which alluded to Howard Baker of Tennessee's now-famous question of Nixon at the Watergate hearings: "What did the president know and when did he know it?"

This is not to say that the Enron-as-Watergate analogy wasn't sloppy; it was. Still, its recurrence points back, again and again, to an implied sinister connection between the company and Washington politics.[6] Unlike some 9/11 conspiracy theories, which as Michael Truscello argues in this volume were often simplistic or easily dismissed, it was harder to discount some Enron conspiracies. Even if Enron conspiracy theories, such as those found on the Web site Here in Reality, were textbook examples of what Richard Hofstadter has famously described as the "Paranoid Style," their tactic of connecting politicians and corporations was a legitimate critique of contemporary political economy. For example, Here in Reality featured a frantic schematic with lines that linked icons such as Enron's logo to George Bush's or Dick Cheney's head. Clicking on an icon took users to a list of events or details, each bullet point a damning connection. In effect, conspiracy theories involving Enron and Bush were more or less populist expressions of a profound unease with the confluence of business and government.

Interestingly, a graphic in the January 21, 2002, issue of *Time* paralleled the site's iconography. An insert titled "The World of Ken Lay," featured the embattled executive's head at the center, with pipelines snaking throughout the page as if they were diabolical iron tentacles of influence and intrigue. Between the pipelines were postage-stamp photographs of figures such as George W. Bush, his father, Dick Cheney, John Ashcroft, and Karl Rove.[7]

THE MORAL SERIOUSNESS OF ENRON GAGS

Still, the deep unease present in all of this—the idea that there is simply something sordid about a too-close relationship between political and corporate power—needed a conduit beyond conspiracy theories and journalistic glosses of Watergate. Here, humor of various stripes stepped in to fill the void, and were powerful vehicles for such critiques. As Gray, Jones, and Thompson maintain: "Satire's calling card is the ability to produce social scorn or damning indictments through *playful* means and, in the process, transform the aggressive act of ridicule into the more socially acceptable act of rendering something ridiculous" (Gray, Jones, and Thompson 2009, 12–13, emphasis in original). These pieces of satire, then, were freighted with moral seriousness.

Though cartoons and humorous essays pointed to the particularly cozy relationship between Bush and Enron, they also hinted at a wider condition of a radical free market regime that was now in power.[8] Rather than the apocalyptic and dark mutterings of online conspiracy theorists, or the ominous specter of Watergate, humorists presented a far more withering attack since they portrayed the connection between business and government not as a secret cabal, but as casual and ordinary, a particularly devastating critique since free market ideology denies any kind of role for government in economic life. These early political jokes about Enron were instances of what scholar Paul Lewis characterizes as "intentional humor." For Lewis, moments of intentional humor "contribute to a butt shift," a shift in the joke's target, and "can highlight a point or blow smoke on it, call attention to a problem or cover it up" (Lewis 2006, 7–8).

11.1   Tom Tomorrow, "Your Comprehensive Cartoon Guide to the Enron Collapse!" (2002). Reprinted by permission of Tom Tomorrow.

Many of these pieces focused on the relationship between the company and both the Bush administration and the Republican Party in general. The popular political cartoon strip *This Modern World*, for example, skewered both Enron's penchant for deregulation (a value the company's managers shared with the Bush White House) and the more overt connections between the two (see figure 11.1). The 2002 strip, titled "Your Comprehensive Cartoon Guide to the Enron Collapse!," featured five panels, four of which directly related to the company's political connections and deregulation. The text accompanying the images was highly ironic and sarcastic, framing Lay, Skilling, and various Republican politicians as dishonest charlatans. For example, the second panel, "Deregulation Mania," began with the phrase: "Oops! As it turns out, corporations **can't** always be trusted to police themselves. Who **knew?!**" (Tomorrow 2002, emphasis in original). The very next panel went even further in painting deregulation as a conservative political project. It featured illustrations of Phil and Wendy Gramm and text noting that Wendy Gramm helped Enron avoid specific regulations while working for the Commodities Futures Trading Commission before joining the company's board of directors.[9] "What an **unexpected** turn of events!" a cartoon Phil Gramm exclaimed, while his wife remarked: "It's certainly funny how life works out sometimes!" Other panels pointed to Ken Lay's involvement in Cheney's infamous Energy Task Force. Throughout, the strip's creator, Tom Tomorrow, made a point that mirrored the argument implicit in Watergate references and conspiracy theories. This cultural artifact connected the Bush administration and Enron in a way that directly contradicted the idea of a "free" market. However, it was the humor itself that added bite. The lighthearted tone in the cartoon framed both the executives and conservative politicians as flim-flam artists. While this piece of "intentional humor" shared the sympathies of conspiracy theories, in Tomorrow's rendering, there was nothing exceptional about the relationship between Enron and Bush; it was simply business as usual.[10]

Another, more biting example could be found on the political site whitehouse.org, which compared Bush's denials of his connection to Enron with the Monica Lewinsky scandal of the late 1990s. Disguised as the talking points for a presidential press conference, the page had a number of bullet points such as one that read:

> Finally, just several months ago, as Miss Enron repeatedly arrived at the White House bearing her full complement of eco-political implements of gratification, I DID NOT feverishly satisfy myself upon learning of her energetic servicing of not only my partner Vice President Richard Cheney, but also *every last member* in his Energy Task Force club! ("Newsroom" 2002, emphasis in original)

To be sure, this particular piece of satire was lewd, but this was precisely the point. Both the Bush administration and Enron executives had framed their devotion to free markets in almost moralistic terms.[11] For example, Lay's constant push for deregulation frequently centered on consumer rights and choices. In addition to mocking both corporate and political power, these depictions of Enron buying politicians in the name of deregulation reclassified such actions as inherently undemocratic.

However, such forums—cartoons and parody Web sites—were limited in the depth of their criticism simply by being short form genres. By contrast, satirical essays could extend these arguments. One of the most articulate skewerings of both Bush and Enron came (perhaps unsurprisingly) from the late Texas-based liberal writer and humorist Molly Ivins, who had long been a critic of George W. Bush—or "Shrub," as she often referred to him. While other pieces of humor implicitly framed Enron as a political scandal, it was Ivins who did so explicitly. Writing in the March 1, 2002, edition of *The Progressive*, Ivins started out her brief piece: "Admit it, you're wallowing in Enron. Aside from the fact that it wrecked a bunch of people's lives, it is a beautiful scandal" (Ivins 2002, 3). What made this a "beautiful scandal" for Ivins was that it was a *political* scandal. After detailing Enron's connections with Texas governor (and Bush protégé) Rick Perry, she turned her attention to the company's connections with both George W. Bush and Dick Cheney. As she stated: "The funniest line so far about Enron is, 'This is not a political scandal.' It was totally coincidental that they made all those political contributions. Disinterested public service was their only motive, putting high quality people in public office. And they never got a thing for it" (3). Here, Ivins offered the same link and complaint that the cartoons did. Enron was more than a business scandal specifically because its leadership involved itself in politics. Even beyond the personal connections between Enron and Bush, the company itself devoted considerable funds lobbying both the federal and state governments for legislation that would lead to a favorable business environment.

In and of itself, this connection did not seem too damaging. After all, Enron was certainly not alone in corporate contributions to and ties with politicians. Yet it was Enron's (as well as Bush's) ideological commitment to deregulation that made salvos like Ivins's particularly devastating. In her typically acid and derisive style, she wrote that Enron had nothing but good intentions in making political contributions—it was just another case of corporate altruism—stating: "And they never got a thing for it. Not natural gas deregulation, or deregulation of the energy futures market when Wendy Gramm was chair of the Commodities Futures Trading Commission, or a new chairman of the Federal Energy Commission, or calling off the pressure on off-shore banks, or exemption from oversight on derivatives" (Ivins 2002). Echoing other pieces of humor, Ivins recast deregulation as a government action—the presence of government interference in the market, rather than the absence of it. Taken as a whole, the piece offered a rejoinder to free market ideology. In effect, Ivins removed the modifier "free" from the phrase, revealing an *undemocratic* market.

In short, these early pieces of Enron humor performed important cultural work, serving as popular protests against a free market ideology that found its purest and most extreme proponent in George W. Bush. Philosopher Simon Critchley (among others) has argued that humor can be a danger to power since mocking it "exposes its contingency" (2002, 11). In this sense, Enron humor was radical in the way that it sharply criticized the Bush administration and was a voice of dissent in a hostile climate. These "anti-jokes," as Paul Lewis might call them, were efforts "to turn thoughtless mirth into grim reflection by insisting" that factual (if inconvenient) connections were "too serious, too dangerous, too depressing . . . to laugh at" (Lewis 2006, 13). These cartoonists, Web creators, and writers demanded that the connection between Enron and Bush be taken seriously.

Still, Tom Tomorrow was open about his progressive leanings, and Ivins was publishing in a liberal forum; surely, their audiences were predisposed to these arguments about Enron and Bush (indeed, Ivins all but acknowledged this in her winking, knowing asides, framing the Enron scandal as a guilty pleasure—a bit of schadenfreude). More surprisingly, a similar sensibility also appeared in more mainstream outlets. In early 2002, *Newsweek*'s "Perspectives" page (featuring a smattering of pithy, newsworthy quotes, as well as political cartoons) frequently featured Enron. Some of these pieces worked to connect Enron to the Bush administration. For example, in the magazine's January 14, 2002, edition, the page featured a cartoon that depicted an aide (or perhaps reporter) approaching Bush at his desk. "Critics say your administration has deep ties to Enron. What does Enron's collapse mean?" the man before the president asks.[12] Seemingly unfazed, the cartoon Bush replies: "We have to find a new undisclosed location for Dick Cheney . . ." (Luckovich 2002, 19). To be sure, this was mild stuff in comparison to Tom Tomorrow and Molly Ivins, but the public mocking and linking of Bush (and Cheney) to Enron in a widely read forum was a problem for the administration. While 9/11 cast a patina of stoicism around Bush, Enron was almost immediately a point of ridicule. The cartoon in *Newsweek* was literally surrounded by pithy quotes, many of which—far from humorous—were dark references to 9/11.

Numerous factors contributed to Enron's status as a national joke: its fall was widely known, its connections to the Republican Party were so direct, and its logo provided an easy visual gag.[13] As I have argued, instances of political humor immediately following Enron's collapse can be read as powerful critiques of free market ideology in a manner that, unlike humor that directly engaged 9/11, had wide appeal.

THE DEPOLITICIZATION OF ENRON HUMOR

However, by the middle of the decade, Enron humor had, by and large, lost its political baggage. Jokes about the company persisted, but the connections to George W. Bush mostly fell by the wayside. When references to the president did appear, they were often an afterthought. For example, in 2006, when Enron executives stood trial, Andy Borowitz wrote a short humorous piece on *Newsweek*'s Web site. The comic conceit Borowitz used throughout was that Lay was opting for the "Gilligan Defense" in court, claiming that a coconut fell on his head, causing him to lose his memory (Borowitz 2006). To end the piece, Borowitz did introduce Bush as an element, writing, "Elsewhere, President Bush expressed confidence about Iraq's future, and added that he thought that Brad Pitt and Jennifer Aniston would get back together" (Borowitz 2006). This was hardly critical political humor. While the piece did reference the Iraq war, Bush figured here as a hopeless optimist, not as sinister or cynical.

Indeed, despite the incisive commentary offered by early Enron humor, the linking of the two did not have the political impact that it first seemed it would. Bush made it a point to distance himself from Lay and the company, and a close look at humor from later in the decade even suggests that the ultimate, hegemonic acceptance of free market ideology trumped criticisms of the abuse endemic to that ideology.

The Motley Fool's elaborate Enron spoof comprising the whole of the Web site on April 1, 2006 (April Fool's Day), was one instance of late Enron humor failing to include a critique of free market ideology.[14] While the writing on this Web site was frequently irreverent, in this case the satire deviated strongly from earlier critiques of close connections between government and business; in fact, it functioned in much the opposite way. Although the Web site appeared to savage the corporation and its principal players, it did so in a way that also called into question the legitimacy of government regulating business. As evidenced by the angry and perplexed responses by some readers, the intended satire was also read as a free market manifesto.[15]

In contrast to earlier pieces of Enron humor, *The Motley Fool* never singled out Bush and, in fact, effectively demonstrated how pervasive Bush's ideas had become, particularly the president's invocation of an "ownership society," a phrase used frequently during Bush Jr.'s time in office.[16] On one level, the president was acknowledging a fundamental feature of the postindustrial economy—a radical instability brought on by the unrestricted movement of capital.[17] The "ownership society," however, did not represent a way to find safety in this instability. For Bush, the ownership society really meant a full acceptance of that instability through privatization on an individual level. Specifically, it entailed measures such as: individual, private health care accounts, individual, private retirement accounts (a concept that Enron's collapse exposed as risky), lower taxes, and even tort reform. In another speech, even after Bush implicitly referred to Enron's executives as "irresponsible citizens," he declared that the U.S. had to work to be "the best place in the world to do business. That means less regulations on our business owners [sic]. That means legal reform, so frivolous lawsuits don't make it hard to hire" (Bush 2004). Here, Bush connected three themes that would come together in *The Motley Fool's* April 1, 2006, edition—individual investors, tort reform, and free markets—all important building blocks for the ownership society and of neoliberalism.

The first "story" that greeted visitors that day carried the headline "Motley Fool Sues the U.S. Government." The piece's authors, David Gardner and Tom Gardner (the Web site's founders), facetiously claimed that in the spirit of championing shareholders' rights, the organization was "preparing a class action lawsuit against the federal government on behalf of the former executive leaders of Enron, all of the company's shareholders, and anyone whose investments were adversely affected by the fall of Enron" (Gardner and Gardner 2006). Of course, this was tongue in cheek, but the stance the authors took towards the government, as well as the formal qualities of the gag, failed to carry the same import that was central to satirical pieces from the first part of the decade.

The site, with its mishmash of parodic articles, chiding asides and inane visual images, was a semiotic mess. Though Enron was clearly the satirical target, the rhetorical modes and tropes the authors used throughout the issue only served to reaffirm neoliberalism's basic premises. Perhaps the most problematic gag was the "Million Ken March" the authors proposed, encouraging their readership to don masks of Ken Lay for a march on Washington, referencing years of protest in the capital (though, most obviously, the Million Man March).

Here, the "Million Ken March" ridiculed the very notion of genuine people's movements, social protest and solidarity as a concept (or, generally, any oppositional tactics of the Old Left). The idea of a class action lawsuit was simply preposterous, dovetailing with one of the ownership society's tenets—tort reform. Additionally, by mocking the idea of a people's movement, the joke seemed to be in line with neoliberalism's commitment to and valorization of the *individual* instead of groups.

Indeed, the way the article's authors described the company's mission throughout the 1990s mirrored Lay's conception of deregulation as a force that benefits consumers, even liberating them. The Gardners scoffed at the very idea of a company intent on helping people, noting, with more than a dash of irony: "Its mission was to save you money. Its mission was to increase the stock price for shareholders, and management would stop at nothing in pursuit of that goal" (Gardner and Gardner 2006).

Such statements also reflected an ambivalence that pervaded the April Fool's issue. Even in the more or less carnivalesque environment of *The Motley Fool*'s Web site, the 2006 April Fool's edition was particularly extreme. In Bakhtinian terms, such humor is not focused solely on an outside target, but rather, "it is also directed at those who laugh" (Bakhtin 1984, 12). The various authors of the site frequently turned a satirical eye on their own past exultation of Enron, and even to the presumed ideological predispositions of their readership. Journalists and investors alike found no solace here for failing to interrogate the company in any real way. However, these prevarications were no laughing matter since they declined to place any meaningful blame on the corporation. Sure, Enron was greedy, but unlike Tom Tomorrow's or Molly Ivins's work, the *Fool*'s joking did not call for systemic change.

In an odd way, the tone and humor throughout the articles on the site chastised the *Fool*'s audience, individual investors. For example, in another article, "The Tyranny of the Individual Investor," Chris Hill, the author, proclaimed that investors, acting as a "violent" mob, had become tyrannical, and that they had "gone too far," pressuring the company for higher and higher gains. The accompanying image of a car set ablaze underscored the idea of an unruly mob that was a threat to social order (Hill 2006). The logic in this piece was particularly contorted, full of internal contradictions, but the overriding message was unmistakably antidemocratic.

Of course, *The Motley Fool*'s writers were not actually insisting Enron executives hadn't done anything wrong. However, the site was rife with odd slippages that undercut the intended satire and actually reified many of the Bush administration's economic premises. Thus, even though the gags were ridiculous, it is not entirely surprising that some took the story seriously. Not too long after the *Fool* resumed publishing its typical fare, the Gardners also posted a follow-up to the April Fool's issue. In their follow-up letter, "Motley Fool Withdraws April 1 Lawsuit!," the Gardners wrote that they hoped their joke called attention to a serious issue, but they failed to specify what that issue was; they also reported that many readers did not seem to understand it was a joke, going so far as to publish some of the angry letters they received.

Most of these letters were expressions of shock and disappointment. One self-described "long-term" reader was "concerned by what appears to be a crusade on behalf of Enron executives." The reader even went on to wonder "whether you or other Fools are friends with Ken Lay. Are you? Related to him? Business dealings? Did you lose money on Enron stock? See what I mean? You are failing in the fundamental standard of disclosure that you promote to others. I don't know (and you haven't told us) whether you are interested or disinterested, whether you are enraged in a spirit of public service, or whether you have a dog in the fight" (JW).

Another reader expressed an open attitude to the idea of the lawsuit before realizing that the whole issue was a joke. Though the reader felt the site's authors were being unfair to whistleblowers, he or she was generally willing to hear out the Gardners' "arguments" in defense of Enron, writing, "I do, however, have alot of repsect [*sic*] for what the fool has done to date, so I have not just junked you into the same bin as the guy who stands on the corner downtown trying to make us all realize that we were duped and that the world is really flat. I perused the information you have offered to date, however, and other than trying to drive the elephant of Enron's misconduct through the loop hole of rule 346(a-7.2), I have not seen much to cause me to cast aside my pitchfork and torch." Perhaps the readers could not be blamed for taking the site seriously. Some articles barely suggested themselves as humorous, and instead read almost as free market libertarian screeds about innovation.

In effect, *The Motley Fool*'s April Fool's joke, through its use of satirical treatment of Enron, failed to fulfill the political threats implicit in earlier bits of humor that linked Enron and the Bush administration. Rather (and bizarrely), they bolstered many of the central tenets of Bush's ownership society.[18] In this sense, *The Motley Fool* suggested a good amount of acceptance of neoliberal philosophy. Indeed, the rampant inconsistencies in the jokes' targets evinced a "contradictory consciousness," which historian T. J. Jackson Lears (in his essay on Gramsci) describes as a mix of "approbation and apathy, resistance and resignation" that accompanies the presence of cultural hegemony (Lears 1985, 570). While the *Fool*'s writers took aim at a crooked corporation, they did so in a way that offered no real alternative. Though, by their own statements, the Gardners intended the April Fool's issue to be intentional humor, writing that they wanted to create an "indefensible argument based on self-interest" in the manner of Enron, the overall message of the site simply (if somewhat resignedly) rearticulated many of the basic assumptions of a neoliberal world view (Gardner and Gardner 2006).

If, as other essays in this collection suggest, 9/11 humor became more political throughout the decade, Enron jokes followed an inverse trajectory. The quietly, though undeniably conservative, humor of the *Fool's* site hinted that the ownership society and neoliberalism had achieved some sort of hegemonic victory. If some political jokes treated Bush as a warmonger or reckless cowboy, they did not offer systemic critiques of neoliberalism. Even if criticism of the Bush administration grew throughout the decade, it was of a different political stripe than the decade's early Enron jokes.

NOTES

1. Rosalie Genova (2007) has noted the linguistic connection between Enron and 9/11.

2. In truth, this attitude has long been pervasive in Houston's business community.

3. In his typically acidic writing style, Thomas Frank (2001) describes this brand of ideology as a "zealous, cult-like love of free markets."

4. Many present-day scholars tend to discuss neoliberalism in tandem with a consideration of transnationalism. Here, I take a broad view of neoliberalism, seeing it as an ideology that also includes deregulation and privatization in the United States.

5. Frank is, to a degree, exaggerating here. Still, it is true that Ken Lay found a friend and ally in the Texas governor's mansion.

6. The popular writer Malcolm Gladwell (2007) has argued that Enron, rather than a replay of Watergate, was its inverse. Instead of hiding information from the public, Gladwell insists, Enron was a flood of information that obscured understanding (Gladwell 2007).

7. To be fair, not all the figures here are Bush administration officials.

8. Certainly, I am not implying that neoliberalism or an extreme free market stance is unique to the Bush administration. Indeed, as Brenner and Theodore (as well as others) have pointed out, as a project, deregulation goes as far back as the late 1970s. However, the fervor for markets has, since then, waxed and waned. George W. Bush and Dick Cheney were certainly the most enthusiastic proponents to inhabit the White House. Perhaps it took a scandal as glaring as Enron to give this ideology visibility, and satirists a target.

9. Both of the Gramms figure prominently in many Enron narratives, since Wendy Gramm's appointment to the board is about as close to a tit-for-tat arrangement as one can find in the Enron story.

10. Though this a withering critique, it bears noting that Bush himself is absent as a satirical target. Rather, Dick Cheney and various conservative politicians stand in synecdochically for the president.

11. Indeed, both Ken Lay and George W. Bush frequently referenced their religious faith in public.

12. The cartoon, apparently, originally ran in the *Atlanta Journal Constitution*. However, I point to its appearance in *Newsweek* instead, since it would have reached a wider audience this way.

13. Despite this connection, readers should not take this to mean that Enron did not cultivate a relationship with Democratic administrations and politicians. Even though Lay

and Bush shared a particularly close relationship, Lay wrote to Clinton appointees, such as Bill Richardson (who was energy secretary during the latter half of the 1990s). In short, Enron, and Ken Lay in particular, cultivated ties with both parties.

14. *The Motley Fool* itself has its roots in the early Clinton years, having been founded by two brothers in 1993. Later in the decade, the *Fool* (as it is sometimes called) became closely associated with "new economy" stocks and companies. It even published a list of the "Fool 50" of "innovative" forward-thinking companies. Naturally, Enron was on the list—a fact the company took great pride in. As the site's title might suggest, its writers often employ an irreverent tone as it dispenses investment advice and news. In some ways, stylistically, the Gardners operate in the same vein as Molly Ivins and Thomas Frank—more or less engaging in "serious" discourse (e.g., personal finance) through the use of humor. As part of its irreverent ethos, on the first of every April, the site publishes an April Fool's edition—essentially a hoax.

15. *The Motley Fool* is not the only instance of this mistaken identity. Ted Gournelos (2009) identifies numerous instances of journalists taking *The Onion*'s parodies of news stories seriously.

16. In a stump speech at a northern Virginia community college in 2004, for instance, Bush noted that people could not depend on spending their entire lives under an umbrella-like security of one company: "Now people are moving around. It's a different world. And there is some uncertainty in that kind of world. Moms and dads are both working, sometimes out of the house. And the economy is changing. And, therefore, government policy ought to change with the times. And one way to bring stability and security into a person's life is to encourage ownership" (Bush 2004).

17. Significantly, this instability is brought on, encouraged, or at least extended by the dismantling of regulatory frameworks that both Enron and Bush worked for in Texas.

18. On some level, this should hardly be surprising. It is worth noting that the *Fool*'s origins are not located in the Bush years, but rather during the 1990s. Indeed, Bush and the ownership society should not be read as a radical break from Clinton-era economic thinking, but rather as the logical (if extreme) expression of a neoliberal sentiment that goes back as far as the 1970s and 1980s and that was allowed to progress unmolested (and, in many cases, aided) throughout the supposedly liberal Clinton years.

WORKS CITED

Bakhtin, Mikhail. 1984. *Rabelais and His World*. Trans. Helene Iswolsky. Bloomington: Indiana UP.

Borowitz, Andy. 2006. Ken Lay Claims Amnesia After Coconut Fell on His Head. *Newsweek* , March 14. http://www.newsweek.com/id/47196 (accessed February 23, 2010).

Brenner, Neil, and Nik Theodore. 2003. Cities and Geographies of "Actually Existing Neoliberalism." In *Spaces of Neoliberalism*, ed. Neil Brenner and Nik Theodore, 2–32. Malden, MA: Blackwell, 2002.

Bush, George W. 2004. "President's Remarks in Ask President Bush Event," campaign speech, August 9. http://georgewbush-whitehouse.archives.gov/news/releases/2004/08/20040809-3.html (accessed August 14, 2009).

———. 2004. "President's Remarks at a 'Focus on Ownership' Event," Campaign Speech, October 2. http://georgewbush-whitehouse.archives.gov/news/releases/2004/10/20041002-9.html (accessed August 14, 2009).

Critchley, Simon. 2002. *On Humour*. London: Routledge.

Duffy, Michael, and John F. Dickerson. 2002. Enron Spoils the Party. *Time*, February 4.

Frank, Thomas. 2001. The Enron Outrage. *Salon.com*, December 14. http://dir.salon.com/ politics/feature/2001/12/14/enron/index.html (accessed February 23, 2010).

Gardner, David, and Tom Gardner. 2006. The Motley Fool Sues the U.S. Government. *The Motley Fool*, April 1. http://www.fool.com/specials/2006/06040100ene.htm (accessed July 26, 2009).

———. 2006. Motley Fool Withdraws April 1 Lawsuit! *The Motley Fool*, April 3. http://www .fool.com/specials/2006/06040300sp.htm (accessed August 14, 2009).

Genova, Rosalie. 2007. "How Enron Collapsed at Ground Zero: Tangled Narratives in the New Century." Master's thesis, University of North Carolina at Chapel Hill.

Gladwell, Malcolm. 2007. Open Secrets: Enron, Intelligence and the Perils of Too Much Information. *The New Yorker*, January 8. http://www.newyorker.com/ reporting/2007/01/08/070108fa_fact_gladwell (accessed February 21, 2010).

Gournelos, Ted. 2009. *Popular Culture and the Future of Politics: Cultural Studies and the Tao of South Park*. Lanham, MD: Lexington Books.

Gray, Jonathan, Jeffery P. Jones, and Ethan Thompson. 2009. The State of Satire, the Satire of State, in *Satire TV: Politics and Comedy in the Post-Network Era*, ed. Jonathan Gray, Jeffery P. Jones, and Ethan Thompson, 3–36. New York: NYU Press.

Hill, Chris. 2006. The Tyranny of the Individual Investor. *The Motley Fool*, April 1. http:// www.fool.com/specials/2006/06040104ene.htm (accessed August 14, 2009).

Ivins, Molly. 2002. I Love Enron. *The Progressive*, March 1, 66 (3), www.factiva.com (accessed July 31, 2009).

Lacayo, Richard, and Amanda Ripley. 2002. Persons of the Year. *Time*, December 30. http:// www.time.com/time/subscriber/personoftheyear/2002/poy intro.html (accessed February 23, 2010).

Lears, T. J. Jackson. 1985. The Concept of Cultural Hegemony: Problems and Possibilities. *The American Historical Review* 90.3: 567–593.

Lewis, Paul. 2006. *Cracking Up: American Humor in a Time of Conflict*. Chicago: University of Chicago Press.

Luckovich. 2002. Cartoon (image), *Newsweek*, January 14.

Morrow, Lance. 2001. The Case for Rage and Retribution. *Time* Special Issue, September 11.

"Newsroom." 2002. *Whitehouse.org*, January 11. http://web.archive.org/web/20021203122322/ www.whitehouse.org /news/2002/011102.asp (accessed July 22, 2009).

"Perspectives." 2002. *Newsweek*, January 14.

Pooley, Eric, and Karen Tumult. 2001. Bush in the Crucible. *Time*, September 24.

Smith, Rebecca, and John R. Emshwiller. 2003. *24 Days: How Two Wall Street Journal Reporters Uncovered the Lies That Destroyed Faith in Corporate America*. New York: HarperBusiness.

Spigel, Lynn. 2005. Entertainment Wars: Television Culture after 9/11. In *The Selling of 9/11: How a National Tragedy Became a Commodity*, ed. Dana Heller, 119–154. New York: Palgrave MacMillan.

Tomorrow, Tom. 2002. "Your Comprehensive Cartoon Guide to the Enron Collapse" (image). *Salon.com*, January 7. http://dir.salon.com/story/comics/tomo/2002/01/07/tomo/index .html (accessed August 14, 2009).

CHAPTER TWELVE

WHAT'S SO FUNNY ABOUT A DEAD TERRORIST?

Toward an Ethics of Humor for the Digital Age[1]

—Paul Lewis

One problem with writing a book about rapidly changing trends in politics or popular culture is that the demands of publication compel authors to stop writing while the trends they have been studying continue to evolve. Hardly seems fair. And yet if one has accurately plotted the trajectory of these trends, found useful explanatory frames for the events studied, respected the lessons that seemingly anomalous occurrences can provide, and taken into account the way new facts can both challenge existing theories and guide future empirical research, then some or most of the events that occur after the final draft is in the hands of the press should be susceptible to (and therefore confirm the validity of) the analyses developed in the book.

I speak from experience. Since completing the final, precopyedited draft of *Cracking Up: American Humor in a Time of Conflict* (2006) in the comparatively quiet month of August 2005, I have followed what has been a veritable cavalcade of the kind of stories discussed in the book. From the publication of the Danish Muhammad cartoons in September 2005 through the appearance of Barry Blitt's July 2008 *New Yorker* cover that depicted Barack Obama as a terrorist, U.S. politics and culture have been impacted by 9/11-inflected jokes, satires, and parodies. A timeline of these stories would include: the global and still-ongoing response to the Muhammad cartoons, the International Holocaust Cartoon Contest sponsored by the Iranian newspaper *Hamshahri* (2006), Ann Coulter's mocking of 9/11 widows (June 2006), the proactive defense of the government of Kazakhstan to the impending release of Sasha Baron Cohen's *Borat* (September 2006), the release of a video showing two 9/11 terrorists (Ziad Jarrah and Mohammed Atta) laughing and joking before recording their suicide messages (October 2006), the release of Albert Brooks's *Looking for Comedy in the Muslim World* (2006), the Axis of Evil Comedy Tour (March 2007), al Qaeda's second-incommand, Ayman al-Zawahiri, ridiculing a bill calling for a timetable for withdrawing U.S. troops from Iraq and mocking President Bush, whom he invited to a meeting to be held in the recently bombed Iraqi parliament cafeteria (May 2007), Jeff Dunham's posting of "Achmed, the Dead Terrorist" on YouTube following its broadcast on Comedy Central and release as part of the *Spark of Insanity* DVD (September 2007), and John McCain's singing "Bomb Iran, bomb, bomb Iran" at a campaign appearance in New Hampshire (April 2007). Unlike most professional comedy and canned jokes, these stories feature mockery and ridicule used not only (or even primarily) to amuse but also to shock, persuade, relax, insult, impress, soothe, taunt, and/or denigrate.

What the events on this representative, but far from exhaustive, list have in common is that they all seemed to matter far beyond the mirth provided by their comic materials. At the same time, the way they mattered, or seemed to matter, varied. Some added new scripts to the ongoing, familiar culture wars of recent decades. Some affected how individual jokers were seen in light of their joke(s). Some seemed (or threatened) to influence public opinion on pressing issues. Some were fueled by changes in communication technology, some provoked waves of negative response and/ or intense debate, and in some, the revulsion seemed to rise to the level of *gelotophobia,* a recently discovered social anxiety disorder that afflicts sufferers with a fear of being laughed at.

In chapter 4 of *Cracking Up,* I follow the evolution of ridicule and satire directed at George W. Bush before and after the 9/11 attacks. Rejecting excessively general assumptions about humor—including the widely shared belief that it (singular) is both a panacea and a heroic virtue—made it possible for me to refute the claim that terrorists are necessarily humorless, to highlight the role of humor in the Abu Ghraib abuses, and to consider the possibility that humor operated fallaciously (*argumentum ad mirth*) to boost public support for destructive policies, e.g., invading Iraq and ignoring the threat of global climate change. Humor controversies since 2005—including the Muhammad cartoon fiasco, ex-senator George Allan's "Macaca" moment (2006), the Don Imus "nappy-headed" blunder (April 2007), and John Kerry's botched joke about the stupidity of the Iraq War (October 2007)—ramped up the expectation in the U.S. that the wrong or right joke can have powerful effects that run from amusement and appreciation to resistance and outrage. The stories listed above from the worlds of politics and entertainment suggest that widely shared humor can not only reveal smoldering anxieties, but also reduce or intensify them.

While the history of humor theory is rife with sweeping claims (that is, sentences that begin *Humor is X* or *Humor does Y*), and while humor promoters assume that humor should be broadly seen as having positive functions, nuanced models being developed by social psychologists support a more flexible and complex approach to the impact of comedy, ridicule, satire, and mirth in politics and culture. Most notably, Nicholas A. Kuiper and his colleagues (2004) have identified three dimensions and four styles of humor, only some of which are adaptive and, therefore, beneficial. Concluding that generalizations about the benefits of humor conceived as a unitary construct are untenable, Kuiper et al. suggest that people who are able to use humor effectively to "elicit laughter from others and . . . maintain and bolster relationships" (139) are likely to feel better, while people who use humor to attack others or in failing efforts to promote themselves are likely to feel worse. Similarly, studies of humor within couples (Martin et al. 2003; Campbell et al. 2008) have found that "when people use more affiliative humor during a conflict discussion, their partners feel closer to them and feel that they were more successful at resolving their conflicts, but that when they use more aggressive humor their partners feel less close and . . . that the discussion did not contribute to resolving the conflict" (Campbell et al., 53). On the broad stages of comic performance and political ridicule, this complex view of humor functions (positive vs. negative, adaptive vs. rigid, affiliative vs. alienating) highlights the importance of tact. That is, humor creators who traffic in potentially provocative images and ideas need to think in new ways about how audiences—that can now spread from local to national to global with the click of a cell phone video camera—will react.

By providing frames that clarify the dynamics of humor response (from amusement to indifference to taking offense), Thomas A. Veatch (1998) explains why specific individuals and groups respond differently to the same comic materials. Whether one will be amused or outraged by a joke, cartoon, or other comic work will, according to Veatch, be determined, in part, by the interplay between one's sense of (1) what is normal and proper, and (2) how this is being violated in the work. For people to be amused, the principle being violated must seem important, but not so important in context as to be seen as morally inviolable. In one example, Veatch discusses the unamused response of a new mother to a dead-baby joke she used to find funny. Life experience, he argues, has strengthened her attachment to the principle that babies need to be protected, to the point at which she can no longer take its violation lightly. As complex as this fluidity is in individuals, Veatch notes that different "cultures have extremely different moralities"

(168). The implication for humor exchange across national, ethnic, and religious lines is profound: groups cohere around shared principles that can be safely violated only by a humorist who has a profound, though in most cases intuitive, appreciation of levels of attachment. In a world of transnational and instantaneous communication, the stakes have never been as high or the need for tact as great.

Two stories, each of which features humor about terrorists and terrorism, demonstrate the nature of the challenge and the contrast between tactless and tactful treatments of potentially explosive materials. In simple exchanges of canned jokes between friends, much can be taken for granted and transgressions often pass without harm. But public joking about potentially sensitive topics has recently become riskier as insensitive jokers can not only damage their own standing, but stir destructive passions beyond the first circle of reception. As the contrast between the Danish cartoon story and Jeff Dunham's "Achmed, the Dead Terrorist" routine suggests, the first rule for satirists may now be, if not do no harm, then do as little harm as possible.

THE MUHAMMAD CARTOON CONFLICT: NATIONAL SATIRE, TRANSNATIONAL RESPONSE

At the 2004 conference of the International Society for Humor Studies in Dijon, France, then-president of the organization John Morreall contrasted the mindset that supports terrorism with having a sense of humor. Terrorists are rigid, fanatical, serious, he argued, while humor is playful, flexible, balanced. In a similar vein, Malcolm Kushner (2001), who described himself as "America's favorite humor consultant" in a *USA Today* op-ed piece that ran three weeks after the 9/11 attacks, argued that the conflict of our time was between humorous America and its humorless Islamic fundamentalist enemies: "The act of laughing itself is symbolic of an open society. And it's antithetical to the entire social structure of terrorists' rigid conformity and control." Coming from a leading humor researcher and a leading humor advocate, these assertions inadvertently highlight myopic tendencies in the field: how easy it can be to conclude that someone (or group) that does not find your (or your group's) comic materials funny has no sense of humor, while at the same time failing even to recognize humor directed at oneself or one's group as humor.

Soothed by upbeat assessments of humor, few in the West were prepared for the violent reaction to the twelve cartoons published by the Danish newspaper *Jyllands-Posten* on September 30, 2005 (Timeline). In response to a call to create images that featured Muhammad, the cartoonists produced a range of work, including some that mocked the conservative editors and others that responded to anxieties about Islam and terrorism. From the start, the images provoked anger. Nonviolent protests sprang up in Denmark, and, after a delegation of Danish Muslims traveled to the Middle East to denounce the cartoons, angry protests broke out across the Muslim world, resulting in scores of deaths, burning of embassies, and boycotts of Danish products.[2]

Two of the most controversial *Jyllands-Posten* images were both comic and satirical: Jens-Julius's cartoon depicting the prophet at the gate of heaven shouting "STOP, STOP WE HAVE RUN OUT OF VIRGINS!" to a line of smoking suicide bombers waiting to get in, and Kurt Westergaard's representation of Muhammad's head wearing a black bomb/turban with a lit fuse. Both of these incongruously shift Muhammad out of his seventh-century time frame and associate him with contemporary acts of terror. While any visual representation of this figure would offend many Muslims, these two cartoons were most often seen either as insensitively provocative and profane or as tellingly pointed and liberating. Given the enhanced communication technologies that helped to internationalize this story, it is interesting to note how much it was driven by multiple failures to communicate, understand, and empathize. To many non-Muslims, a key irony was the way outrage over the association of Muhammad with violent terrorists seemed to motivate acts of violent protest. To many Muslims, a key irony was the hypocrisy of free-speech doctrines that restrict Holocaust deniers while allowing anti-Islamic blasphemy.

If humor were, indeed, a universal and positive form of communication, it would be the perfect way to bridge these divides. However, the impulse to celebrate humor and laughter requires modification if it is to accommodate this story of global ridicule and outrage—unprecedented, perhaps, in the intensity of the response with its attendant carnage and high body count. Offered originally by the newspaper as an assertion of one editor's, country's, or culture's privileging of free speech through a celebration of irony and irreverence, it was received as aggressive and impious slander across the Muslim world, and quickly morphed into what Giselinde Kuipers aptly called the "first transnational humor scandal" (Lewis 2008, 7). On the advocacy side, consultants like Kushner, Allen Klein (1989), and Annette Goodheart (1994)—who hype the value of humor and/or laughter in entertainment, relaxation, play, creativity, its role in communication, education, persuasion, intimacy, community building, and its support of sanity, well-being, and physical health—appear to have run into a tsunami of counter-evidence. Of course, these and other boosters generally concede that humor can be hurtful or aggressive, but they tend to view such uses of humor as secondary or in contradiction with what they see as its intrinsically positive functions. This cartoon controversy should remind them that humor can intensify (rather than vent) hostility and contribute to the perceived harm of its targets. Indeed, it's not just that jokes can be cruel: it's that they're perfect weapons for heaping insult on top of injury. Will we, then, as Dr. Madan Kataria tells his thousands of Laughing Club followers, achieve "world peace through laughter"? Or, as this story suggests, are we just as likely to achieve world war this way? To paraphrase T. S. Eliot, is this the way the world ends? Not with a bang but a guffaw?

At best, *Jyllands-Posten*'s project was an experiment in community building that went fatally awry. Looking back, Fleming Rose, the culture editor who managed the cartoon project, explained, "The cartoons did nothing that transcends the cultural norms of secular Denmark, and this was not a provocation to insult Muslims" (Bilefsky 2006). But the response, even among European Muslims, suggests that far more community building needs to precede a constructive sharing of such rough and irreverent humor. Without a preexisting common affiliation, the very playfulness of satire directed at minority subgroups can easily seem like the taunting of an oppressive, bullying majority. In Veatch's terms, secular Danes were far less attached to the view of Muhammad as sacred than were pious Muslims, and this difference lent itself to exploitation by outraged clerics across the Islamic world. The fact that so many Muslims were offended undercuts Rose's assertion that the cartoons were neither provocative nor insulting. A tactful approach to the project of reaching out to Danish Muslims would have paid less attention to a forceful projection of the cartoonists' values and more to those of Muslim readers/viewers. Attempting to do this would have made it possible to mock terrorists without drawing down the wrath of terrorist-opposing but Muhammad-revering Muslims.

In general, humor research has paid more attention to joke appreciation (what kinds of jokes are favored by specific individuals and groups) than to its opposite, which I have called the "antijoke" response (Lewis 1987, 2006), that is, resistance to humor seen as witless, distasteful, or outrageous. But in this story we see two powerful rhetorical forces at work: first, the force of ridicule, which is particularly painful when it seems to mock the suffering of its butts, and second, the global wave of outrage in what was arguably the most powerful antijoke response in human history. If cartoons produced in one country as political commentary and satire can be distributed worldwide and spark global protests that express and intensify intragroup hostility, adversely impact international trade and diplomatic relations, and lead to scores of deaths, then we are not dealing with ethnic joke exchanges as they have been understood in the past. In the comparatively tranquil contexts that provided Christie Davies (1990, 2002) with his comparatively harmless materials, it was possible to argue (as Davies did) that ethnic jokes (based on religion or other identity-group markers) express and perhaps vent the anxieties or concerns of the joke teller's group by associating undesired traits (stupidity, filthiness, etc.) with other groups (defined by their proximity to and similarity with the joke teller's group). In the world of ethnic–joke telling Davies posits, a speaker shares a canned joke with a member or members of her own group about failures (of intelligence, cleanliness, etc.) important to the joking group and projected by way of the joke onto the target group. But this triangular model (teller-listeners-target) has little explanatory force in the world of viral communication across national, ethnic, and religious boundaries. It no longer describes a world in which every wag with a cell phone can film and upload comic material and gaffes, satire produced in one country is rebroadcast or otherwise distributed around the planet, and everyone with computer access can join discussions about the impact of controversial humor.

Elliott Oring (2003) has insisted that the playful and ambiguous nature of jokes makes it difficult for them to convey a single, serious or hostile thought to all listeners/interpreters. But this story demonstrates that the very playfulness and ambiguity of humor can intensify its perceived hostility. To Fleming Rose, the bomb-turban cartoon was about the way extremists have taken control of Islam; to many Muslims, extreme and moderate, this nuanced point and other possible interpretations got lost in what struck them as a blasphemously playful representation of Muhammad. Far from reducing the potential insult, the possibility of multiple interpretations ("see how many ways we can play with the image of your prophet?") added fuel to the fire. Oring has argued that even the most hostile jokes are less harmful than physical attacks (Lewis 1997, 471–72), but does anyone believe that the beating of a Muslim immigrant by an anti-immigration thug in, say, Hillerod, Denmark, would have generated anything like the violent spasm unleashed by these ambiguous, playful cartoons? If not, then it looks like mere cartoons can in some situations do more harm than "real violence." Indeed, when ridicule accompanies torture or other forms of violence, jokes can apply the most cutting lash: pouring the salt of contempt on bleeding wounds. While virtually everyone in the West denounced the savagery of the Abu Ghraib guards, few noted that they used ridicule as a torture technique (Lewis 2006, 8-13). But, with the images of these laughing sadists firmly established across the Muslim world in the run-up to the appearance of the cartoons, it's no wonder that millions of protesters took offense, seeing the irreverent images of Muhammad through the cruelly comic lens of Abu Ghraib and its killing jokers.

In general, the Danish cartoons look like a case in which humor was used to communicate between groups separated by suspicion and fear (secular Danes and Islamic fundamentalists), to reprimand, instruct, and provoke. That the response spiraled out of control is an indication not just of the new world of global communication we inhabit, but also of the largely unnoticed fact that, far from always lubricating and tamping down potential intragroup conflict (an adaptive function), humor can also serve maladaptively as lighter fluid. The outraged Muslim masses had a large list of background grievances—including their comparatively low economic and political status, Israel-Palestine, the Iraq War in general, and the vivid images of the smiling American torturers at Abu Ghraib in particular. Can we blame them for the context in which cartoons that seemed risible and only moderately provocative to most in the West were received as taunting, degrading, and outrageous by Muslims from Denmark to Indonesia?

From a methodological perspective, it seems clear that studies of humor production and reception on a far smaller scale have relevance to this global, transnational event. In addition to the general sense of positive and negative humor functions developed by Campbell et al. and Kuiper et al., four areas of research are relevant: (1) Studies of audience reception and interpretation of humor and satire. Early models for this kind of work—Rokeach and Vidmar (1974) and Jhally and Lewis (1992)—raised concerns about the transmission of intended messages in comedy. Just as jokes mean different things to different listeners, so humor intended to make one point can convey any number of ideas. In a starkly divided world, studies of humor response across cultural fault lines have an unusual urgency as part of the effort to heighten awareness and respect. (2) Studies of the role of humor in intensifying hostility and relaxing prohibitions against violence and discrimination. While both Oring and Davies have argued that jokes lack persuasive force, Thomas E. Ford and Mark A. Furguson (2004) have found that disparaging jokes about disadvantaged subgroups can move listeners already prejudiced against these groups toward a greater tolerance of discrimination and violence. Empirical data suggest that this effect is based on the way jokes tend to shift the disparagement of target groups into a "non-serious mindset" that can weaken external norms against discrimination. In pushing back against the cartoons, were the Muslim crowds expressing their determination to reject nonserious disparagement, insisting rightly (if also in self-destructively violent ways) that anti-Islamic contempt and satirical expressions of it in Europe be taken seriously? (3) Studies of responses to harsh ridicule. In situations of control and intimidation—from forceful tickling to schoolyard bullying to the abuse of prisoners and inmates—ridicule can inflict pain on victims/butts while pressuring onlookers to become coconspirators through the deployment of what Leslie M. Janes and James M. Olson (2000) call "jeer pressure." By emphasizing the power of humor to inflict pain, weaken resistance to cruelty, and inspire vengeful feelings, studies of this kind of harsh joking seem most directly relevant to the story of how these cartoons were received. (4) Studies of gelotophobia. It turns out that gelotophobes have difficulty distinguishing between situations in which they are the butts of gentle mockery and those in which they are being subjected to harsh ridicule (Platt 2008). Perhaps because they were teased roughly in childhood, gelotophobes fail to see the "safe and non-threatening quality of" "good-natured teasing." Missing the presence of reassuring cues, they "think the presence of laughter signals hostility" (122). It is important to consider whether large groups of people can act out of shared gelotophobia, perhaps in the same way that groups can act out of a sense of shared trauma or oppression. In other words, to what extent were offended Muslims in Denmark and elsewhere failing to see that the cartoons were harmless, and to what extent were they justified in feeling attacked?

The production and distribution of the cartoons was frequently cast as an issue of free speech, especially in the West, but the freedom to say or publish something does not resolve questions about whether it should be said or published. While the riots were ongoing on February 5, 2006, the Organization of Islamic Conference insisted that "the intention of Jylland Posten [*sic*] was . . . to incite hatred and violence against Muslims" (OIC Condemns). Two weeks later Fleming Rose explained his purpose in commissioning the work: "The cartoonists treated Islam the same way they treat Christianity, Buddhism, Hinduism and other religions. And by treating Muslims in Denmark as equals they made a point: We are integrating you into the Danish tradition of satire because you are part of our society, not strangers. The cartoons are including, rather than excluding, Muslims" (Rose). But how welcoming is this statement if the satire-creating group (we) gets the active verbs and the satire-enduring group (you) is meant to go along passively?

DUNHAM'S ACHMED: BEYOND FEAR IN POST-9/11 AMERICAN HUMOR

Posted on YouTube on September 29, 2007, following its broadcast on Comedy Central and release as part of the *Spark of Insanity* DVD, Jeff Dunham's "Achmed, the Dead Terrorist" sketch was viewed over twenty-eight million times and commented on approximately thirty-nine thousand times by the end of January 2008. A year later it was the fourth most watched YouTube video (Luscombe). While it would take a team of critics to read through all the responses, a brief review suggests that most are appreciative: "lol" appears frequently as do favorite quotes from the act. Achmed's absurdly unthreatening appearance suggests that many viewers have recommended the clip because it both amuses and soothes. Little more than a redecorated Halloween skeleton, Achmed is dummy short and decked out with a thin, long beard and turban made out of underpants. His remarkably expressive but also hilarious bug eyes alternate between staring fiercely and darting back and forth to emphasize a shift in his focus. His bushy eyebrows move up and down as he issues his commands. And his arms and legs dangle and shake loosely as his torso moves. Asked by Dunham early on to say what kind of terrorist he is, Achmed replies, "A terrifying terrorist." But all of his attempts to scare the "infields" fall flat, and his repeated exclamations of "Silence, I kill [keeel] you" become more shrill and receive louder laughter from the studio audience with each iteration.

Insecure enough to ask Dunham whether he is frightened yet, Achmed is, then, a pathetically ineffective image of radical Jihadism. A suicide bomber whose fuse went off in four seconds rather than thirty minutes, he is confused about whether he is dead or alive. "I need some ligaments," he admits as Dunham lifts him up and tries to adjust his rattling bones, but he also says, "I feel fine. It's a flesh wound." Finally convinced that he is dead, Achmed eyes the audience, looking for his seventy-two virgins and complaining that many of them seem to be "ugly ass guys." "If this is paradise," he whines, "I've been screwed." As the act goes on, Achmed starts to tell jokes, some conspicuously not politically correct, based on U.S. popular culture and stereotypes. For example, he alludes to Clay Aiken, Lindsay Lohan, Jews, and Catholic priests, all the while laughing along with the audience. After a particularly offensive wisecrack, he exclaims, "I'm killing, *so to speak*," an expression that highlights his utter harmlessness.

The comic appeal in the U.S. of this diminutive "terrorist," whose greatest threat is an offensive joke, suggests how much the culture had relaxed since the period immediately after 9/11. In the aftermath of the attacks, following a week or two in which joking seemed inappropriate to many, song and cartoon parodies directed at Osama bin Laden and the Taliban began to appear online, supplanting the virulent strain of anti-Bush satire in circulation pre-9/11. The work of Ron Piechota—an amateur musician and songwriter who was inspired by a radio station's call for songs to put on a CD honoring twin tower survivors—is typical. An instant Internet hit, Piechota's "Fifty Ways to Kill Bin Laden" rewrote the Paul Simon classic around violent images of the enemy leader's termination ("Lop off his face, Grace . . . Pop open his heart with a dart . . . Just rip off his balls, Paul"), while his version of a Christmas song had "Bin Laden's head roasting on an open fire."

The shift from this angry and frightened first wave of dead-terrorist humor to the milder Dunham routine can be seen in two ways. On the one hand, by reducing the image of the terrorist bomber to that of a limp, leering, almost charming puppet, the act can be seen as appealing to a desire for distraction and denial. On the other hand, as the Bush administration demonstrated, by narrowing options to fight or flight, war or surrender, too much fear can lead to poor decision-making. To the extent that "Achmed, the Dead Terrorist" helped us relax, one could argue, it supported a mood in which a more balanced approach—including an emphasis on international law enforcement, cooperation with allies, domestic security, and global outreach—could gain support. Seen through either of these political lenses or through both, "Achmed" became popular not only because it was clever, but also because it transformed a still-but-less feared figure into a diminutive, bug-eyed loser.

Beyond the appeal of Achmed in the United States lurks a broader and comparative question: why did the Danish cartoons stir global outrage while Dunham's routine attracted virtually no criticism here or abroad? It's true that a small minority of people who posted comments on YouTube and other sites complained about what they saw as an anti-Muslim bias in the act. It's true that the South African Advertising Standards Authority in October 2008 banned the use of an advertisement for a ringtone based on the act after receiving one complaint about how Achmed "was offensive to the Islamic religion and created an impression that all Muslims were terrorists"

(Miller). And it's true that the Islamic Human Rights Commission, a controversial group based in London, recognized Dunham in 2009 for "outstanding Islamophobia" (Armstrong). Still, these are mere ripples of concern in comparison with the tsunami of outrage that pushed back against the Danish cartoons. As of this morning (January 17, 2010), the Danish cartoonists are still subject to violent physical attack while Dunham's greatest concern is that his Comedy Central program was not renewed.

Defenders of the cartoons could argue that most of the differences in these responses were based on the sinister motives of anti-Western clerics and opinion leaders in Denmark and elsewhere who seized on and even distorted the episode to incite Muslim masses to strike back, but this begs the question: what about the cartoons made them more useful to this end than the Dunham routine? At least in the case of the Jens-Julius cartoon that shows a line of dead and smoking terrorists at the gate of heaven, the images are similar. And yet the differences are also striking and revealing. Context and genre were important factors, as editorial cartoons generally convey serious messages often without comic framing, whereas puppet acts performed by comedians are generally intended to be funny often without raising serious issues. In both the Jens-Julius and Westergaard cartoons, Muhammad himself appears. Where the depiction of an ineffective and indeed ridiculous terrorist could offend some Muslims, the image of a discombobulated (Jens-Julius) or bomb-toting Muhammad (Westergaard) was far more widely resented. The former seems (at least in retrospect) likely to divide Muslims, the latter to unite them against the West.

The role of humor in both cases is key. In the Danish cartoons, simple incongruities (bomb-turban; disconcerted prophet; dead, standing but still smoking terrorists) carry without elaborating the comic point. Even people who approve of the cartoons and support the ideas they convey have not tended to argue that they were particularly funny. Because Muhammad is central to the comedy, any amusement is about him. By contrast, in the Achmed routine a single, failed terrorist is the object of brilliantly elaborated satirical premise based on his obviously foolish and immediately contradicted belief that he is frightening. Like conservatives who enjoy Stephen Colbert's reductio ad absurdum version of their own worldview, even Muslims who support terrorism as a tactic could find Achmed amusing. How much more, then, is he likely to entertain a wide audience? How much less likely to provoke outrage, shock, condemnation? If the *Jyllands-Posten* editors and cartoonists wanted to use humor to reach across cultural and religious divides, they would have been well advised, first, to be funny and, second, to work with, and not against, the core values of their audience.

Intentions matter little in these stories. It was fine for Westergaard to reject interpretations of his cartoon as "incorrect," noting that it was aimed not at "Islam as a whole . . . [but at] terrorist acts [that] stem from interpretations of Islam" (*Jyllands-Posten*: Bomben's). And it was fine for *Jyllands-Posten* to publish an open letter on January 30, 2006, saying that "serious misunderstandings . . . of some drawings of the Prophet Muhammad have led to much anger . . . They were not intended to be offensive." Perhaps, but striving harder to avoid such misunderstandings would not be a capitulation to intolerance or a form of self-censorship. It would be an exercise of craft grounded in a new, transnational sense of audience and purpose responsive to the fluid distribution of material in the digital age.

NO MORE "MACACAS"

"Are you content now?" said the Caterpillar.
"Well, I should like to be a *little* larger, Sir, if you wouldn't mind,"
said Alice, "three inches is such a wretched height to be."
"It's a very good height indeed!" said the Caterpillar angrily,
rearing itself upright as it spoke (it was exactly three inches high).
"But I'm not used to it!" pleaded poor Alice in a piteous tone. And she
thought to herself, "I wish the creatures wouldn't be so easily offended."
—Lewis Carroll, *Alice in Wonderland*

What happens when a joke goes wrong? When satire misfires? When listeners won't put up with a putdown? Freud, the first major humor theorist who saw the importance of situations in which jokers encounter resistance, developed a model of adult humor-sharing based on the expression or venting of repressed impulses. While innocent (or silly) jokes can make adults smile, only tendentious or purposive ones, he noted, inspire "sudden bursts of laughter" (1905, 96). Or not. Because the interpretive process of getting a joke allows the teller to slip generally repressed (aggressive or sexual) images or ideas into conversation, it's always possible that the listener will find the content or message too blunt to enjoy. Avoiding such resistance, Freud implied, required a tactful sense of who the listener is. He observed, for example, that more refined or educated women who would be repulsed by explicitly smutty images tended to prefer more subtle jokes about sex.

Also, Freud observed, the listener's connection to the butt needs to be taken into account, as people are less likely to enjoy even half-concealed expressions of sexuality or hostility directed at their "highly respected relatives" or "devoted friends" (145). Because jokes, like dreams, do serious work, knowing one's audience is essential for the artful humorist.

✦ ✦ ✦

In Freud's model, joke sharing involves three people: the teller, the target or butt, and a somewhat detached third person (100). But what if the audience in particular situations is less finite, less predictable, less knowable? What if the third person is taping the exchange on his cell phone? What if the joke told quietly at a cocktail party to conjure erotic enthusiasm is heard and seen not only by the teller's immediate interlocutor but by her parents, grandparents, teachers, friends, and community leaders? What if something about it is unusual or striking enough to create a buzz, migrate from YouTube to cable news, get played and replayed, debated by pundits? Welcome to the digital age, in which amusing the expandable audience requires an expansive awareness and sensitivity—a new kind of tact. As Alice finds when her assumptions about the creatures she meets in Wonderland prove wrong, one needs to do more than wish that others not "be so easily offended."

On February 2, 2008, the patron sinner of political gaffes in the United States, Earl Butz, died at the age of ninety-eight. In its obituary two days later, the *New York Times* noted that the dead Republican would be remembered less for his contributions to farm policy as secretary of agriculture under both Richard Nixon and Gerald Ford than for the racist joke that led to his resignation. As Butz was the first U.S. politician brought down by an unacceptable joke told in what seemed like a private conversation, his experience provides a model of the kind of myopia that has become increasingly dangerous in our time.

The joke that brought the secretary down was not his first comic lapse. Two years earlier, he was forced to apologize for having ridiculed the pope's opposition to birth control by telling reporters that "[h]e no playa the game, he no maka the rules." Then, in October of 1976, during a conversation aboard a commercial airline flight, Butz responded to a question about why the party of Lincoln had so much trouble attracting blacks: "The only things the coloreds are looking for in life [he said] are tight pussy, loose shoes, and a warm place to shit." Twenty-one years after Rosa Parks refused to move to the back of a bus in Montgomery, Alabama, sixteen years after the

Greensboro sit-in, nine years after the Selma-to- Montgomery marches, and within eight to twelve years of the enactment of the major civil rights laws that were a response to persistent protest, Butz's joke was not only racist and tasteless but also remarkably in denial about what black Americans were then and had been looking for. And yet the soon-to-be-humiliated secretary insisted at the time that he was just kidding. In announcing his resignation, Butz, clearly surprised by the storm he had raised, said this "is the price I pay for a gross indiscretion in a private conversation" (Hannifin). In a story about the firing, *Time* reported that Butz remarked wistfully, "I've paid a tremendous price. . . . You know, I don't know how many times I told that joke, and everywhere—political groups, church groups—nobody took offense, and nobody should. I like humor. I'm human."

A repeat offender, Butz went not for the insanity but the comedy defense by positing a social world in which jokers have (or should have) the widest scope. Though he claimed that taking pleasure in derisive wit is a "human" propensity, it's true that taking offense is similarly human. Indeed, the positive reception his earlier tellings of the what-the-coloreds-are-looking-for joke reveals almost nothing about the potentially negative impact jokes like this can have and quite a bit about the limited range of people with whom the secretary shared it. Were the members of his political and church groups all white, conservative, and male? Were they at least somewhat resentful of the evolving demands of the civil rights movement? Were jokes like this familiar to them, part of a culture of assumed superiority? Butz's implicit claim that because jokes are meant to be playful and enjoyable, they are necessarily harmless and "should" therefore be inoffensive acquires no real support from the fact that prior tellings were deemed unobjectionable by like-minded listeners. On the contrary, the secretary's stunning fall was based on his lack of exposure to diverse perspectives. In spite of his earlier transgression ("he no playa the game . . ."), nothing in the secretary's experience compelled him to temper his joke telling with concerns about the likely responses of listeners who might not share his worldview and values. Nothing alerted him to the possibility that sharing the joke with a reporter in private might test the established limits of the personal-public transmission of humor. Within the frame of his superior positions (cabinet secretary, dominant speaker, back-slapping joke sharer), Butz's inaccurate sense of control led to his fall. No wonder the surprising reversal left him emotionally breathless, gasping for oxygen: "nobody took offense, and nobody should." Like Mary Shelley's monster, his joke went rogue, bursting out to a wide audience and returning to harm its teller. Was it, then, the first Frankenjoke? And was the secretary Butzed-out?

Remarkably enough, a similar complacency about subject and audience undermined another Republican thirty years after the Butz resignation. Running ahead of Democrat Jim Webb in the race for the Virginia Senate seat in August 2006, then-Senator George Allen inflicted a fatal wound on his own reelection campaign when he twice called an American of Indian descent "Macaca" at a rally in Breaks, Virginia. "This fellow here over here [he said, pointing to the only person of color at the event] with the yellow shirt, Macaca, or whatever his name is. He's with my opponent . . . Let's give a welcome to Macaca, here. Welcome to America and the real world of Virginia" (Craig and Shear). Although his audience responded positively to the comment, laughing and applauding, once the clip got onto YouTube and cable news, Allen's poll numbers plummeted. Unable to explain away the clear racial implications of the slur, Allen went on to lose by 9,329 votes, .4 percent of the 2,370,445 cast. For all the work that still needs to be done on the impact of political humor (Compton), this is a clear example of its potency, demonstrating that even a single joke or putdown can determine the outcome of a political race.

Perhaps the greatest, though certainly unintended, value of these humor fiascos, like the far more costly Danish cartoons, is that they highlight attitudes and assumptions that support tactless humor sharing. Within closed circles of like-minded people, insults and slurs, rough joking and ridicule, especially directed at out groups and out-group members, can go down pleasantly enough. But in these times when audience expansion is increasingly difficult to control and when building a sense of shared purpose is essential to human survival, public humorists need to find ways not to incite outrage that can harm both themselves and others.

Thomas Veatch's example of the new mother who no longer enjoys dead-baby jokes is apt. Telling such a mother to lighten up would miss the point that everyone is unwilling to laugh about some images and ideas, that the impulse to be amused is no more universal than its opposite. Though a series of dead-baby jokes traded back and forth by adolescents could seem funny, someone who told them to new parents on a maternity ward would be a tactless clod. Similarly, as anyone who has been embarrassed or harmed by inadvertently sending an e-mail containing an off-color witticism or bit of ridicule to many people via the unintended use of the Reply All function can attest, tact begins with a knowledge of one's audience. Not all dead terrorist humor is, then, created equal. In a world of viral communication— in which local events can suddenly be dispersed, in which the listeners you amused can be superceded by a larger delighted, unmoved, or irate crowd—the challenge is knowing your audience well enough to work with, and not against, it even as it expands exponentially. Earl Butz exclaimed, "I told that joke . . . *everywhere* [and] *nobody* took offense." But these concepts of place and personhood, much to his surprise, were changing. Satirists and wags who find themselves explaining what their cartoons, jokes, parodies, and putdowns really meant, what they intended to achieve, and how others should interpret them have already failed. A week after his Macaca moment, George Allen was asked to explain what looked to many like a racial, xeno-phobic slur: "Let's give a welcome to Macaca here. Welcome to America and the real world of Virginia." His considered defense was as revealing as the offhand piece of ridicule that got him in trouble: "There was no racial or ethnic intent to slur anyone [he said]. If I had any idea that, that that word, and to some people in some parts of the world, world, was an insult, I would never do it, because it's contrary to what I believe and who I am" (*Meet the Press*). While this revealingly smug utterance undermined Allen's cam-paign, its value today is cautionary. The "people" he took for granted and the "world, world" within which he was operating were more diverse and far less amused than he supposed.

NOTES

1. Some ideas for this chapter have evolved over the past few years, appearing first in papers delivered at conferences of the International Society for Humor Studies, then in Lewis (ed.), "The Muhammad Cartoons and Humor Research: A Collection of Essays" by Christie Davies, Giselinde Kuipers, Paul Lewis, Rod A. Martin, Elliott Oring, and Victor Raskin. *Humor: International Journal of Humor Research* 21–1 (2008): 1–46, and "Jeff Dunham: *Spark of Insanity*," *Tikkun* July–August 2008.

2. "*Jyllands-Posten* Muhammad Cartoons Controversy." This article provides access to the original cartoons, a detailed timeline of events following their publication, and arguments about the controversy. For an overview of how the reception of these cartoons fits into the history of satire and its reception in the Middle East, see Leonard Freedman, *The Offensive Art: Political Satire and Its Censorship around the World from Beerbohm to Borat* (London: Praeger, 2009), 140–55.

WORKS CITED

Armstrong, Dennis. "Giving Voice to Controversy." *Ottawa Sun,* January 17, 2010. http://www
    .ottawasun.com/entertainment/thescene/2010/01/12/12440516.html (accessed January 17,
    2010).
Association for Applied and Therapeutic Humor. E-mail, March 4, 2009.

Bilefsky, Dan. "Cartoons Ignite Cultural Combat in Denmark." *New York Times*, Sunday, January 1, 2006. http://www.nytimes.com/2005/12/30/world/europe/30iht-islam9.html (accessed March 2, 2010).

Campbell, Larne, Rod A. Martin, and Jennie R. Ward. "An Observational Study of Humor Use While Resolving Conflict in Dating Couples." *Personal Relationships* 15 (2008): 41–55.

Cann, Arnie, and Lawrence G. Calhoun. "Perceived Personality Associations with Differences in Sense of Humor: Stereotypes of Hypothetical Others with High or Low Senses of Humor." *Humor: International Journal of Humor Research* 14-2 (2001): 117–130.

Cann, Arnie, Lawrence G. Calhoun, and Janet S. Banks. "On the Role of Humor Appreciation in Interpersonal Attraction: It's No Joking Matter." *Humor: International Journal of Humor Research* 10-1 (1997): 77–89.

Compton, Josh. "When Voters Laugh: Reviewing Research on Political Humor Effects." Paper presented at the conference of the International Society for Humor Studies, Long Beach, California, June 24–27, 2009.

Craig, Tim, and Michael D. Shear. "Allen Quip Provokes Outrage, Apology." *Washington Post*, August 15, 2006.

Davies, Christie. *Ethnic Humor Around the World: A Comparative Analysis*. Bloomington, IN: Indiana University Press, 1990.

———. *The Mirth of Nations*. New Brunswick, NJ: Transaction Publishers, 2002.

Ford, Thomas E. "Effects of Sexist Humor on Tolerance of Sexist Events." *Personality & Social Psychology Bulletin* 26-9 (2000): 1094–1107.

Ford, Thomas E., and Mark A. Ferguson. "Social Consequences of Disparagement Humor: A Prejudice Norm Theory." *Personality & Social Psychology Review*, 8-1 (2004), 79–94.

Freud, Sigmund. *Jokes and Their Relation to the Unconscious*. James Strachey, trans. New York: W. W. Norton & Co., 1905; 1963.

Hannifin, Jerry. "Exit Earl: Not Laughing." *Time*, October 18, 1976.

Janes, L. M., and J. M. Olson. "Jeer Pressures: The Behavioral Effects of Observing Ridicule of Others." *Personality & Social Psychology Bulletin* 26(4): 474–485.

Jhally, Sut, and Justin Lewis. *Enlightened Racism: The Cosby Show, Audiences, and the Myth of the American Dream*. Boulder, CO: Westview Press, 1992.

"Jyllands-Posten: Bomben's Ophavsmand." *Jyllands-Posten*, February 2, 2006.

"Jyllands-Posten Muhammad Cartoons Controversy." http://www.search.com/reference/ Jyllands-Posten_Muhammad_cartoons_controversy (accessed January 15, 2010).

Klein, Allen. *The Healing Power of Humor: Techniques for Getting Through Loss, Setbacks, Upsets, Disappointments, Difficulties, Trials, Tribulations, and All That Not-So-Funny Stuff*. New York: Penguin Putnam Inc., 1989.

Kuiper, Nicholas A., M. Grimshaw, C. Leite, and G. A. Kirsh. "Humor Is Not Always the Best Medicine: Specific Components of Sense of Humor and Psychological Well-Being." *Humor: International Journal of Humor Research*, 17: 1–2 (2004): 135–168.

Kuipers, Giselinde. "The Muhammad Cartoon Controversy and the Globalization of Humor." In "The Muhammad Cartoons and Humor Research," ed. Paul Lewis, 7–11.

Kushner, Malcolm. "Unleash America's Secret Weapon: Humor." *USA Today*, October 4, 2001.

Lewis, Paul. *Cracking Up: American Humor in a Time of Conflict*. Chicago: University of Chicago Press, 2006.

———, ed. "Debate: Humor and Political Correctness." *Humor: International Journal of Humor Research* 10 (1997): 453–513.

———, ed. "The Muhammad Cartoons and Humor Research." *Humor: International Journal of Humor Research* 21–1 (2008): 1–46.

———. "Joke and Anti-Joke: Three Jews and a Blindfold." *Journal of Popular Culture,* 21–1 (1987): 63–73.

Luscombe, Belinda. "The Puppet Master." *Time,* June 8, 2009. http://www.time.com/time/magazine/article/0,9171,1901490,00.html#ixzz0h2abupgb (accessed March 3, 2010).

Martin, Rod A., P. Puhlik-Doris, G. Larsen, J. Gray, and K. Weir. "Individual Differences in Uses of Humor and Their Relation to Psychological Well-Being: Development of the Humor Styles Questionnaire." *Journal of Research in Personality* 37 (2003): 48–75.

"'Meet the Press' Transcript for September 17, 2006." http://www.msnbc.msn.com/id/14815993// (accessed January 30, 2010).

Miller, Joshua Rhett. "Comedian Defends 'Achmed the Dead Terrorist' Puppet Routine Against South African Ban." Fox News, October 2, 2008. http://www.foxnews.com/story/0,2933,431866,00.html (accessed January 17, 2010).

"OIC Condemns Publication of Cartoons of Prophet Muhammad." Islamic Radio News Agency, February 5, 2006 (http://www.workablepeace.org/Cartoons/oic.pdf (accessed March 2, 2010).

Platt, Tracy. "Emotional Responses to Ridicule and Teasing: Should Gelotophobes React Differently?" *Humor: International Journal of Humor Research* 20:1 (2008): 105–128.

Rose, Fleming. "Why I Published Those Cartoons." *Washington Post,* February 19, 2006. http://www.washingtonpost.com/wpdyn/content/article/2006/02/17/AR2006021702499.html (accessed March 2, 2010).

"Timeline: The Muhammad Cartoons." *Times Online.* February 6, 2006. http://www.timesonline.co.uk/tol/news/world/article725158.ece (accessed March 2, 2010).

Veatch, Thomas A. "A Theory of Humor." *Humor: International Journal of Humor Research* 11–2 (1998): 161–215.

Vidmar, Neil, and Milton Rokeach. "Archie Bunker's Bigotry: A Study in Selective Perception and Exposure." *Journal of Communication* 24 (1974): 36–47.

Coda
Humor, Pedagogy, and Cultural Studies

Arthur Asa Berger is one of the most well-known and prolific scholars work-
ing at the intersection of humor, critical cultural studies, cultural anthropol-
ogy, communications, humor studies, and sociology. He has published dozens
of books, on topics as varied as politics and advertising, anthropologies on
U.S. commodity culture, pedagogy and cultural studies, media theory, and
humor studies. As he is an interesting case study himself of a scholar who
can at once be prolific and incredibly dedicated to his students (and other
people's students!), and as he was an early participant in the debates that have
now become the field known as "humor studies," we asked him to share some
thoughts on 9/11 as a cultural phenomenon, and the important place it (and
humor) has in the classroom.

> Media events can be defined as occurrences that, because of their importance
> or the amount of interest people have in them, are given considerable coverage
> by television as they unfold. A media event, then, involves television coverage of
> something that is happening; the coverage is simultaneous. In addition, the media
> event deals of core values and society, with fundamental beliefs and the events
> either reinforce our belief in those values or lead to some alterations in them.

> . . . . [E]veryone feels uneasy in this world of "choice," for no matter what we have,
> there is more to be had. There are newer versions of everything and there all are new
> products—new styles of clothing, new lifestyles—to be consumed (and new politi-
> cians to be elected and dumped when we get bored of them as well).
> —Arthur Asa Berger, *Manufacturing Desire* (131–32)

ON HUMOR THEORY

In my work on humor I elaborated a typology with forty-five different
techniques of humor that generate laughter. I found, after I had listed these
techniques, that they fit in four categories—techniques basically involved

language (e.g., allusion, exaggeration, irony, puns), logic (e.g., absurdity, repetition, reversal, unmasking), identity (e.g, burlesque, caricature, exposure, parody), or action (e.g., slapstick and speed). This list can be used to study humor in different groups and countries to see what techniques dominate and what patterns of techniques emerge, and are particularly useful for studies of cultural politics (e.g., racism) because they abstract us so much from the difficult questions of what humor *is* and, even more difficult, what it *does*. I contrast these forty-five techniques that deal with *what* makes us laugh with what I call the four dominant *why* theories of humor, that have been elaborated since Aristotle's time.

Superiority Theories of Humor

Aristotle's theory is the oldest theory of humor. He wrote that comedy involves "an imitation of men worse than average," or more correctly "made worse" by the playwright.

Another superiority theorist, the political philosopher Hobbes, offered one of the most famous statements about humor and superiority. He wrote in his *Leviathan* that "the passion of laughter is nothing else but sudden glory arising from a sudden conception of some eminency in ourselves by comparison with the infirmity of others or with our own formerly." What superiority theorists argue is that we laugh at people who we see as inferior to ourselves (or ourselves as we once were) and who are ridiculous or have been made ridiculous by the authors of comedies, jokes, and other humorous texts.

Psychoanalytic Theories of Humor

We can consider Sigmund Freud to be the father of the psychoanalytic approach to humor. It suggests that humor is based on masked aggression, frequently involving human sexuality, and that this humor offers us gratifications we all desire. As Freud explained in *Jokes and Their Relation to the Unconscious* (2003, 101), which has some wonderful Jewish jokes in it, "and here at last we can understand what it is that jokes achieve in the service of their purpose. They make possible the satisfaction of an instinct (whether lustful or hostile) in the face of an obstacle that stands in its way." There are numerous other gratifications that humor provides, and Freud and other psychoanalytic theorists of humor have explicated a number of them.

Incongruity Theories of Humor

Incongruity theories are probably the dominant or most widely accepted theories of humor. Incongruity theorists all suggest that all humor is based on the difference between what people expect and what they get in some kind of humorous text or encounter. Jokes offer a good example of incongruity. The punch line of the joke is "funny," incongruity theorists argue, because it offers an unexpected but acceptable resolution of the events described in a joke. The punch line "surprises" us because it is incongruous and generates laughter—if the joke is a good one. Jokes are traditionally defined as short stories that are meant to amuse people—that is, to generate mirthful laughter—and which have a punch line.

The philosopher Schopenhauer wrote that that humor is based on incongruity: "The cause of laughter in every case is simply the sudden perception of the incongruity between a concept and the real object which have been thought through it in some relation and laughter itself is just the expression of this incongruity" (as cited in Piddington 1963, 171–72). Incongruity, then, is what generates of laughter and laughter is a signifier of something humorous. All humor is based on incongruity, but not all incongruity is humorous.

Communication Theories of Humor

What I describe as communication theories (a category not often foregrounded in traditional studies of humor) deal with the way the human mind processes information and deal with such matters as play frames and paradoxes in communication and the way they generate humor. The work of Gregory Bateson and William Fry can be classified as these sorts of cognitive theories. For example, in his book *Sweet Madness*, William Fry writes (1968):

> During the unfolding of humor, one is suddenly confronted by an explicit-implicit reversal when the punch line is delivered. The reversal helps distinguish humor from play, dreams, etc. . . . But the reversal also has the unique effect of forcing upon the humor participants an internal redefining of reality. Inescapably, the punch lines combine communication and metacommunication. (153)

Humor, for communication theorists, is a form of communication that forces us to confront paradoxical aspects of reality. One way we deal with the paradoxical nature of reality, Fry suggests, is to laugh at it.

The Problematic of Why Theories

All of these grand theories, I would argue, lack one important thing—the ability to consider, with, in any degree of detail and with any degree of specificity, what it is in humorous texts that generates laughter. They deal with the nature of humor, at a high level of abstraction, but do not help us understand the way texts generate laughter. Let me offer an example that I have used in many of my writings on humor. This joke I call "The Tan":

> A man goes to Miami for a vacation. After four days he notices he has a tan all over his body, except for his penis. So the next day he goes to a deserted area of the beach early in the morning, takes his clothes off, and lies down. He sprinkles sand over himself until all that remains in the sun is his penis. Two little old ladies walk by on the boardwalk and one notices the penis. "When I was twenty," she says, "I was scared to death of them. When I was forty, I couldn't get enough of them. When I was sixty, I couldn't get one to come near me . . . *and now they're growing wild on the beach.*"

I believe we can find (at the very minimum) the following techniques of humor at work in this joke: eccentricity, the man must have every bit of his body tanned, even his penis; mistakes, the old lady thinks that penises are growing wild on the beach; exposure, the exhibitionism of the man and the sexual desire of the woman; repetition, the woman at twenty, forty, and sixty.

What this list of techniques suggests is that jokes should be seen as complex texts that have many different techniques of humor in them. The techniques approach allows us to get more out of the joke than using the why theories: it involves *superiority* (our feelings about the silly people in the joke); it involves *masked aggression* (ridiculing the man and the elderly women); it involves *incongruity* (the punch line surprising us); or it involves *play and paradox* (recognizing that this is a joke and not reality). "The Tan" joke is essentially about identity (eccentricity, exposure) and logic (ignorance revealed, repetition).

I should add that proponents of each of the "why" theories spend a great deal of time and effort arguing with proponents of other "why" theories and asserting the supremacy of their particular "why" theory. I recall seeing a statement by an aggression theorist that read "I defy any humor scholar to show me an example of humor that does not involve aggression." That statement, in itself, I found humorous. Rather than spending time and effort debating the nature of humor, I prefer a more practical and pragmatic approach that focuses on humorous texts and tries to figure out how they work.

As I showed in my book *The Art of Comedy Writing* (1997), we have had marvelous humorous texts from the times of the Greeks and Romans, who wrote superb comedies, to the present. There is, in human beings, it would seem, a need to laugh at ourselves and this need takes many different forms—from plays and poems to cartoons, comic strips, and jokes. A joke, we must remember, has a definite form: a narrative with a punch line meant to cause mirthful laughter. There are many other forms of humor, such as wit, puns, riddles, and so on. I recall reading somewhere that the average person in America laughs fifteen times a day, though much of this laughter is not based on responses to jokes but in response to simple statements people make to one another such as "how are you?"

As Robert Provine, a psychologist who has done some extremely interesting work on humor, writes in his article "Laughter":

> Contrary to our expectations we found that most conversational laughter is not a response to structured attempts at humor, such as jokes or stories. Less than 20 percent of the laughter in our sample was a response to anything resembling an effort at humor. Most of the laughter seemed to follow rather banal remarks, such as "Look, it's Andre," "Are you sure?" and "It was nice meeting you, too." (41)

Laughter, Provine adds, is to a great degree a social phenomenon and people are "about 30 times more likely to laugh when they are in a social situation than when they are alone" (41).

A Note on 9/11 Jokes

If we can use the German concentration camps such as Auschwitz and the Holocaust to create humor, and there are many humorous texts on these topics, we can tell jokes and create humorous texts about anything. So it is not surprising that we make jokes—more literally, not jokes but for the most part "humorous" riddles—about disasters of all kinds, including 9/11. We make humorous responses to tragedies because doing so has some kind of a therapeutic value for us, collectively speaking, even if the humorous texts are repugnant. It strikes me that using riddles to deal with tragedies is, psychoanalytically speaking, a kind of regression—to a period in our childhood when we were innocent and where the countless tragedies of the world did not mean anything to us. These 9/11 texts (as Giselinde Kuipers points out in chapter 2 of this volume) are examples of what we might call "sick humor" cycles that circulate after every tragedy and possibly help us to deal with the anxiety we face, ultimately, about our own deaths. Making light of 9/11 or other tragedies doesn't make them disappear, but does seem to help us get on with our daily lives.

HUMOR, PEDAGOGY, AND CULTURAL POLITICS

We all like to bite the hands that feed us and there's nothing like being tenured and well paid at a respectable university to make one want to bring the whole decadent bourgeois system crashing down. Nothing better, that is, except getting a grant to do research and show how the media conglomerates are destroying or are a threat to our democratic institutions. If we get some grant money from the media conglomerates, all the better.

One of the problems is that many students who may, in some cases, be taking courses in communications, radio and television, media arts and similar departments to fulfill requirements (and would be much happier dollying in and out in some television studio) don't understand what we are talking about. I've found that sometimes students can grasp the concepts we teach, but can't apply them on their own. You can ask them to define the terms and they can do that tolerably well, in some cases. But using the concepts is a different matter. There's a kind of gap between understanding concepts and applying them.
—Arthur Asa Berger, *Manufacturing Desire* (33–34)

Humor has a role in everything, so it is quite natural that it would have a role in cultural politics, and it certainly does with pedagogy. For one thing, having a sense of humor helps people deal with the crazy things that go on in the political world. If you take everything that our politicians say and do seriously, you'll be a good candidate for a nervous breakdown. (Of course, what they do shapes our lives, but that's another matter...where a sense of humor helps.) And of course, the various comedians who satirize news shows do a wonderful job of cutting politicians down to size. Politicians are like moths who can't resist the "flame" of being on the shows the news comedians have, even though they know it is perilous.

Though I have spent many years studying humor and trying to figure out what it is that generates mirthful laughter, I still find the process of humor an amazing thing. This leads to an imperative that has shaped my career (such as it is) as an academic. When I faced the problem of teaching a course on media, pop culture, etc., I decided that it made sense to empower my students and teach them techniques that they could then use to make their own analyses of various aspects of pop culture rather than reading what some scholar had written. So cultural criticism, which is what American studies and pop culture studies seem to have morphed into, should focus on methods that can be used to process media, culture, and politics with an eye to students' everyday lives. I've always thought that methods tend to stay with students, because once they learn a methodology (such as semiotics, psychoanalytic theory, etc.) they start applying it to various aspects of their lives and to experiences they have. So it stays with them. On the other hand, students who read large "readers" and are asked to remember the contents of the chapters they read probably forget what they've read and memorized once they have taken a test on this material. That is a bit of an oversimplification, but I think that, in general, it is correct.

This notion, that it pays to teach concepts and methods of analysis, has political and social and cultural implications, because students who learn methods start seeing the world differently from the way they used to see it. I've had students who have graduated from my courses send me letters and sometimes clippings from newspapers that reflect the way the methods they've studied have influenced their decision-making and world view.

When I taught I always looked for examples of the way concepts can be applied that were "far out." That is, I used humor to amuse the students and create a bit of puzzlement on their part. I even injected humor in a book I wrote on communication research methods (Berger 2000), even though I know that any number of professors who use the book don't appreciate (to put it in a positive way) my sense of humor or my use of humor in a "serious" book.

In one of my classes a student raised his hand to ask a question. When I called on him he said, "Could you please raise your left hand when you are being serious so we'll know when to take notes?" I explained to him that because of his limited experience, some topics that I discussed that seemed "ridiculous" were really part of mainstream intellectual thought. Many of my students found semiotics curious but intriguing. They thought psychoanalytic theory was "ridiculous," though some students really liked it and read more on the subject on their own. The students tended to like Marxist theory, because it seemed to be relevant to their lives and the social problems that impinged on their lives. And they found sociological theory, and topics such as uses and gratifications, mildly interesting.

I'd like to think that my years as a professor and my academic writings had some impact on some people; if they didn't, I wasted a lot of time preparing for an academic career and writing books. Professors who write academic books and textbooks have no way of knowing what kind of an impact their works have, since they seem to vanish into a dark void once they are published. But every once in a while, someone who has read one of my books sends me a letter (when people wrote letters) or an e-mail. Let me end by quoting from a letter that I received a number of years ago.

Dear Dr. Berger
    While wandering through the stacks of Central Library, looking for a book for my freshman composition class, my eyes fell on your book "Pop Culture." I took it out and read it the same night. It was wonderful. You brought out many things which are always on my mind, always disturbing me . . . However hard I try to remain aware of popular culture, and criticize it continually, I am nevertheless sucked in. There is no way not to be drawn into the flow of it. It is the easiest way to live—complacently. Southern California, especially (I was raised in Massachusetts) is ideal for a leisurely, material oriented existence.
    My reason for writing to you is (actually, I'm not quite sure why I write to you but you seemed a suitable person to turn to) to ask if there is a line of study one can follow in order to understand these strange phenomena, such as chewing gum. It is all so disturbing, there must be somebody equally disturbed as I, possibly a group of them, already studying it. But where are they? And is it possible for them to have any noticeable effect on the American public? Before we bury ourselves in McDonald's hamburgers and pet rocks, perhaps we shall see the light. But what does the light consist of, and how do we extricate ourselves from this mess? It doesn't seem very possible.

That letter was written in 1976. Since then, the study of popular culture, media, and everything else that ends up as part of cultural studies has progressed and now there are many people studying popular culture and, in some ways that are not always clear to me (and maybe this is a matter of wishful thinking), actually having an impact upon individuals and upon society at large.

✦ ✦ ✦

From the editors:
Arthur, from the black hole of academic books we thank you, and we hope that our work will similarly be a source of inspiration, confusion, challenge, temptation, and entertainment—for our students, our colleagues, our tenure committees, and ourselves.

WORKS CITED

Berger, Arthur Asa. 1997. *The Art of Comedy Writing*. Piscataway, New Jersey: Transaction Publishers.

———. 1996. *Manufacturing Desire: Media, Popular Culture, and Everyday Life*. New Brunswick: Transaction Publishers.

———. 2000. *Media and Communication Research Methods: An Introduction to Qualitative and Quantitative Approaches*. Thousand Oaks: Sage Publications.

Freud, Sigmund. 2003. *The Joke and Its Relation to the Unconscious*. Translated by J. Carey. New York: Penguin Books.

Fry, William. 1968. *Sweet Madness: A Study of Humor*. Palo Alto, California: Pacific Book Publishers.

Piddington, Ralph. 1963. *The Psychology of Laughter*. New York: Gamut Press.

Provine, Robert. 1996. Laughter. *American Scientist* 84 (1): 38–47.

Contributors

Gavin Benke, a doctoral candidate in American studies at the University of Texas at Austin, researches the intersections of business and culture in the United States. His dissertation, "Electronic Bits and Ten Gallon Hats: Enron, American Culture and the Postindustrial Political Economy," uses Enron as a case study to examine the cultural and spatial implications of postindustrial political economy in the late twentieth and early twenty-first centuries.

Arthur Asa Berger is professor emeritus of Broadcast and Electronic Communication Arts at San Francisco State University. He has published more than one hundred articles in publications such as *The Journal of Communication, Society, Rolling Stone, The San Francisco Chronicle,* and *The Los Angeles Times,* and more than sixty books on media, popular culture, humor, and tourism. Among his books are *Media Analysis Techniques, What Objects Mean, Bloom's Morning, Pop Culture, Television in Society, An Anatomy of Humor, Ads, Fads and Consumer Culture,* and *Shop 'Til You Drop.* He has also written a number of darkly comic academic murder mysteries. He is married, has two children and four grandchildren, and lives in Mill Valley, California.

Ted Gournelos is an assistant professor in the Department of Critical Media and Cultural Studies at Rollins College. His monograph *Popular Culture and the Future of Politics* was released in 2009 by Lexington Books, and he has published essays on a variety of film, television, and digital media productions as well as cultural and policy issues. He is currently working with David Gunkel (Northern Illinois University) on an anthology on oppositional politics in the digital age called *Transgression 2.0,* as well as articles on contemporary U.S. and Japanese media and politics. He is a practicing artist working in Orlando, Florida.

Viveca Greene is a visiting assistant professor of cultural studies at Hampshire College. Her work has appeared in *The Nation, In Media Res,* and *We* *the Media: A Citizen's Guide to Fighting for Media Democracy.* She teaches courses on consumer culture, audience studies, popular culture, and media irony. Her current research is on irony, cultural politics, and "hipster racism," and for ten years she worked at nonprofit organizations that focused on media issues, including Children Now, The Institute for Alternative Journalism/Alternet, and The Center for Media Literacy.

David Gurney is an assistant professor of communications and theater at Texas A&M Corpus Christi, with his Ph.D. from Northwestern University's screen cultures program. His dissertation research focused on the growth in popularity of online video, the role of humor in that growth, and in particular what the term "viral video" means as a cultural category. He has published his writing in the online journal *Flow* and has a piece in the *Flow* anthology, *Flow TV: Television in the Age of Media Convergence* (2010).

David Holloway is a professor of American studies at the University of Derby in England. His books include *Cultures of the War on Terror: Empire, Ideology, and the Remaking of 9/11* (Montreal: McGill Queen's University Press, 2008) and *The Late Modernism of Cormac McCarthy* (Westport, CT: Greenwood, 2002), and he is contributing coeditor *of American Visual Cultures* (New York: Continuum, 2005). He has written for journals including *The Southern Quarterly, Comparative Literature Studies,* and *PUBLIC,* and has contributed chapters to a variety of edited book collections on American cultural and intellectual history.

Lanita Jacobs is an associate professor of anthropology and coaffiliated with the Program in American Studies and Ethnicity at the University of Southern California. Her research has explored African American linguistic and cultural practices around hair, notions of truth and authenticity in African American stand-up humor, and African American families raising children with acquired and/or traumatic brain injury. She is author of *From the Kitchen to the Parlor: Language and Becoming in African American Women's Hair Care* (Oxford: Oxford University Press, 2006), as well as several articles and book chapters on race, gender, community, and language.

Giselinde Kuipers is an associate professor of sociology at the University of Amsterdam, as well as holder of the part-time Norbert Elias Chair in sociology at Erasmus University Rotterdam. She is the author of *Good Humor, Bad Taste: A Sociology of the Joke* (Berlin/New York, 2006), as well as numerous articles in English and Dutch on humor, popular culture, media, and cultural globalization.

Paul Lewis is a professor of English at Boston College. The author of *Cracking Up: American Humor in a Time of Conflict* (2006), *Comic Effects: Interdisciplinary Approaches to Humor in Literature* (1989), and articles on American literature and culture, he is a member of the editorial board of *Humor: International Journal of Humor Research,* the vice president of the Poe Studies Association, a freelance writer, and the neologist who coined the word Frankenfood.

David Monje is an assistant professor in the Department of Communication Studies at Northeastern University. His research focuses on the intersection of politics, culture, and the media. He received his Ph.D. in Communication and Cultural Studies from the Institute of Communication Research at the University of Illinois, Urbana-Champaign.

Michael Truscello is an assistant professor in the Department of English at Mount Royal University in Calgary, Alberta, Canada. His publications appear in journals such as *Postmodern Culture, Technical Communication Quarterly, Rhetoric Review, TEXT Technology,* and *Cultural Critique,* and in *The Postanarchism Reader,* forthcoming from Pluto Press. He is currently at work on a book-length study of the role of technology in the anarchist tradition.

Jamie Warner is a professor of political science at Marshall University where she teaches political theory. She is particularly interested in the function of political humor and parody in a democracy and has written on the Radical Cheerleaders, Billionaires for Bush, *The Daily Show with Jon Stewart,* as well as *The Onion.* Her work has appeared in both communications and political science journals including *Polity, Popular Communication, Politics & Gender,* and the *Electronic Journal of Communication.*

Aaron Winter received his Ph.D. in English from the University of California Irvine in 2008. More recently, he has been a Taiwan National Science Council postdoctoral fellow and visiting lecturer in American literature at National Tsing Hua University. You can learn more about his research at http://laughingdove.net and read his parodies of academic culture at http://mlade.org.

Index